D0754411

STRATEGIES FOR
PROTECTING
WEALTH

STRATEGIES FOR PROTECTING WEALTH

DARRELL AVISS

EDITED BY LARRY CHAMBERS

McGraw-Hill

New York Chicago San Francisco Lisbon London
Madrid Mexico City Milan New Delhi
San Juan Seoul Singapore
Sydney Toronto

JUL 2 6 2007

DOUGLAS COLLEGE LIBRARY

*The **McGraw·Hill** Companies*

Copyright © 2007 by Darrell Aviss. All rights reserved. Printed in the United States of America. Except as permitted under the United States Copyright Act of 1976, no part of this publication may be reproduced or distributed in any form or by any means, or stored in a data base or retrieval system, without the prior written permission of the publisher.

1 2 3 4 5 6 7 8 9 0   DOC/DOC   0 9 8 7 6

ISBN-13: 978-0-07-147812-0

ISBN-10: 0-07-147812-4

This publication is designed to provide accurate and authoritative information in regard to the subject matter covered. It is sold with the understanding that the publisher is not engaged in rendering legal, accounting, or other professional service. If legal advice or other expert assistance is required, the services of a competent professional person should be sought.
> *--From a declaration of principles jointly adopted by a committee of the American Bar Association and a committee of publishers.*

McGraw-Hill books are available at special quantity discounts to use as premiums and sales promotions, or for use in corporate training programs. For more information, please write to the Director of Special Sales, Professional Publishing, McGraw-Hill, Two Penn Plaza, New York, NY 10121-2298. Or contact your local bookstore.

CONTENTS

As you begin perusing *Strategies for Protecting Wealth*, please understand that this book is not for everyone. Rather, it's geared toward those in high-net-worth, high-liability, high-risk professions, such as physicians, attorneys, and business owners exposed to liability and risk of litigation. If you find yourself faced with this exposure, this text will give you tools you can use to protect your personal assets and to build wealth in a protected environment.

In Part 1 of *Strategies for Protecting Wealth,* we have consulted attorney Jacob Stein, Esq., a specialist in taxation and asset protection law with the law firm of Boldra, Klueger & Stein, with offices in Los Angeles, California. The firm's practice is limited to domestic and international tax planning, asset protection, and structuring complex business transactions.

In the arena of asset protection, Mr. Stein assists high networth individuals and successful businesses in protecting their assets from potential creditors by focusing on properly structuring asset ownership and business structures and operations.

Jacob is an instructor with the California CPA Education Foundation, National Business Institute, and Lorman Education Services, teaching courses on advanced tax planning and asset protection. He is the Chair of the Tax Section of the San Fernando Valley Bar Association, and a member of the tax sections of the American, California and Los Angeles County Bar Associations.

He has provided an in-depth investigation into the traditional methods of asset protection and favorable foreign jurisdictions. But this book goes beyond the obvious legal shields to examine how portfolio structure and choice of investments will help fortify your wealth against erosion and loss.

In addition to providing you with straightforward wealth protection tactics, this text answers advanced questions, such as:

- What are the three factors you should consider when protecting your wealth?
- How does an academic approach to structuring an investment portfolio improve asset protection?
- Why should foreign-currency-backed investments be included in a risk-management strategy?
- What is the gold standard of all asset protection vehicles?

You don't have to become an expert to create your own asset protection strategy, but for a more comprehensive education, be sure to read McGraw-Hill's best-selling *Asset Protection, Concepts and Strategies for Protecting Your Wealth* by Jay Adkisson and Chris Riser, covering the legal, technical, and theoretical aspects of asset protection.

WHAT IS WEALTH PROTECTION?

Wealth protection is the long-established process of arranging your financial affairs through the use of asset-protection strategies to minimize the risk of loss against numerous unforeseen circumstances—such as seizure by potential litigants or future creditors. A creditor can be anyone with a claim on your assets: your business partner, the bank, the Internal Revenue Service, and even your children or former spouse.

Asset protection does not involve doing anything illegal or unethical. It is neither a means nor an excuse to avoid or evade U.S. taxes, nor for making a fraudulent conveyance. Rather, it is simply the process of structuring the ownership and location of your assets in advance so as to safeguard them from potential future risks.

Protecting your assets is instinctive.

This asset-protection tactic is used by the male stickleback to protect his nest from raiding females (top). After the guardian male sees a group of egg-eating predators, he swims away from the nest, poking his snout into the ground several times (middle). This action resembles a feeding movement; it is a distraction used by the male stickleback to lure the attacking females away from the nest (bottom).

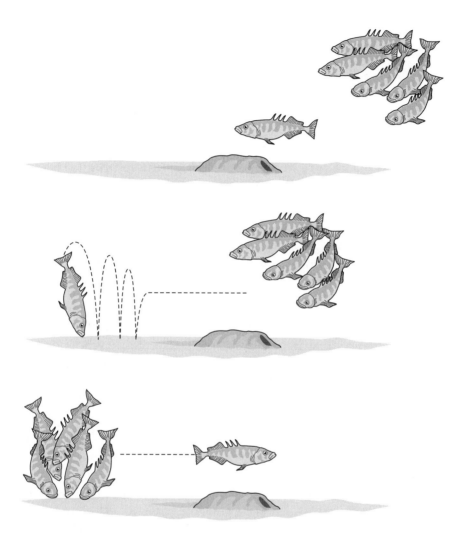

- Although the laws of nature allow for a natural depletion through attrition, efficiency, and balance, the current litigious environment in the United States demands a more aware, proactive approach to protecting your wealth. If you are successful and are perceived as wealthy, consider this: The United States is host to 95 percent of lawsuits filed worldwide.

- A new lawsuit is filed every 30 seconds and, as a business owner, you have a one-in-four chance of being sued over the next year.

- The United States has 5 percent of the world's population and 70 percent of the world's lawyers. Litigation is a $300 billion drain on the economy."Since 1994, the average jury award in tort cases as a whole has tripled to $1.2 million; in medical malpractice, it has tripled to $3.5 million; and in product liability cases, it has quadrupled to $6.8 million, according to just released data from Jury Verdict Research."—quote from *Forbes Magazine*, May 13, 2002.
- "The toll of just one lawsuit can be so great that, guilty or innocent, many firms shut their doors, lay off their employees, and vanish into legal graveyards."—quote from Jack Fans, president of the National Federation of Independent Businesses.

You could be sued for something you weren't directly involved in and lose everything. This is demonstrated by the following true story. In Michigan, in 2002, a nanny who worked for a wealthy business owner was driving the children to their school, talking on her cell phone, when she ran a red light and crashed into a car containing a family of three. The family was killed. Michigan law stipulates that in cases such as this, both the driver and the owner of the vehicle are liable.[1] Unfortunately, both the business owner and his wife were named on the car's registration—as they were on all of their assets. Because of the lack of any wealth protection planning, the accident ultimately put almost all of the business owner's assets in jeopardy.

Would your wealth survive the cost of a catastrophic loss? Are you a prime target because of your profession or public stature? Have you taken any effective measures to protect yourself? Do you even know how or where to begin?

Part 2 of *Strategies for Protecting Wealth* provides a short course on investment structures, understanding investment theory, and how to insulate your assets as they continue to grow.

Part 3 combines entity and structure within a jurisdiction of natural litigation protection into one gold standard.

---

1 Bloomberg Wealth Manager, Asset Protection, March 2005.

Utilizing these strategies and tactics can actually deter potential lawsuits due to the solid structure of protection you build. Let this book become your eye-opening guide that will decrease your exposure and increase your comfort level—for life.

DISCLAIMER

This book was written solely for informational and educational purposes. It should in no way be construed as an offer by the author of this book to sell Swiss annuities, Swiss life insurance, or any other Swiss investment.

We urge readers to follow all applicable U.S. tax and retirement plan rules and regulations. We in no way endorse the use of Swiss annuities and life insurance as a method to evade payment of taxes to the Internal Revenue Service (IRS).

This book is not intended to give legal, accounting, or tax advice. We urge you to consult your legal, accounting, or tax professional for advice in those areas.

For U.S. citizens: Please note that some Swiss investment opportunities are not available in some U.S. states. Please consult your advisor for details.

This book is written for investors who have a truly global outlook and wish to protect their hard-earned wealth against the uncertainties of a volatile stock market, a falling dollar, and a legal system that appears to encourage plaintiffs to sue wealthy individuals.

My goal is to educate the reader about a new and unique strategy that is both simple and powerful in the protections it provides. This "process" can diversify your overall investment portfolio using methods you have never considered before—allowing you an opportunity to invest in the world's strongest currency, thus increasing returns while lowering risk.

This "Wealth Protection Strategy," when implemented properly, can preserve your privacy, protect your assets, and reduce taxes—all legally and safely in Switzerland, the world's third largest financial center and the private banking capital of the world.

Let me tell you how I came to learn of the remarkable opportunities that are available to savvy investors in Switzerland. As a financial consultant for over 23 years, I thought I had seen and heard everything in the world of investing. And then by chance, I met Dr. Walter Jorgensen.

Dr. Jorgensen was 70 years old and invited me to his home to review his investment portfolio to see if he could improve his results. At his age, I knew he would know a thing or two about the ups and downs of the financial markets. Upon entering his home, I could see that he was very frugal, and he proceeded to tell me he was very conservative in his financial affairs and liked to keep things simple. "Simplicity is very important to me," he told me. "One of the things I've noticed is the degree to which people love complexity."

And then Walter did something completely unexpected. He brought out a cardboard box, the contents of which he dumped on the floor in front of me. I picked up what appeared to be a contract, one of about a dozen or so, and discovered that I was holding in my hand a Swiss annuity contract, something I had never seen or heard of before—and much to my embarrassment, knew nothing about.

What I did know is that I felt I was about to discover something very important, a feeling that was confirmed when Walter told me he had amassed over $4 million in these contracts over the years.

"You see," he continued, "I get a great return on my money, much more than my CDs, not much less than my stocks in fact, with none of the risk. What's more, my money cannot be taken by anyone, for any reason. Have you noticed that wealthy people are hounded by lawyers and a legal system that determines guilt by one's ability to pay?" he asked me. "Hmm" I pondered, "asset protection, something else I didn't know about investing in Switzerland."

"Weren't you worried about sending your money to another country?" I asked. "Not at all," he immediately responded. "My car is Japanese, the gasoline in it is Dutch. The stereo over there is from Germany. We are already global persons—all of us—why not personal financial globalization?" he answered, displaying a wisdom I was now beginning to see clearly.

And so began my education. I immediately went back to my office and began researching this new and exciting opportunity and soon discovered that information on Swiss annuities and other foreign offerings has largely been unavailable to the American public due to a very restrictive regulatory environment.

I then began a journey that would take me to Switzerland dozens of times over the course of nearly three years. This quaint little country at the top of Europe—land of chocolates, of fine watches, the beautiful mountains and lakes—was a delight to visit. I met with the Gnomes of Zurich, which is their slang for Swiss bankers, insurance company executives, and private money managers.

At first, information was difficult to come by. The Swiss are a very private and discreet people. They take their reputation as money managers to the world's elite very seriously and do not easily reveal their secrets to foreigners. In fact, the Swiss consider the right to privacy as important as Americans consider the Bill of Rights.

Eventually, I earned their confidence and they began to share with me the strategies that have made Switzerland a financial superpower for hundreds of years. After extensively researching every unique investment opportunity in Switzerland, I concluded that certain types of Swiss investments are the safest and most powerful tools for asset growth and financial protection I had ever seen.

Through this process, I uncovered what I believe to be some of the most powerful wealth protection strategies and tactics available for high-risk professionals such as physicians, real estate developers, attorneys, and private business owners. These readers will find the information contained within these pages especially compelling.

One caveat: I have taken great pains to debunk some popular myths pertaining to "offshore" investing and asset protection. There is no such thing as a "secret" Swiss bank account, and many of the complex structures and tactics you've seen promoted on exotic islands in faraway places you can hardly pronounce do nothing more than make their promoters wealthy, usually at your expense.

But if you are an investor concerned about the turbulent and volatile markets that exist today, corporate accounting scandals, investment banking conflicts of interest, and widespread mutual fund abuses that have rocked investor confidence in U.S. markets, then this book can provide you with some safe, simple strategies to protect the wealth you've taken a lifetime to accumulate.

I know that it takes people a while to warm up to new ideas, so I offer you this bit of closing advice: The best investment method for you is one that turns procrastination into participation.

I therefore strongly encourage you to contact your professional advisors to explore how *Strategies for Protecting Wealth* can enhance your existing financial plans and investment portfolios.

The world is changing; don't be left behind.

STRATEGIES FOR PROTECTING WEALTH

PART ONE

Asset Ownership Protection

In 1975, when less than one half of 1 percent of the American population had a net worth in excess of a million dollars, asset protection was primarily for the ultra-wealthy, who kept an attorney and business manager on retainer. Their names were recognizable for their "estates," "foundations," and "trust funds" that insulated them from common liability. They benefited from tax shelters and advantages that required a certain "entry level" of wealth. Today, with a reported astounding 8.9 million U.S. millionaires, asset protection has become an everyday topic for average professionals who are concerned about how to hold onto their assets in this litigious society and insulate their wealth from unfavorable tax laws and the effects of the financial markets.

CHAPTER 1

Unbundled Wealth

Protecting your assets is a bit like herding cats—buttoning up one vulnerability leaves three others unattended. The affluent don't have just one asset; they have a variety. No single line of defense will cover everything they own. Those assets need to be unbundled and may require an individual entity for each.

Take the case of Mr. William Reilly, who owns a large manufacturing company in Ohio. This single asset dominates his net worth. His stock has a very low tax basis and he has a large tax liability. As the business owner, losing a lawsuit would have a major impact on Reilly and his entire family. Businesses like Mr. Reilly's have many component assets, including the market value and rental value of real property, his company's equipment, customer contracts, customer lists, patents, copyrights, trademarks, key employees' contracts, even vendor contracts, etc. Each of these component parts are assets that can be valued, monetized, and are best protected separately. (See Figure 1.1.)

For instance, one entity might own Mr. Reilly's customer list and rent it to the operating business. Real property and equipment might be contributed to other entities and leased to the operating business. Trademarks could be housed in another entity and licensed to the operating business. Yet another entity

FIGURE 1.1

Unbundling Components

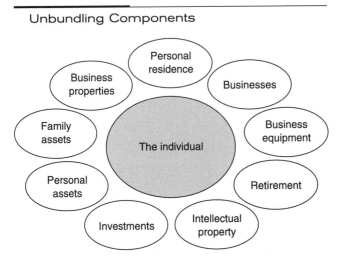

might contract with the employees and lease their services to the operating business. Each contract would allow funds to flow from the operating business to each of the separate entities, where those funds are protected from the creditors of the operating business and from the creditors of the other component entities.

How does that help a professional, such as a doctor? Dr. Lynder is an emergency room physician and, like many doctors today, he is not only concerned about being sued and the amount of time he would spend defending himself, but is also concerned that the potentially devastating liability exposure might greatly exceed his very expensive malpractice insurance coverage.

"You try to save somebody's life and oftentimes have to resort to some extreme procedures to do that, but in the back of my mind is the nagging realization that if I fail, the family will sue. I earn a lot of money and I've accumulated some personal assets. I really don't know how to protect myself."

That is exactly what happened to one of his colleagues, an obstetrician-gynecologist who was sued over a baby's birth defect. Although the doctor did not believe she caused the baby's problem, a nightmare scenario resulted that put the doctor's entire $10 million net worth at risk and consumed all of the doctor's time and attention, effectively putting her practice on hold.

Many malpractice polices now contain a provision called "the hammer," which stipulates that if the carrier decides to seek a pretrial settlement (which in a way translates into taking responsibility for the claimant's loss) and the insured refuses, then the insured assumes personal liability for any amount awarded in excess of the suggested settlement offer—even if otherwise covered by the policy. Of course, judgments against you not only take a big chunk of your accumulated wealth, but also affect your future cost of insurance, future earnings, loss of client/patient confidence, credit ratings, employability, etc. In addition, what happens to your personal residence, rental real estate, brokerage accounts, and retirement plans?

Dr. Lynder's best defense is to use a combination of estate-planning tactics, techniques, and entities to insulate her family and personal assets from claimants. In the process, her assets become unattractive to claimants or it becomes too difficult to attach or place a lien on them.

Consider, for instance, the accounts receivable. A physician could forestall creditors by using his or her accounts receivable as collateral for a loan from the bank. This is a simple strategy because a creditor can't take an asset that's already encumbered. If the doctor owns a medical office building in his or her name, this means a victorious plaintiff could claim it. But, putting the title into an entity such as a limited liability company (LLC) could possibly put that asset out of reach. Other defenses include assigning a deed to a family limited partnership or similar entity (not always ideal, since you could risk losing valuable tax breaks), or creating a qualified personal residence trust, or even fully leveraging an asset so that it holds no equity value. Again, all of these tactics must be planned ahead of time, and tax implications must be thoroughly examined.

What often happens is that people don't realize their exposure until challenged, then react after the fact by trying to hide assets. The same actions undertaken during estate planning, most experts say, will have a better chance of holding up in court because it won't look as if you were only trying to stiff creditors or avoid paying possible judgments against you. From an asset-protection perspective, the method of transferring assets into a structure is often more important than the structure itself. Transferring or attempting to move your money *after* a lawsuit is anticipated or filed will generally be struck down in court as a "fraudulent conveyance." If a court finds there has been a fraudulent conveyance, it can declare the transfer void and the assets available to creditors.

Perhaps the first step in asset protection is a thorough assessment of your assets so that you have a complete picture of what is at stake. Inventory and calculate the value of your assets—personal, family, and business. This list may help stimulate the process:

- Individual retirement accounts
- 401(k) plan or other workplace retirement accounts
- Pensions
- Insurance policies
- Annuities
- Inheritances
- Trust income
- Business assets and insurance policies
- Royalties, patents, and copyrights
- Bank, brokerage, and mutual fund accounts
- Home equity
- Other real estate
- Valuables such as jewelry, cars, and boats
- Household furnishings and possessions, such as art and silver

Once you've compiled an inventory of your assets, gather an understanding of asset-protection entities and any current rules that might have an effect on what strategies you might want to implement. For instance, when you establish a trust, you are required to notify the IRS, and just by doing that you may become a target for examination by the IRS.

No single asset-protection strategy fits all, and for every individual seeking asset protection, a custom-tailored plan should be designed. Our legal consultant, Jacob Stein, suggests that the nature of the assets to be protected should be the primary driver of asset-protection planning.

Protecting cash and securities is usually the hardest. It is also of the utmost importance, because cash and securities will be the first asset a creditor will pursue. Protecting rental or investment real estate or a part-time business is usually accomplished through the use of a limited partnership or a limited liability company. The same limited partnership or limited liability company that is so commonly used for estate planning (they are usually referred to as *family limited partnerships*) provides great protection benefits for the assets within the entity from the lawsuits directed against the individual personally.

Although a limited liability company may protect rental or investment real estate, it is a weak tool for protecting personal residences because it doesn't meet the "business purpose" criteria. For a personal residence, a common estate-planning tool known as a *residence trust* may be the best protection. Married couples should be aware that in community-property states, like California, all of the community property is liable for the debts of either spouse. This means that a lawsuit against either spouse will reach all of the couple's assets if they are not properly protected.

In non-community-property states such as New York or Florida, a creditor of one spouse can only reach the assets of that spouse. Let us assume that one spouse is a plastic surgeon, and the other one grows orchids. Obviously, the surgeon is exposed to a lot more risk. This means that some form of reallocation of assets between the two spouses should be considered, where ownership of some of the assets is moved from the high-risk spouse to the other.

The elements of effective and ethical wealth protection begin with timing, then consideration of governing laws (state, federal, and foreign), tax laws, and a good working knowledge

FIGURE 1.2

Traditional Creditor Protection Techniques

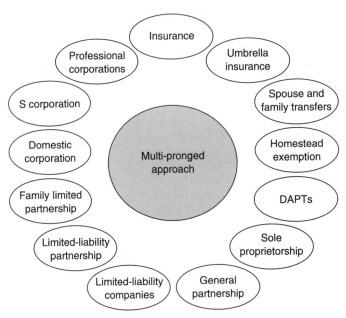

of protection strategies. The result is a multi-pronged approach encompassing a wide variety of entities, structures, and jurisdictions. (See Figure 1.2.)

A general understanding of each entity is necessary to ensure that you are indeed getting the best tax advantages, along with protection from seizure by a creditor/claimant, which is the focus of the next chapter.

CHAPTER 2

Traditional Entities

The preliminary entities of asset protection begin with the basics of necessary insurance, issues of correct title, the decision of whether or not to incorporate, which type of retirement plan is best, writing a will, and tax considerations.

The second tier involves proper utilization of entities such as living trusts, irrevocable life insurance trusts, and marital, family, or gifting trusts, along with risk management of assets that can be invested. Most people don't need to go beyond the second tier until they achieve an ultrahigh net worth.

INSURANCE

When an insurance company is on the hook for at least a portion of your liability to a creditor, you should make every attempt to transfer the onus of payment to the insurance company and away from yourself. At the very least, every business should have a general liability insurance policy; every professional should maintain malpractice coverage; and every household should have umbrella coverage, in addition to homeowner and auto liability policies. Note that life insurance is considered an asset, rather than a protection. Although most states make proceeds from a life insurance policy unavailable to creditors, the cash surrender value does not enjoy the same protection.

An *umbrella personal liability policy* provides coverage beyond normal liability policies. For example, a homeowner's policy may offer $300,000 in liability coverage against a negligence claim, and an umbrella policy may provide $1 million of additional coverage. An umbrella policy will begin to pay claims only after the liability coverage limits have been exceeded. An umbrella policy also protects in situations not covered by the liability clause found in the homeowner's and automobile insurance policies.

Umbrella insurance is not meant to act as a substitute for the professional's malpractice insurance; but, it can play an important role in improving asset protection insofar as it can often be taken into account if a court attempts a "solvency analysis" to determine whether a fraudulent transfer has occurred. Also, if litigation does arise, a plaintiff's attorney may well become fixated on chasing the limits of the umbrella insurance policy, to the exclusion of the professional's other personal assets.

Malpractice insurance was designed to transfer the risk of loss away from the insured person and to the insurance company. To the extent that it makes economic sense, malpractice insurance should always be the primary risk-management method, and asset protection should play only a secondary role.

SPOUSE AND FAMILY TRANSFERS

Married professionals occasionally put all of their worldly goods in their spouses' names for safekeeping. That tactic may or may not always work, depending on where you live. In many states, signing property over to a spouse is better than owning it together, because a creditor can force a couple to liquidate jointly held assets to collect the debtor's share. Of course, letting a spouse own everything puts the other spouse in a vulnerable position if that spouse should die or the couple later gets divorced. If the spouse is merely holding assets that the other spouse still controls—by writing checks on a bank account, for example—a creditor still has a good shot at those assets. To qualify for protection, the transferred assets must truly become the spouse's property.

In addition, shifting assets to a spouse may be in vain in states that have community-property laws, such as California and Texas. In these states, a married couple jointly owns all property acquired during the marriage, even if the property is titled in only one spouse's name. Exceptions are made for gifts, bequests, and the like. Generally, a creditor of one spouse can pursue the entire value of community property to satisfy a judgment.

In Florida, Ohio, Pennsylvania, and a number of other states, an option is a formidable version of joint ownership known as *tenancy by the entirety*. In most states that offer this option, a creditor cannot grab property unless there is a judgment against the spouse as well. However, this protection disappears if the couple gets a divorce or if the spouse dies.

Tenancy by the entirety (TBE) is a form of individual (versus corporate or partnership) co-ownership in which ownership passes automatically at the death of one co-owner to the surviving co-owner. Tenancy by the entirety ownership interests are limited to ownership by two persons who are husband and wife at the time the property is acquired. If the married couple then divorces, the form of ownership automatically changes to *tenancy in common* (TIC). Generally, tenancy by the entirety ownership is limited to real estate, although about a dozen states permit the ownership of personal property.

Tenancy in common is defined as ownership of real or personal property by two or more persons in which ownership at the death of one co-owner is part of the deceased owner's disposable estate and does not pass to the co-owner(s). Tenants in common have no right of survivorship, meaning that if one owner dies, that owner's interest in the property will pass by inheritance to that owner's devisees or heirs, either by will or by intestate succession. There is no limit to the number of persons who can acquire property as tenancy in common, and those persons could be, but need not be, married to each other.

Joint tenancy with right of survivorship occurs when two or more people maintain a joint account with a brokerage firm or a bank and it is normally agreed that, upon the death of one account holder, ownership of the account assets passes to the remaining account holder(s). The benefit of this arrangement is that the transfer of assets escapes probate, but estate taxes may still be due, and there is no creditor protection.

THE WILL

In terms of asset protection, what a will does is put a deadline on creditor claims. Imagine this nightmare: your father's estate was settled two years ago. The estate went to probate, debts were paid, and the heirs split what was left. Now a long-lost creditor surfaces and the heirs are facing a lawsuit.

When a will is probated, creditors usually have just a few months to come forward and demand payment. If the proper procedures are followed, an estate won't be liable if a creditor surfaces much later. You typically can't enjoy the benefits of this shorter time period with a living trust.

The major drawback of the will is that it is a public document. Outsiders don't know how much money you have in the bank or what else you own, but that kind of privacy can disappear upon death. Strangers may stroll into a courthouse and scrutinize anybody's probate records. They can easily learn who the heirs are, what they inherited, where they live, and many other private details.

HOMESTEAD EXEMPTION

Homestead exemptions, once considered the strongest bastion against creditors, are now subject to exceptions under the Consumer Protection Act of 2005.[1] Before the act was passed, states such as Kansas, Florida, Iowa, South Dakota, and Texas allowed unlimited homestead exemptions. The new law was originally designed to protect against abuse by corporate executives charged with financial crimes, but a last-minute revamp of the rules concerning asset protection now affects investors beyond these corporate criminals.

---

1 The key areas of the Bankruptcy Abuse Prevention and Consumer Protection Act of 2005 came from an interview by Andrew Gluck with Gideon Rothschild, a partner at the New York law firm of Moses & Singer. Mr. Rothschild is also a CPA and the former chair of the American Bar Association Committee on Asset Protection. *Investment Advisor Magazine*, 2005.

DOMESTIC ASSET-PROTECTION TRUST (DAPT)

Domestic Asset-Protection Trusts (DAPTs) cost $10,000 or so to set up, plus $2,000 to $3,000 per year to maintain, making them rather pricey, and there are other limiting caveats that may make this form of protection unfavorable. For starters, all assets must be located within the state and managed by an advisor in that state. For example, an investor from Oklahoma must have all Oklahoman assets that are managed by an Oklahoman manager. Plus, the trusts are capped at $1 million.

About 30 states that permit this form of ownership limit it to real estate. It cannot be used for assets like stocks and bank accounts. Florida and Texas allow it for both real estate and other assets. In January 2004, an asset-protection trust law took effect in Utah, enabling people to put money into an asset-protection trust, with the trust document drafted in such a way that creditors cannot gain access to the money. Since then, other states—including Oklahoma and Alaska—have joined the party, putting similar trust laws on the books.

The 2005 changes to the Bankruptcy Code have created a new 10-year limitation period for transfers to self-settled trusts that are meant to hinder, delay, or defraud creditors. (If you create a trust for your own benefit, you have established a "self-settled trust.") This effectively means that all transfers to domestic asset-protection trusts will be suspect for the 10 years prior to the date that a bankruptcy petition is filed.

Because DAPTs haven't yet been seriously tested in the courts, the big question remains whether a plaintiff who wins a judgment in New York, for example, can enforce it against a DAPT drafted in Alaska. After all, Article IV of the U.S. Constitution says states should honor other states' decisions.

SOLE PROPRIETORSHIP

A *sole proprietorship* is the most common form of business ownership. By definition, it is an unincorporated trade or business owned by an individual. Thus, a sole proprietorship is not a legal entity separate and apart from its owner. As such, *personal assets of the owner are exposed without limitation to any and all liabilities related to the conduct of this type of business.* This unlimited liability exposure is the most significant difference between sole proprietorships and other types of businesses.

Sole proprietorships are easy to establish. No special forms need to be completed. In fact, when filing your tax return, all you would need to complete in addition to your 1040 is a Schedule C (sole proprietorship). The owner can use this structure to employ family members in order to shift income among family members. However, the downside is that the practitioner would have *unlimited liability* since, under this format, all the practitioner's assets are "at risk."

GENERAL PARTNERSHIP

A *general partnership* is basically two or more owners doing business together with the intent to divide the income and profits from the undertaking. The legal aspects of partnerships are governed by state partnership statutes, most of which are in conformity with the Uniform Partnership Act (UPA) and the Revised Uniform Limited Partnership Act. Partners in general partnerships are *jointly and severally liable (without limitation) for all the debts and obligations of the partnership.* General partners can also be legally bound (and thus held financially responsible) for actions taken by any of the other partners who appear to be acting on behalf of the partnership.

Because a partner is liable for the acts of the other partners even beyond his or her ownership interest, this kind of liability exposure makes forming a general partnership extremely risky and not appropriate for protecting assets.

THE LIMITED LIABILITY COMPANY

The *limited liability company* (LLC), a relatively recent creature of state statute, is a noncorporate entity that combines the flexibility of a partnership with limited liability for all of its members, even if they participate actively in its management. It has become the entity of choice for investors worth $10 million or more. Limited liability companies and limited partnerships closely mirror foreign limited partnerships in form and function.

The state statutes generally grant limited liability company members much flexibility in determining how their business will be run. Many statutory provisions operate only by default, when the members fail to provide different ones by agreement. Most of the rules governing the internal operations of a limited liability company are contained in the members' private operating agreement, comparable to a partnership agreement or corporate bylaws. To further reinforce the asset-protection values of an LLC interest, it is advisable to include a buy-out provision in the LLC agreement allowing the entity to buy out an assignee's interest for a nominal amount.

The LLC can also be a separate legal entity (apart from its members) that owns its own assets and is liable for its debts. Therefore, the personal assets of LLC members generally are beyond the reach of LLC creditors or the other members' creditors. Likewise, a judgment against an individual member would only allow a creditor to collect from the debtor-member without disturbing the partnership business.

LLCs also have flexible ownership (some states require two members, others require only one), capital structure, and centralized management. However, some states may not recognize one-person LLCs, nor will they permit certain lines of business to use the LLC structure. Because LLCs allow members to participate fully in management without risk of losing limited liability protection, they are ideal for closely held financial-planning practices.

LIMITED LIABILITY PARTNERSHIP

The *limited liability partnership* (LLP) is a relatively new entity format that was designed as a result of the enormous personal liability problems faced by partners in legal and accounting firms. These problems arose primarily from claims of professional malpractice after the series of thrift and financial institution failures of the 1980s. The laws were written for professional practices. Because LLPs are partnerships, they are subject to partnership legal and tax considerations. The major advantage of LLPs is the ability to benefit from pass-through taxation without having to satisfy S Corporation qualification rules. However, not all states and/or professional standards of organizations (such as some state board of accountancy rules) allow certain professionals to set themselves up in this capacity. In addition, because they are partnerships by definition, LLPs must have at least two co-owners. LLP protection is not available in all states, and it may not look as attractive in states that do not offer LLC-like liability protection to LLP partners.

Beware that both LLPs and LLCs carry hefty fees: you can count on spending $2,000 to $10,000 to create one, and $500 to $2,000 a year afterward to maintain it.

A FAMILY LIMITED PARTNERSHIP

A *family limited partnership*, more recently referred to as *family limited-liability companies* (FLLCs), can be used to insulate one group of assets from others, but this takes proper planning. Jacob Stein cautions if you put all of your properties into one LLC, it could cause a domino effect. That is, if a creditor can get to one of the properties, he or she can get to all of them. Conversely, if you insulate each asset, you might lose one property, but are not likely to lose all of them.

An FLP has traditionally been one of the popular ways to hold real estate, mutual funds, bank accounts, and other possessions. One spouse may be the general partner with a 1 percent interest and managerial rights, while the couple would own the remainder as limited partners. Or one spouse may be the general partner, with the other spouse and the couple's children serving as limited partners. The general partner may then reduce the estate by gradually transferring assets to heirs in the role of limited partners.

Before you implement a family limited partnership, however, consider the following scenario. Say your spouse retains control of the assets. If you die, his or her partnership interest could be discounted for tax purposes. For one thing, it's not marketable. So $500,000 in FLP assets might be taxed, for instance, as only $300,000. The same principle also applies to gifts made to limited partners to avoid or reduce gift taxes.

On the other hand, to reach your partnership assets, your creditor must obtain a *charging order* from the court. This order entitles the creditor to any income generated by FLP assets and paid to your client. However, you or your spouse as the general partner is not obligated to distribute this income to a limited partner and won't be in any rush to do so. The creditor will be liable for taxes on the income whether it is actually received by the creditor or not. If the general partner does not release the funds, the result is a tax bill to the creditor on phantom income!

If you are thinking about establishing family limited partnerships, be aware that the IRS has lately been quite successful in attacking these. It is of the utmost importance to have them regularly reviewed by competent legal advisors, especially if you have an old partnership.

DOMESTIC CORPORATIONS

Historically, the most commonly used means of asset protection in the United States has been the *domestic corporation*. Even mutual funds, some of the largest repositories of wealth in the United States, are structured as domestic corporations. When used properly and in conjunction with other asset-protection techniques, the standard, for-profit, state-formed "C" Corporation can provide substantial asset protection for the business, but, most importantly, provides personal asset protection for the owners.

Corporate law in the United States is well developed and over time has proved largely successful in insulating shareholders from corporate liabilities. A corporation is a legal entity and separate from its stockholders, its officers, its directors, and its employees. So long as the corporation's separate identity is maintained and the corporation is not used to perpetrate a fraud, shareholders have little reason to fear that the corporate shell will be penetrated by the corporation's creditors to make the shareholders personally liable for the corporation's debts. Even corporate officers and directors are shielded from corporate liability to a significant degree.

Just the simple act of incorporating your business can protect your personal assets, reduce your taxes, and provide a universe of "fringe benefits" such as retirement plans, deferred compensation, life insurance, and medical reimbursement plans.

THE S CORPORATION

The *S Corporation* is a small business organization that qualifies for and has made the election to be treated as a pass-through entity under the federal income tax laws. This enables S Corporation shareholders to receive the profits from the business as dividends and have them escape taxation by flowing through directly to the individual shareholders' income tax returns. This avoids the double taxation of dividends.

Disadvantages include the filing of a Form 2553 to make the S Corporation election (after you have become incorporated), limited flexibility to select tax year, and no ability to retain income at lower current tax cost. In addition, S Corporations are subject to strict eligibility requirements with failure to meet these requirements resulting in profits being subject to double taxation. S Corporations only permit one class of stock.

THE PROFESSIONAL CORPORATION

The *professional corporation* encapsulates the liability from claims, such as employment practices claims made by staff, certain toxic materials claims, etc.

Just as with any other corporation, a professional corporation does not protect an individual from liability for her or his own personal actions. Just as a shareholder who is at fault in an auto accident that occurs on company property is not protected from personal liability, neither is a professional who commits negligence. A professional corporation only shields the professional owner from the ordinary liabilities of the business, such as contractual liabilities for office supplies, equipment leases, etc.

In an attempt to attract new business, some states have adopted new corporation laws that claim to offer certain asset-protection benefits. In many ways, states are no different than some offshore countries who tout asset-protection advantages. Nevada has by far been the most aggressive state in promoting its enticing corporate laws. Indeed, within only 10 years, Nevada's corporate industry has grown to rival Delaware's, the traditional asset-protection refuge. There is no corporate income or franchise tax, but this applies only to the business conducted in Nevada. Nevada law may make it difficult for creditors seeking judgments to discern the ownership of a corporation, but there simply is no absolute secrecy or confidentiality associated with Nevada corporations. Because of aggressive and often fraudulent marketing by corporate Nevada promoters, the state is slowly acquiring the same shady reputation that has adversely affected offshore debtor and tax havens. Some promoters market these corporations as a secret vehicle that will save taxes and protect assets from the Internal Revenue Service (IRS)—and none of that is true. The bottom line is that if you're a doctor in California, a Nevada corporation will do very little for you in any way. Nevada does not have an agreement with the IRS to share information. But if you're sued and you're under oath to give information about your assets, you have to tell somebody about your Nevada corporation; otherwise you're under penalty of perjury. There are legitimate jurisdictions, legitimate products, and legitimate vehicles for a given situation.

INTERLOCKING OWNERSHIPS

Ideally, you could create *interlocking ownerships* through a holding company structure. In a simple holding company structure, two tiers of companies exist. The lower tier is comprised of companies that are actively conducting business, holding business assets, employing people, etc. These are the liability-prone companies. The upper tier is comprised of one or more companies with few employees that conduct no business other than owning stock in the lower-tier companies.

Holding companies have in the past been utilized by tax planners to create situations involving interlocking ownership. That arrangement drives down the percentage of ownership held by a taxpayer, yet still allows the taxpayer to retain control. For

U.S. persons, the Internal Revenue Code has attribution rules that seriously restrict the effectiveness of these structures. Interlocking ownerships may offer some asset-protection advantages.

Once you have distinguished the proper application of these elementary creditor protection means, your next consideration is the trust, both domestic and foreign.

CHAPTER 3

Redefining Safe Harbors— The Use of Trusts

Our legal expert Jacob Stein believes that trusts are the heart and soul of asset-protection planning, due mostly to the fact that trusts separate beneficial ownership of assets from legal ownership. The beneficiaries of a trust are the beneficial owners of the assets, but they do not hold legal title to the assets. The legal title is vested in the trustee of the trust. The trustee of a trust thus stands in the position of a fiduciary to the beneficiaries. The trustee holds title to the trust assets for the benefit of the beneficiaries.

A creditor holding a judgment against a debtor can generally reach any asset owned by the debtor, with certain exceptions such as retirement plans. To the extent the debtor does not own an asset but does possess beneficial enjoyment of the asset, the creditor can also gain access to that beneficial enjoyment of the asset. Finally, even if the debtor does not own the asset or have beneficial enjoyment of the asset, if the debtor can, at his or her discretion, gain access to that asset, so can the creditor.

In the world of asset protection, debtors thus strive to achieve two incompatible goals:

- They want to possess the beneficial enjoyment or control of assets, whether through direct ownership or otherwise.

- They also want to distance themselves from the ownership and control over the assets, to make such assets
  inaccessible to creditors.

In this obvious dichotomy, trusts come to the rescue. However, trust documents are becoming increasingly intricate, and their powerful hold over heirs is tending to last for longer periods of time. Because trusts often exist for many decades, a great deal of thought must go into their creation.

Most legal jurisdictions allow us to specifically provide for a trustee's powers, duties, and obligations. A trustee's powers can be broadly or specifically defined in the trust; they can be enlarged or limited. For example, a trust may allow the trustee to take any action necessary to provide for a productive investment of assets. By the same token, the trust may prohibit a trustee from making certain distributions, such as a distribution to a beneficiary that would be attached by a creditor.

By (1) properly structuring a trustee's powers and allowable actions, (2) properly identifying the appropriate trust partici-pants, and (3) picking the right jurisdiction, the asset-protection benefits of trusts can be successfully utilized.

CREATING A LIVING TRUST

For many Americans, the living trust has replaced the will. A *living trust* is a document that allows an estate to pass its assets directly to the deceased's heirs instead of going through probate court. However, although a living trust will avoid probate and will allow the trust owner to specify how certain assets will be distributed, it will not save taxes and it will not protect the deceased's assets. The avoidance of probate—and of having one's assets made public and placed at the risk of creditors—is the living trust's most important feature. But don't let anyone tell you that a living trust will save you taxes or protect your assets in any way.

Living trusts are difficult to challenge and harder to contest than a will. A will can be disputed without even hiring an attor-ney. The open nature of the probate process also makes it easier for creditors to challenge a will. Trust administration is a much more private and, therefore, more protected process.

Challenging a living trust's provisions is tough because assets can typically be divided up much more quickly. By the time somebody protests, the checks may already have been mailed out. At this point, the challenger would face the daunting prospect of separately suing the beneficiaries and the trustee.

The secrecy of a living trust could also cut down on potential challenges. Family members, for instance, may never discover that a special friend or a charity was given a generous bequest. A living trust can also be handy for those who wish to give unequal inheritances to their children.

The more sophisticated *AB trust*, also known as a *living trust with marital life estate*, lets a couple pass the maximum amount of property to their children. The assets are owned inside the trust and are thus protected from creditors or lawsuits, plus you get a federal estate tax benefit because taxation to a nonspouse beneficiary is eliminated. Another creative form is the *irrevocable life insurance trust* (ILIT).

Here's a simple example of how this works for both tax benefits and asset protection: Max Brendan, a local real estate developer and contractor, has $3 million in life insurance, and upon Max's death that money would go to his spouse, Bernice. There would be no tax on that death benefit because the irrevocable life insurance trust is the owner of the life insurance, so upon Max's death the $3 million goes into the trust. Bernice was made trustee of the trust, so she still has access to the interest, dividends, and corpus, as needed; and at her death, the principal would go to her children/heirs with no federal estate tax. An irrevocable life insurance trust might cost $1,000 to set up, but would save $1.5 million in tax. Now, say, Max had partners in his construction firm, who, for whatever reason, seek monetary contribution or reparation from Max's estate. Because the ILIT owns the insurance policy (not Max's estate), the $3 million is protected for Bernice.

While many factors contribute to the asset-protection benefits of trusts, there are two types of trusts that are of overriding benefit and, thus, importance—spendthrift and discretionary.

Spendthrift Trusts

A *spendthrift trust* is a type of irrevocable trust that either limits or altogether prevents a beneficiary from being able to access the principal or the income of the trust. The income and the principal are not paid to someone else; the beneficiary simply has no discretion as to when and how much will be distributed from the trust to him or her.

For example, an oil tycoon, who is worried that his daughter will spend her entire inheritance on a shopping spree in Paris, will provide in the trust for periodic distributions of cash to the daughter, and at the same time remove the daughter's ability to invade the trust and, thus, anticipate her distributions.

Spendthrift trusts have traditionally been used to provide for beneficiaries who are incompetent or improvident. However, a spendthrift trust can be established for any type of a beneficiary, without that requirement. Today, almost every trust incorporates a spendthrift clause, but there is no mandatory language that needs to be used to create a spendthrift trust. The only two requirements are a valid trust and a clear intention by the settlor to make the trust spendthrift.

The beneficiary's inability to transfer his or her interest binds the creditor, making it impossible for the creditor to attach the beneficiary's interest. [1]

The ability of a settlor to create a spendthrift trust, thereby defeating a beneficiary's creditors, is grounded in the high value our society places on property ownership rights.

Property owners are allowed to dispose of their assets in any manner they see fit. Allowing a creditor of a spendthrift trust's beneficiary to override the settlor's intent to provide for a beneficiary would negate the settlor's property rights. Further, a settlor has no obligation to make his or her wealth available to a beneficiary's creditors; consequently, such creditors have no basis on which to object if the settlor declines to do so.

The protection of the spendthrift trust extends solely to the property that is in the trust. Once the property has been

---

1 In California, the spendthrift trust is recognized in California Probate Code Sections 15300 and 15301.

distributed to the beneficiary, that property can now be reached by a creditor. Even if the beneficiary refuses such distribution and elects to retain money in the trust, the spendthrift protection of the trust ceases with respect to that distribution and the beneficiary's creditors can now reach that money. As in all other instances, whenever a debtor gains control over property (control that allows the debtor to use the property for his or her own benefit, not someone else's), the creditors can reach that property.[2]

The next type of trust solves that problem by removing the requirement that the trustee make periodic distributions to the beneficiary. As a matter of fact, discretionary trusts remove any requirement that a trustee may be subject to with respect to distributions.

Discretionary Trusts

A trust is called *discretionary* when the trustee has "discretion" in making distributions (as to the timing, amount, and the beneficiary). Because the trustee is not required to make distributions, a beneficiary is less likely to receive a distribution that would be reachable by a creditor. While protection from creditors may be the primary concern, little will be accomplished if the beneficiary, while being protected from creditors, is left at the mercy of the trustee.

For any trust that is drafted with pure asset protection in mind, the trustee's powers must be fully permissive. Permissive powers are those that are exercisable in a trustee's discretion, and a court will generally not substitute its judgment for the trustee's (provided that the trustee acts in good faith and reasonably). Property that may be distributed to a beneficiary pursuant to a permissive interest is not recognized as a future (and certainly not present) interest. Consequently, such property is outside the reach of the creditor.

In a discretionary trust, there is no need to impose a spendthrift restriction on the beneficiary. Because the beneficiary's

---

2 In California, this is also recognized by statute. See California Probate Code Section 15301(b).

interest in the trust is so tenuous, the beneficiary has no ability to anticipate distributions or alienate his or her interest in the trust.[3]

However, similar to spendthrift trusts, once a distribution has been made to the beneficiary, such a distribution is reachable by a creditor.

Fortunately, most state jurisdictions offer the beneficiaries some protection, even from the trustee. An example is that in California the Probate Code Section 16080 provides that the trustee must exercise his or her discretion reasonably. Even if the trustee's discretion is "sole and absolute," the trustee's duty of care prevents the exercise of the discretion from being arbitrary and capricious.

I asked Jacob Stein what, if any, limitation is on the protection afforded by a discretionary trust. He pointed to the rule against self-settled trusts, "The greatest restriction on the asset-protection benefits of trusts, in most jurisdictions, is the prohibition against the so-called self-settled trusts."

Self-Settled Trusts

A *self-settled trust* is a trust where the settlor of the trust is also a beneficiary. A *settlor* is any person who "settles" a trust, that is, contributes property to the trust. The settlor does not need to be the sole contributor of property to the trust, just one of the contributors. This means that any time a beneficiary of a trust contributes property to that trust, the trust becomes self-settled as to that beneficiary. For example, a husband and wife establish a trust for their own benefit, and each one contributes half of community property. The trust will be self-settled as to each spouse.

The ability of the settlor to control his or her own property is of paramount policy concern, which is the reason why spendthrift trusts protect beneficiaries from creditors. However, allowing a person to set up a trust for his or her own benefit and

---

3 California Probate Code Section 15303(a) provides that in a discretionary trust, a creditor of the beneficiary may not compel the trustee to pay any amount. Furthermore, the limitations placed on the protection of spendthrift trusts (creditor's ability to reach 25 percent of distributions and piercing for support payments) do not apply to discretionary trusts.

thus defeat the claims of creditors would be blatant. Historically, self-settled trusts never afforded the beneficiaries any protection from creditors, and in many jurisdictions that continues to be true even today. If a trust is self-settled, that means only that the interests of the beneficiary in the trust are not protected from creditors. It does not mean that the trust is invalid, nor does it offer other benefits. The trust may still allow the settlor to avoid probate and to provide for beneficiaries.

Mr. Stein also points out that a self-settled trust can be the result of a direct settlement by the beneficiary (i.e., the beneficiary contributes property to the trust), or an indirect settlement. For example, if the beneficiary provides consideration to settle a trust, such trust will be deemed self-settled even if the beneficiary did not directly contribute the money to the trust. Thus, if the beneficiary settles the lawsuit and causes the other party to contribute money to the trust, the beneficiary will be treated as settling the trust. Similarly, if the beneficiary uses an intermediary or an agent to settle the trust, the trust will be deemed self-settled by the beneficiary. The courts will not allow beneficiaries to circumvent the self-settled trust rules by employing any roundabout tactics.

The prohibition against allowing self-settled trusts to afford creditor protection in most U.S. jurisdictions has been one of the contributing factors to the rise of foreign trusts that are sited in the jurisdictions that do not strip self-settled trusts of their spendthrift protection. In reaction, several U.S. jurisdictions recently entered the lucrative asset-protection trust market by striking their self-settled trust statutes and affording creditor protection to self-settled trusts.

These trusts are usually formed in Alaska, Nevada, or Delaware ("providing states"). The providing states' statutes allow that self-settled trusts funded with assets of the settlor will still qualify for certain levels of creditor protection from the creditors of the settlor. They are essentially the domestic versions of foreign asset-protection trusts (FAPTs). Some even have "flight" provisions, wherein, in the case of creditor attack, the assets are relocated offshore. Flight provisions are provisions that allow the trustee to move the domicile of the trust as well as the assets from one location to another under certain circumstances. For instance, someone finds out that you have an offshore trust in Antigua. Then your creditor's lawyer notifies the trustee in Antigua that he or she is going to come to file a lawsuit. With a flight provision, you could move the assets to another location to avoid the lawsuit.

The topic of offshore or foreign trusts is so steeped in predisposition and confusion that the next two chapters are devoted to evaluating their contribution to asset protection.

Glossary of Trust Terms

Whether you are creating or inheriting a trust, you should know the terminology:

Bypass trust (also known as a shelter trust)—If you're married and your estate has any chance of being smacked by federal estate taxes, you'll want a bypass shelter trust. A bypass shelter trust allows a husband and wife to each enjoy what's rightfully theirs: a limited free ride on estate tax obligations. If you're smart enough to claim it, the federal government offers each person an estate tax credit.

Executor—Person or institution named in a will to carry out its instructions. A woman selected for this job is called an executrix.

Fiduciary—Person who holds a position of trust. Trustees and executors are called fiduciaries because the law requires that they responsibly carry out a will and/or trust's dictates. A bank or trust company that serves this role is called a corporate fiduciary.

Grantor—Person who creates a trust; also can be called a settlor or trust creator.

Irrevocable trust—A trust that can't be canceled or changed by its grantor after it's established.

Remaindermen—The people who receive what's left of a trust when it terminates.

Revocable trust—A trust that can be changed or dismantled while the grantor is still alive (such as a living trust).

Successor trustee—Person or institution that takes over as trustee when the original trustee(s) has died or become incapacitated.

Testamentary trust—A trust created by a will.

Trust corpus—Name for property that's put into a trust.

Trustee—A trustee holds legal title to the trust assets for the benefit of the beneficiaries.

CHAPTER 4

Riches Out of Reach— Use and Domestication of Foreign Trusts

A foreign trust differs from a domestic trust because of the following characteristics:

1. Increased ability of the settlor to retain benefit and control
2. Less likely to be pursued by a creditor
3. Foreign jurisdictions usually are more beneficial to the debtor statute of limitations, burden of proof, and other important provisions
4. No full faith and credit, comity, or supremacy clause issues
5. Favorable to the debtor spendthrift provision laws
6. Provides confidentiality and privacy
7. Flexibility

Transfers of assets to the "foreign" trust will be treated as a sale for tax purposes. To avoid the sale treatment on the funding of the trust, most foreign trusts are drafted as grantor trusts. Being grantor trusts, they avoid sale treatment on funding and remain tax neutral during their existence.

For nearly two decades, the U.S. government has attempted to discourage people from moving assets offshore. The Treasury Department requires that offshore asset-protection strategies be as transparent as possible and, under IRS rules, every creation of every offshore foreign trust by a U.S. person must be reported. There is virtually no income tax advantage to a foreign trust, and the "offshore" aspect alone may make you a target for examination by the agency. The trusts are usually somewhat expensive to set up and maintain properly, but failure to maintain them properly can lead to disastrous U.S. tax consequences. Unscrupulous advisors sometimes recommend trusts as "tax savings plans." Under most circumstances, over the years, the IRS and Congress have closed most of the loopholes. There are no ways to legally save taxes with an offshore asset-protection trust.

There are also significant annual reporting requirements for all parties involved (including the foreign trustee). Offshore trusts have been especially affected by the Patriot Act, causing many wealthy investors to bring their money back to the United States because of the new time-consuming reporting requirements for international investing. With broad powers born out of policy wars against drugs, terrorism, and money laundering, the United States can now unearth and examine the most private financial matters of its citizens almost anywhere in the world.

So, why bother?

The primary advantage of foreign trusts derives from "jurisdictional immunity." This means, essentially, that courts in other countries do not recognize U.S. legal judgments. Offshore trusts in general do not protect assets from creditors, but they do shield money from the gaze of perfunctory investigations while providing jurisdictional immunity.

THE OFFSHORE ASSET-PROTECTION TRUST (OAPT)

The offshore trust is the investment vehicle that the fewest number of creditors are going to go after because they know it's going to cost time and money. Those trying to seize an individual's offshore assets must relitigate in the country where their target has his or her money. They must hire a legal team in that country and navigate the entire administrative process of presenting a case from scratch. By the time they litigate their claim in the other jurisdiction, they will probably have wasted most or all of the money they might have received. Instead, they may want to negotiate a settlement.

While a deep discussion is beyond the scope of this chapter, the chosen jurisdiction and the choice of trust law must be examined carefully by an experienced advisor as there are other risk factors to be considered (e.g., foreign revolution, government seizure of foreign assets, risks of local taxes, history of English Common Law in the jurisdiction, etc.).

Still, foreign trusts are not panaceas. They are not for everyone, nor should they be marketed en masse. You should own enough vulnerable assets to justify spending the $20,000 or more in fees for the legal structures, plus the annual maintenance and associated costs of rigorous compliance notices. If you have less than $5 million of investable assets, if you live in the United States, if the assets are going to remain in the United States, and if you have no intention of ever leaving the United States, it probably doesn't make sense for you to set up a foreign trust. Although from a practical standpoint this might be true, everyone's circumstances are different. Depending upon the facts and circumstances of your situation, there might be a different outcome.

Generally, a foreign trust is most effective when it holds foreign assets. Foreign trusts are truly efficient for asset-protection purposes only if liquid assets are used to fund the trusts, and such assets are, at some point, transferred offshore. While a foreign asset-protection trust can hold any property, including personal and real property in the United States, the ability of a U.S. court to reach U.S. property suggests the benefits of holding only offshore assets in the foreign trust. This would be appropriate if you have a viable business offshore. But if you're a doctor delivering babies in California, for instance, an offshore trust isn't going to do a lot for your U.S.-based assets such as real estate or a business operated within the United States. The best way to ensure protection is by liquidating U.S.-based assets, then investing your cash proceeds through an offshore limited liability company. (For a more detailed discussion, refer to Appendix C, "Foreign LLC and Trust Combos.")

Who is the "right" candidate for a foreign asset-protection trust? Any U.S. person looking for asset protection through diversification of 10 to 30 percent of his or her overall wealth over time while understanding that the professional trustee will make the investment decisions, not the settlor. In other words, you are seeking legitimate *investment diversification*. That being said, there are other offshore vehicles available, such as annuity products, that meet diversification needs and still place assets beyond the reach of investigators and creditors, while complying with U.S. tax and reporting laws. But, we'll take a look at how to manage the risk of the deterioration of your wealth from economic causes in Part Two.

For those readers who do fit the criteria to avail yourself of a foreign trust, the rest of this chapter will supply a sort of safety net to your process.

"Domesticating" the Foreign Trust

There are various practical and legal aspects to structuring the foreign trust. The first consideration is always the choice of the jurisdiction which will govern the trust. Most common law jurisdictions have very similar trust laws based on the English common law system. However, certain foreign countries, in an effort to attract trust business, have modernized their trust laws, with the singular purpose of making such laws more debtor-friendly.

The following factors should be considered when evaluating a foreign trust situs jurisdiction:

- Nonrecognition of foreign judgments
- Recognition of self-settled trusts
- No local taxation
- Debtor-friendly fraudulent transfer laws, including short statute of limitations and high burden of proof
- Availability of competent and reliable trustees
- Availability of competent local attorneys and banks
- British Commonwealth–based culture and legal system
- Trust assets are not reachable by creditors, or in the event settlor files bankruptcy
- Stable political environment

Additionally, it is beneficial if the jurisdiction does *not* have a rule against perpetuities, and thus allows dynasty trusts. (Normally, a trust must have a certain defined period, but with a dynasty trust there is no rule against perpetuities.) While this is not an asset-protection benefit, it can be a valuable estate planning tool.

The foreign trust should also not upset the community property relationship of spouses. Most trusts do not affect the nature of the assets transferred into the trust. This should remain true when a foreign jurisdiction is used and should have a provision respecting the community property or separate property nature of the assets in the trust. (See Table 4.1.)

From an asset-protection standpoint, three jurisdictions stand out from the rest of the pack: the Cook Islands in the South Pacific, Nevis, and St. Vincent and the Grenadines in the West Indies because of having the following provisions favorable to the debtor:

- Nonrecognition of foreign judgments
- "Beyond a reasonable doubt" standard for fraudulent transfers[1]
- A short statute of limitations for fraudulent transfers
- Allowance of self-settled trusts
- Ability by the settlor/beneficiary to retain some control

Interestingly, New Zealand, which is closely tied to the Cook Islands (a former protectorate of New Zealand), has recently been gaining popularity as an asset-protection destination—probably because it is not considered "notorious." While New Zealand does not tax trusts that generate their income elsewhere and does recognize self-settled trusts, it is not an ideal jurisdiction because it will also recognize a U.S. judgment and has a relatively long statute of limitations on fraudulent transfers (four years).

While the choice of the jurisdiction is important, it does not guarantee protection, depending on the actual location of the assets. For instance, offshore bank accounts provide no real

---

1 There are several applicable standards of proof: (1) the lesser standard of "by a preponderance of evidence," (2) the higher standard of "clear and convincing evidence," and (3) the highest standard of "beyond a reasonable doubt."

TABLE 4.1

Asset-Protection Planning Guide

Nation or State	Statutory certainty regarding nonrecognition of foreign judgments	Beyond reasonable doubt standard of proof required in establishing fraudulent intent	Statutory certainty that settlor can be a beneficiary	Statutory certainty that settlor can retain some degree of control
Bahamas	*		X	X
Belize	X		X	X
Bermuda				
Cayman Islands				
Cook Islands	X	X	X	X
Cyprus			X	
Gibraltar				
Labuan	X	X	X	X
Mauritius		X	X	
Nevis	X	X	X	X
St. Vincent & Grenadines	X	X	X	X
Seychelles		X	X	X
Turks & Caicos				
New Zealand			X	X
United States				
Alaska			X	X
Colorado			X	
Delaware			X	X
Missouri				
Nevada			X	X
Rhode Island			X	X

*Bahamas law provides for nonrecognition of foreign judgments unless such a judgment is obtained in France, England, or Gibraltar. While some believe that Gibraltar law provides "instant" protection if the transferor is solvent following the transfers, post-transfers solvency of the transferor and hence the validity of transferor may be subject to a challenge.

asset protection at all. If you have an offshore bank account that has had more than $10,000 in it at any time over the tax year, you must declare it on Schedule B of your income tax return. You are also required to complete a more detailed form (TDF 90-22.1) and file it with the U.S.Treasury Department by June 30 of the year after your reporting.

The United States, working in tandem with a coalition of European tax authorities, established several treaties with the governments of tax havens that soften privacy rules and force banks in these nations to give up tax evaders or freeze accounts when faced with a court order from the U.S. Justice Department. The IRS also signed Qualified Intermediary (QI) agreements directly with banks doing business in offshore havens. In return for collecting and filing information on their U.S.-based customers with the IRS, QI banks gain several regulatory advantages in their dealings with the IRS and the Treasury Department. QI banks also have access to the U.S. financial markets.

Additionally, U.S. judges who favor traditional law may seek ways to undermine the protective benefits of these foreign jurisdictions, or may simply dislike the idea of being unable to exercise their power over these foreign jurisdictions. Such judges are then sympathetic to creditors attempting to overcome the protective benefits of foreign trusts.

Technically, if personal assets are titled in the foreign trust, then the law of the foreign jurisdiction shall control. But this choice of law analysis only works if the existence of the trust is respected. The judge may ignore the foreign trust. If the assets are within the judge's jurisdiction, he or she may exercise the judicial powers directly over the assets. Chances are that domestic financial institutions will cooperate with a judicial order, even if it is attempting to circumvent the trust.

Certain offshore jurisdictions may have trust laws that may be seen as being in violation of a U.S. state's public policy. For example, most states allow creditors to penetrate spendthrift trusts for alimony and child support. If the foreign jurisdiction does not allow any creditor such access, the U.S. judge may seek to do whatever is in his or her power to comply with the state's public policy.

There are two factors influencing whether a settlor of a foreign trust should retain trust assets in the United States. First, it is a possibility—not a certainty—that a U.S. judge may ignore the existence of the foreign trust and go directly after the domestic assets. Although it is just as likely that the creditor may never get to the judge because the mere existence of the foreign trust may (and usually does) dissuade the creditor from attempting to collect.

Second, the location of the assets is relevant only at the time of collection. It does not matter where the assets are located before the judgment comes down and the creditor is able to collect. This means that a debtor can create a foreign trust, but keep the assets of the trust in the United States, so long as the debtor is in a position to move quickly in the event of a collection action.

Moving quickly means transferring liquid assets to an offshore account outside the jurisdiction of a U.S. court. U.S. securities should be sold and the cash transferred offshore. Quickly liquidating real estate is more problematic. Consequently, domestic real estate could be held through a limited liability company (or a limited partnership in some cases), which in turn is owned by the foreign trust. The limited liability company will make it more difficult for the creditor to get to the real estate, possibly giving the debtor time to liquidate the real estate and transfer the cash offshore.

For fraudulent transfer law purposes, it is the timing of the transfer into the trust that controls. It is not relevant what type of assets the foreign trust is holding. In most states, the statute of limitations for bringing a fraudulent transfer action begins running on the date the transfer is perfected (generally, four years, but longer in some states), or on the date of discovery of the transfer if the transfer was secretive (generally, two years).

It is important to note that fraudulent transfers do not require a finding of fraud or any ill intent on behalf of the debtor and do not incur damages, punitive or otherwise. They are valid transfers, but may be voided by a creditor if the transfer diminishes the value of property in which a debtor holds a beneficial interest.

Great care should also be exercised in picking the foreign trustee. Because the trustee will be geographically removed from the settlor, it would be difficult for the settlor to supervise the trustee's actions. Consequently, a reputable trustee, with a long and well established track record should be selected. The trustee should be a financially solid institution. Often, debtors who settle foreign trusts opt for very large institution trustees, like trust departments of large international banks. While such trustees are financially secure and are unlikely to dissipate funds, they may not be as service-oriented as the smaller more specialized trustees. A trustee's flexibility and commitment to the settlor are at least as important as the trustee's financial stability and integrity.

The foreign trustee selected should have no U.S. contacts, directly or indirectly, through affiliates, subsidiaries, agents, or representatives because they might otherwise risk having "minimum contacts"[2] with the United States, thus becoming subject to the jurisdiction of a U.S. court.

Additionally, it is important to properly characterize the trustee's powers in the trust. This is a common dilemma facing settlors. Settlors want to retain control over the trust assets and retain access to the assets, while sufficiently removing themselves from the trust so as not to have any control for the "contempt" analysis (see below).

This is usually accomplished by the use of a discretionary trust, wherein the trustee has full discretion in deciding when, to whom, and how much to distribute from the trust. The discretionary trust is supplemented with a "letter of wishes" which is a nonbinding expression of the settlor's intentions. The letter of wishes can advise the trustee on how the settlor would like the trustee to exercise its discretionary powers. Because the letter of wishes is merely a statement of the settlor's intent and is not binding on the trustee, it is not treated adversely in the "contempt" analysis. The letter of wishes may be updated on an annual basis.

A settlor may also wish to appoint an independent third party as a trust advisor or a trust protector. The job of this independent (but friendly to the settlor) third party would be to assist the trustee in making decisions with respect to distributions from the trust, and other discretionary powers of the trustee.

---

2 The minimum contacts test is the requisite threshold to establish nexus under the due process clause.

Because a trust advisor or a trust protector may be viewed in the same capacity as a trustee, it is inadvisable to have such person in the United States, unless the advisor's/protector's powers are merely passive. If the powers are passive, meaning the advisor/protector can veto a trustee's decision or remove the trustee, but cannot force or advise the trustee to undertake an action, then such person may reside in the United States. There would be no power that such advisor/protector possesses that may be used by a U.S. court to the detriment of the debtor.

Although the trustee will be prohibited from making distributions to the settlor on the occurrence of certain "triggering events," the trustee should be given discretion to make distributions to other beneficiaries. For example, the trustee may be given the power to distribute to the spouse of the settlor (provided that the spouse is not also a debtor, specifically or by the application of community property laws) or to the children of the settlor.

Other threats of an unpredictable and remote nature involving political turmoil or a trustee's dissipating a debtor's fund for its own benefit are a common concern; but the most often encountered risk of the foreign trust is susceptibility to the "contempt" charge.

Creditors usually realize how difficult it would be for them, if at all possible, to retrieve assets from a foreign trust—thus, the efficacy of foreign trusts. In light of that, creditors attempt to find ways to get around the barrier presented by the trust. They turn to the one person who can help them retrieve assets from the trust—the debtor.

Debtors who establish foreign asset-protection trusts will at times retain certain powers over the trusts (see Appendix B, "Estate Planning with Offshore Defective Grantor Trusts"). The powers may be as narrow as a limited power of appointment, or as broad as a debtor acting as the trustee of the trust. Retention of such powers not only poses a risk that the trust will be disregarded as a separate entity, but also subjects the debtor to the risk of being made to exercise such powers.

Creditors will turn to the court to make the debtor exercise whatever power the debtor may have, or be viewed as having, over the trust. If the court buys the creditor's argument, the court will order the debtor to satisfy the creditor's judgment from the trust's assets. If the debtor does not comply with the court order, the debtor may be held in contempt of court.

There are two types of contempt: civil and criminal. The same action or inaction of the debtor may be subject to both types of contempt. Additionally, both types of contempt involve the imposition of similar sanctions: payment of money, imprisonment, or both.

Contempt is generally defined as an act of disobedience to an order of a court or an act of disrespect of a court. A party cannot be held in contempt unless it has willfully disobeyed a court order. Thus, when a court orders a defendant to pay money or produce documents, the defendant must have the present ability to pay the funds or produce the documents requested at the time of the contempt proceedings before an order of contempt will stand.[3]

In a foreign trust situation, the debtor would usually have no money available; therefore the sanction would be limited to imprisonment. In a civil contempt case, the purpose of the imprisonment would be to coerce the debtor to retrieve the money from the foreign trust, or remain in jail. Criminal contempt is nothing more than punishment by the court for the debtor's conduct. Criminal contempt has a high burden of proof, and usually requires a jury trial. It rarely applies to asset-protection cases because criminal contempt cannot be used coercively (i.e., the debtor will spend time in jail regardless of whether any money is retrieved from the trust).

If courts could use civil contempt at will, foreign trusts would not be very effective or, at the very least, debtors would find themselves spending time in jail. Obviously that does not happen. The reason for that is the "impossibility" defense.

The debtor cannot be expected to do what is practically impossible. A court cannot order the debtor to leap the Mississippi River in a single bound and then hold the debtor in contempt until he or she complies, at least not if the debtor attempted to comply. Thus, with one limited exception, impossibility is a complete defense to a contempt charge.[4]

---

3 *Bowen v. Bowen*, 471 So. 2d 1274 (Fla. 1985).
4 *U.S. v. Bryan*, 339 U.S. 323, 330 (1950); *U.S. v. Rylander*, 460 U.S. 752, 757 (1983).

The one limited exception to the impossibility defense is when the impossibility is self-created. However, the impossibility must not only be self-created, but must be self-created in bad faith (e.g., close in time to the court order). Thus, when the defendant destroyed records several days before the court order to produce the documents, that was a self-created impossibility proximate to the time of the order, and thus not a bar to contempt.[5] This is an additional reason to plan in advance.

If contempt is used by the court coercively (i.e., in an attempt to force the debtor to achieve a certain result), if the result is impossible, no amount of coercion will achieve that result. Foreign asset-protection trusts are premised on the impossibility defense.

Foreign asset-protection trusts are drafted as discretionary trusts, with the trustee having full power to make distributions. Additionally, the trustee is specifically prohibited from making a distribution to the settlor or any beneficiary, if such person is being pursued by a creditor (a duress event). A duress event will always serve as an absolute bar on any distribution to the settlor, either by the terms of the trust or by the terms of the applicable trust law of the jurisdiction where the trust is being administered. The trustee is not allowed either to disregard the directions of the trust or to ignore the local trust law statutes.

To have an effective impossibility defense, the settlor-debtor must not have any power to retrieve any money from the trust.

The importance of this is underscored by the now infamous Anderson case.[6] In the Anderson case, the debtors placed the proceeds of their criminal activities in a foreign trust. The court ordered the Andersons to repatriate trust assets and when they failed to do so, they were held in contempt of court.

The Andersons attempted to use the impossibility defense, but were unsuccessful because the impossibility was self-created and very close in time to the court order. The Andersons were

---

5 U.S. v. Goldstein, 105 F. 2d 150 (2nd Cir. 1939).
6 *Federal Trade Commission v. Affordable Media, LLC*, 179 F. 3d 1228 (9th Cir. 1999). The case is commonly referred to as the Anderson case because those were the names of the debtors.

initially the trustees of their foreign trust. They continued to act as trustees throughout the litigation process and did not step down until after the court order. After the court order to repatriate assets, the Andersons stepped down and appointed a foreign trustee. Very clearly, their impossibility to repatriate assets was not only self-created, but with very bad timing.

The debtor bears the burden to prove the impossibility defense. Thus, the Andersons had to demonstrate that they did not retain sufficient control over the trust, which they failed to do in court, but proved six months later from jail.

Although many professionals have been sold on offshore trusts, what happens in real life is that the debtor doesn't want either to flee the country or spend time in jail, so when litigation arises, they end up abandoning the offshore trust that they spent so much to create.

Obviously, building the right structure from the beginning can save you the trouble of trying to hide your assets later. To be truly protected, assets titled in a foreign trust must be located beyond the jurisdiction of a U.S. court long before a judgment against the debtor. If the debtor opens a bank account, the bank must not have any branches in the United States. The same applies to brokerage accounts. If the trust owns a foreign entity, the entity and all its assets must be outside of the United States.

Educate yourself about countries that afford asset-protection features along with estate and investment planning solutions not normally found in typical offshore trusts. In addition, consult with legal counsel about what laws apply in the event of a legal attack and how those laws may differ based on offshore jurisdiction.

Legal options still abound for those seeking to shelter assets abroad. Look for those jurisdictions (such as Switzerland) where asset protection is a part of public policy and has existing laws that have been tested in the courts. Because of Switzerland's strict privacy laws[7], the Swiss annuity by default is creditor and judgment proof. Switzerland does not honor U.S. judgments, nor do Swiss insurance companies issue reports to any governmental

---

7 Article 47, Switzerland Bank Secrecy Act of 1934.

agency of the initial purchase of the policy, or the payments into it, or the interest and/or dividends earned. Also, insurance contracts are viewed completely differently by the IRS because there are legitimate estate-planning reasons for investing in them. Learn more about Swiss annuities, variable annuities, and private insurance portfolios in Part Three.

PART TWO

Investment Protection Theory

In Part One we discussed beneficial jurisdictions, vehicles, and asset-protection strategies, but protecting your assets doesn't stop at just limiting your exposure to legal judgments and various taxes. Maximizing your investments under the umbrella of a qualified retirement plan (in compliance with the Employee Retirement Income Security Act (ERISA) will compound those benefits. But, there are limits to the amount of your pretax contributions.

Since there are many excellent books written entirely on the subjects of both qualified and nonqualified retirement plans and their complex nuances, we won't delve into this area. However, the investments inside the retirement plans are still subject to *market risk*—another major consideration for protecting your wealth.

Using proven investment principles to guide how you invest and distribute your assets can help reduce unnecessary investment risks while maximizing your returns. The following chapters will provide these guidelines that, once understood, should remove much of the guesswork related to investing, with the ultimate goal of protecting your wealth.

The Basic Principles of Successful Investing

Recently, an advisor friend spoke to me about one of his clients. A cardiologist, Dr. Grasmere, for whom he had created an estate plan, wanted to shift a significant portion of his investment portfolio to a "hot" mutual fund manager he had heard on a television interview. It seems the manager's equity portfolio had outperformed Dr. Grasmere's portfolio by almost 50 percent at year-end. My immediate reaction was, "Well, does your client know what the manager's capital-at-risk ratio was?"

The advisor just shook his head. He said the return was based on a portfolio of similar large-cap growth stocks. "Who wouldn't be upset? There's an inherent promise that even a performance of just half that in the coming year would still outdo the doctor's current return. Maybe the doctor should shift his account."

Neither the advisor nor his client was seeing the whole picture. What the fund manager on television didn't explain was that his portfolio had lost 50 percent in year 1, but doubled in year 2. Divided by two years, the manager could honestly tout an average annual return of 25 percent. But, the reality is that if Dr. Grasmere had invested his estate assets of $1,000,000 in the hot fund two years earlier, he would have lost half of its value the first year ($500,000) before doubling the value the following year. At the end of year 2, Dr. Grasmere's investment would amount to his original investment of $1,000,000. That equals zero growth!

On the other hand, even though Dr. Grasmere's actual conservative investment showed a much lower average annual rate of return of 12.94 percent, it was a *compounded* rate of return and his investment grew to $1,275,544. He actually made substantially more money than the hot manager, with lower risk. Once that is explained, it seems almost silly that any investor would fall prey to advertised returns!

The news media promotes what I call "noise." Noise refers to sensationalism and misunderstandings that obscure the facts and manipulate emotions. Unfortunately, the vast majority of individuals who are looking for fast-fix strategies give credence to noise without even knowing it. Not surprisingly, when emotions become part of the mix, anyone can make a misguided investment decision. With this in mind, we begin with a discussion and a short primer on the principles of investing and what you can do to mitigate financial risks.

THE BIG BANG OF MODERN FINANCE

Over 50 years ago, Harry Markowitz, a graduate student at the University of Chicago, developed the principles of Modern Portfolio Theory (MPT) based on his keen insight that risk (which he defined as volatility) must be the central focus for the whole process of investing. Markowitz was awarded the Nobel Prize for Economic Sciences in 1990, along with Merton H. Miller, who called Markowitz's theory, "The big bang of modern finance."

Markowitz observed an investment world blindly living in a paradox. While it was accepted that human beings, by their nature, are risk-averse, investing had essentially ignored the interrelatedness of risk and return—to achieve returns, *risk is necessary*. But how can we control risk? There are many kinds of risks:

- Stock volatility or market risk
- Reinvestment risk

- Liquidity risk
- Inflation risk
- Default risk
- Interest-rate risk

Stock Volatility or Market Risk.   Stock market risk is the risk that the securities you own will fluctuate because of changes in price levels. Most people associate market risk only in relation to the stock market. Stock prices can move up or down randomly.

Reinvestment Risk.   Reinvestment risk is the possibility that the return on your investment will not be reinvested as projected.

Liquidity Risk.   Liquidity risk occurs when you need your money immediately. It may come in the form of early withdrawal penalties or a low return due to a depressed market. The return on various investments may not be immediately available, could be subject to penalties, or you may have to accept a reduced market price.

Inflation Risk.   Inflation risk might be the most devastating risk. Inflation risk affects all investments equally. To combat inflation you must have an investment program that has the potential of providing you with accretionary capital and income. Unless your retirement savings can continue to grow, you run the risk of receiving income with reduced purchasing power. That could mean a declining quality of your life.

Default Risk.   Investments made in specific companies or organizations are subject to default risk. The potential for default due to poor management, economic cyclical swings, or catastrophe will present a level of risk for any investment other than the U.S. government. Default risk can be minimized by purchasing investments in large, financially secure companies. This is no guarantee. But any discussion of investment risk assumes an offsetting reward for a consequent level of risk, including investment risk.

Interest-Rate Risk.   Interest-rate risk is the possibility that a fixed interest investment will incur a decrease in market value due to a change in the prevailing interest rate. Bonds are interest sensitive and particularly sensitive to changes in the interest rate.

Modern Portfolio Theory teaches that there is an easier way to view risk: separate your investment portfolio into two kinds of risk—uncompensated and compensated.

Uncompensated risk (about 70 percent of total risk) is the possibility that economic (and noneconomic) news may impact the market price of a particular stock. For example, the price of Ford Motor Co. stock may go down as a result of the departure of a key Ford executive. An investor who holds only Ford stock can protect himself or herself against this risk by also owning stock in companies that are unaffected by the departure of Ford executives.

Compensated risk (about 30 percent of total risk) reflects the economic (and noneconomic) news that impacts the market price of many (or all) stocks. Since the prices of individual stocks are affected, more or less, by the risk of a general rise or fall in the value of the stock market itself, compensated risk is unavoidable for an investor who invests in the stock market. When investors bear compensated risk, however, they expect to be rewarded for doing so. The question you should be asking then is, How can I protect my portfolio from uncompensated risk while in the pursuit of higher returns?" The answer is found in observing the basic principles of Modern Portfolio Theory. The remainder of this section will show you how to get as much of that reward as you can. The concepts of Modern Portfolio Theory are widely misunderstood and often misapplied or used only when convenient. But they represent a new investment paradigm shift as important to our time as the telescope was to Galileo's era.

THE BASIC PRINCIPLES OF SUCCESSFUL INVESTING

Twenty-five years ago, before the "technology boom," the greatest technology company in the world was IBM. IBM dominated the market; no other company was even close. Logically, IBM should have been the best investment, but other companies were actually better investments. For example, the Clorox Corporation outperformed IBM.

Why can't people who are highly educated in the world of finance consistently pick a superior stock or mutual fund? Because they don't have a crystal ball, and no one knows what will happen in the future. The good news is that a crystal ball may not be necessary.

If you examine your own life, it is the simpler things that consistently work. Successful investing is no different. However, it is easy to have our attention drawn to the wrong issues. These wrong issues can derail us from our journey.

Investing can at times seem overwhelming, but the academic research can be broken down into seven key principles that have stood the test of time:

1. Effective diversification
2. Asset allocation
3. Lower costs
4. Diversification in nondollar-dominated–based assets
5. Investments along the efficient frontier
6. Rebalancing
7. Asset class investing

You can employ these simple principles to put together the hand you've been dealt in a way that gives you a chance to smooth out market volatility and have the highest possible probability for success. These principles work together to level out the roller coaster ride associated with good and bad markets and produce steady results.

The best reason we can give you for learning how to use these basic principles of successful investing is to lessen your fear factor. You will no longer have to play the role of the blind sheep, just following someone else's lead because you're unable to make informed decisions. Nor do you have to get a Ph.D. in finance; simple knowledge is your best protection. Once you have a grasp of how these concepts work, you can take an active role in putting them to work in your favor.

Principle One—Effective Diversification

The first principle you already know—diversification. But diversification is often misunderstood. The object of diversification is to minimize the uncompensated risk of having too few investments. With proper diversification, an investor can eliminate virtually all uncompensated risk from a portfolio.

The biggest mistake most investors make is attempting to diversify within the same asset class. People frequently say, "I'm well diversified; I have four funds." But they're not really diversified because their four funds are all in the same asset class—large growth funds, for instance.

Suppose you are invested in a retirement plan that has many choices, but they're all in the same asset class. How could this happen? Your advisor probably picked them based on best performance, which would have come from the same asset class. So you ended up with three large-cap funds, thinking you're diversified. This is why you have to know what you're doing, or at least have an advisor who does.

Harry Markowitz stated that while almost all diversification is good, there is *effective diversification* and *ineffective diversification.* The reason you need to understand ineffective diversification is because you may think you are diversified when you're not. You may have mutual funds in asset categories that overlap. The overall risk in a portfolio is not the average risk of each of the investments; the overall risk can actually be lower if your investments do not move together. Simply by including investments in your portfolio that don't move in concert, you can reduce the specific risk of individual investments.

An example of ineffective diversification is the investor who holds Microsoft stock and decides to diversify by investing in Dell and six other computer companies. If anything affects the computer software industry, all his investments will move together, either up or down. This is ineffective diversification. Investments that move in lockstep are said to be positively correlated with each other.

Imagine Asset A was your investment in real estate and Asset B represented an investment in stocks. You might see the effect illustrated in Figure 5.1. Over the long term, owning a wide

F I G U R E   5.1

Ineffective Diversification

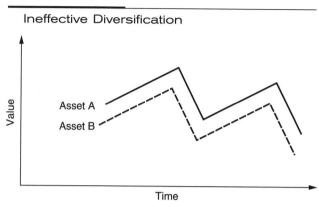

F I G U R E   5.2

Effective Diversification

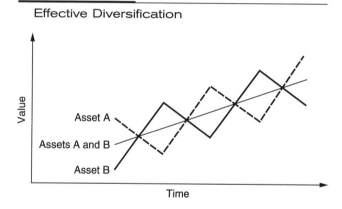

variety of different assets is the best strategy for the investor try-ing to achieve investment success.

Effective diversification reduces extreme price fluctuations and smooths out returns. It is dependent on dissimilar price movements. (See Figure 5.2.)

Dissimilar Price Movement

A portfolio with stocks or asset classes that have dissimilar price movement provides effective diversification. When investments are combined that move differently in time, in proportion, and/ or in direction, you have the basis for effective diversification. *Dissimilar price movement diversification* protects you from having all your investments go down at the same time, thereby reducing risk.

What Harry Markowitz proved in his 15-page dissertation entitled "Portfolio Selection" (also known as Modern Portfolio Theory) is that when two stock portfolios have the same average return, the portfolio with smaller up and down swings in value (less volatility) will have a greater compound return. (Which also explains why, in our earlier example, Dr. Grasmere's conservative investments grew.) Consequently, your prospects for a greater compound rate of return over time could also improve. A reduction in volatility would allow you to be more comfortable, focus on the long term, and not be distracted by the noise of the day.

This phenomenon is reminiscent of the fable of the tortoise and the hare. The hare races like crazy but is out of control, which allows the slow but consistent tortoise ultimately to win the race.

Markowitz didn't discover diversification. Diversification was a well-established practice long before he published his paper on portfolio selection in 1952. What he discovered was a method that evaluated a portfolio as a whole, not just in isolation. Markowitz found that because investors are risk averse, they require extra return from an investment that has greater risk.

Examine your current portfolio recommendations and try to determine which investments you recommend today that do not move in tandem. For example, large-company and small-company stocks do not tend to move at the same rate or direction.

A diversified portfolio provides stability only if you spread your money among the various asset classes that don't always have the same price movements—for example, between value and growth; small and large; international growth and value. Let's assume that we have two mutual funds with different investment goals, which you have owned for two years. Both of them have an average annual rate of return of 10 percent. How would you determine which fund had better performance?

You would expect that the ending value of each mutual fund would be the same, but nothing could be further from the truth. Unless they have the same risk or volatility, that will not happen. If one of the mutual funds took much more risk and was therefore more volatile, their ending values would be significantly different.

In our example, mutual fund A is much less volatile than mutual fund B and, as a result, has a greater compound rate of return and a higher value at the end of two years.

Academics have complex formulas to demonstrate how this works, but maybe it is best explained in Burton Malkiel's best-selling book, *A Random Walk Down Wall Street* (Norton & Company, 1999).

Malkiel asks you to imagine that you live on an island where the entire economy consists of only two companies: one that sells umbrellas and another that sells sunscreen. If you invest your entire portfolio in the company that sells umbrellas, you'll have strong performance during the rainy season, but poor performance when it's sunny. The reverse occurs with the alternative investment, the sunscreen company. Your portfolio will have high performance when the sun is out, but it will tank when the clouds roll in.

This changes when there is a freak weather pattern and it either rains or is sunny all year. If the investor owns shares in the sunscreen company only and it rains all year, he could have a 100 percent loss, while the investor in the umbrella company might have a 100 percent gain.

Chances are you'd rather have constant, steady returns. The solution is to invest 50 percent in one company and 50 percent in the other. By diversifying investments between both companies, an investor makes a consistent return each year.

What makes this work is that while both companies are risky because returns are variable from season to season, each company is affected differently by the weather factor. So long as there is some lack of parallelism in the fortunes of the individual companies in the economy, diversification should reduce risk. In this example, there is a perfect negative relationship between the two companies' fortunes (one always does well when the other does poorly).

Burton Malkiel points out that there is always a rub. When there is a recession and people are unemployed, they may buy neither summer vacations nor umbrellas. Nevertheless, as company fortunes don't always move in a parallel fashion, investment in a diversified portfolio of stocks is likely to be less risky than investment in one or two single securities.

The island economy story illustrates another principle, *asset allocation*, which will be discussed next. Asset allocation refers to the strategy of dividing your total investment portfolio among a variety of assets or asset classes, such as stocks, bonds, and money market securities, to achieve effective diversification. Each asset class has different levels of return and risk attached to it and will behave differently over time. The allocation to diverse assets aims to balance risk for the greatest return. A study by Brinson, Hood, and Beebower showed that 94 percent of performance was attributable to the allocation of the assets.[1] Picking the right individual asset added little value (less than 6 percent). It was the combination or allocation of asset classes that made the most difference.

Some critics see this balance as a settlement for mediocrity, but for most investors, it's the best protection against major loss should things ever go amiss in one investment class or subclass. The consensus among most financial professionals is that asset allocation is one of the most important decisions that investors make.

Principle Two—Asset Allocation

Asset allocation simply means determining what proportion of your money is going to be invested in the different asset classes—stocks, bonds, and cash investments—in order to maximize the growth of your portfolio for each unit of risk that you take. Asset allocation may be the single most important determinant of the long-term performance of any investment portfolio. People often confuse *asset allocation* with *diversification*, but the two are different.

Three separate studies of 91 large pension plans over two different 10-year periods showed that asset class selection accounted for more than 94 percent of investment results and was clearly the most important investment decision made. (See Figure 5.3.)

If all the major academic studies indicate that asset allocation of investments with dissimilar price movement is the answer

---

1 Gary P. Brinson, Randolph Hood, and Gilbert L. Beebower, "Determinants of Portfolio Performance," *Financial Analysis Journal* (July–Aug 1986), pp. 39–44.

FIGURE 5.3

Determinants of Portfolio Performance

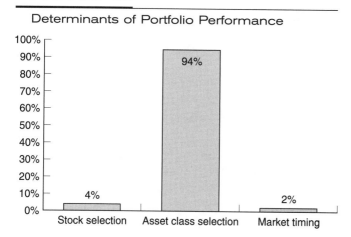

to investment success, it seems prudent to use it. Let's see how we can use dissimilar price movement asset classes to build a portfolio for retirement and its effect on the quality of life for an investor's family.

One way to understand asset allocation is by illustrating where different asset classes fit on an investment pyramid. The pyramid can be thought of as a visual allocation tool that ranks asset classes according to the risk profile of each asset type. (See Figure 5.4.)

The base of the pyramid is the foundation, representing the strongest portion, which supports everything above it. The base should be comprised of investments that are low in risk and have foreseeable returns. It is the largest area and composes the bulk of your assets. At the next level are the moderate to aggressive investments that offer a stable return while still allowing for capital appreciation. Although more risky than the assets creating the base, these asset classes are still relatively safe.

At the top of the pyramid, we find high-risk investments such as currency, options, and hedging. Since the risk is high, these investments tend to have high returns. You can combine these riskier asset classes that have higher expected returns with less risky investments in such a way that they will positively impact your overall portfolio performance.

FIGURE 5.4

The Investment Pyramid

Source: Chambers and Associates.

How do you determine what percentage of each asset class you should own? Academics have actually calculated methods to measure correlation based on risk and return of each investment in a portfolio, thereby enabling the volatility or risk of the whole portfolio to be measured. By using these tools, portfolios can be more systematically created with greater degrees of predictability in terms of risk and return. Because of these measurement tools, it is possible to combine in one portfolio assets that have the potential to generate higher returns due to their volatile nature, but that have a low correlation to one another in market performance. This achieves the result that the portfolio as a whole will actually be less risky than any one of the individual investments, yet will generate a higher overall return than a portfolio made up solely of low-risk investments.

Table 5.1 illustrates the correlation coefficients for each asset class from 1973 through 2002. As you can see, the prices move in different directions. A perfect correlation is +1, and an opposite correlation would be −1. You would want the −1 in your portfolio because it provides you with dissimilar price movement.

TABLE 5.1

Asset Class Corrrelation Coefficients
1973–2002

	MMF T-Bills	Fixed One-Year Fixed	Five-Year Notes	U.S. Large Co. Stocks	Small Co. Stocks	International Large Co. Stocks	Small Co. Stocks
Money Market Fund, T-bills	1.000						
One-Year Fixed	0.852	1.000					
Five-Year Treasury Notes	0.198	0.622	1.000				
U.S. Large Company Stocks	−0.106	0.153	0.253	1.000			
U.S. Small Company Stocks	−0.010	−0.043	0.096	0.666	1.000		
Int'l Large Company Stocks	−0.005	−0.053	−0.009	0.575	0.456	1.000	
Int'l Small Company Stocks	−0.027	−0.114	-0.096	0.278	0.263	0.883	1.000

In the real world, however, there is no −1 correlation. We simply try to get the lowest correlation possible in asset classes. To determine the suitability of an asset, we look at the correlation among the assets, and if they come out low then it provides further diversification. The correlation measures are very good at telling us what asset classes or investments should go into our portfolio, but not necessarily how much we should put into each. To determine how much to put into each depends on time horizon, risk tolerance, and long-term rates of returns for the individual asset classes.

To understand this better, let's examine the correlations among five U.S. investment classes and the Swiss franc as shown in Table 5.2.

This data[2] demonstrates that the Swiss franc is negatively or randomly correlated with virtually all U.S. investments,

2 Wilson Associates of Woodland Hills, California. The table shows the composite correlations among these six major investments during all five-year periods between December 1978 and October 1993 (Dec. 1978–Nov. 1983, Jan. 1979–Dec. 1984, Feb. 1979–Jan. 1984, etc.).

TABLE 5.2

Correlation of the Swiss Franc with Five U.S. Investment Classes*, 1978–1993

	Swiss Francs	T-bills	Money Markets	Govt Bonds	Wilshire 5000	Real Estate Apprec.
Swiss Francs	1.00	−0.84	−0.86	-0.13	−0.01	−0.51
T-Bills	−0.84	1.00	0.99	0.38	0.21	0.83
Money Markets	−0.86	0.99	1.00	0.29	0.16	0.83
Govt Bonds	−0.13	0.38	0.29	1.00	0.59	0.21
Wilshire 5000	−0.01	0.21	0.16	0.59	1.00	0.23
Real Estate Apprec.	−0.51	0.83	0.83	0.21	0.23	1.00

*Dr. William McCord, CFP, and Dr. Donald Moine, *Better Than Gold*, Regency Publishing Inc., 1998, p. 89.

including Treasury bills, money market funds, bonds, and stocks. While Swiss franc annuities have been strong performers for many decades, they tend to be especially strong when U.S. investments weaken.

Now look at each of the five U.S. investment classes relative to one another. There is no negative correlation between any pair of U.S. investments. There are five positive correlations, four of which are extremely strong.

What we often forget is that all our domestic asset classes are traded in U.S. dollars. They are so highly correlated with each other, it is impossible to be truly diversified. This is also an example of ineffective diversification. But you don't have to put your assets into 10 different countries. In this case, because the Swiss franc is so highly negatively correlated with U.S. investments and because it is so strong, simply diversifying into Swiss franc annuities can, by itself, significantly improve the balance of your portfolio (assuming you place enough of your assets into Swiss franc vehicles).

Thus, effective diversification can be achieved by including non-dollar-denominated investments such as currencies as a method of protecting your domestic investment portfolio against the decline of the dollar or the decline in the U.S. markets. When U.S. stock markets fall, or if the dollar falls, in all likelihood foreign

F I G U R E   5.5

Efficient Diversification

currencies and other markets internationally will increase. It is not surprising that this concept is utilized today to manage billions of dollars in the investment world. (See Figure 5.5.)

The center portfolio line combines both euros and U.S. dollars. Since these two asset classes do not move in concert with each other, their individual risks can be effectively diversified away.

In effect, by combining these two currencies, you are hedging your bet by lowering your risk. Our next principle (lower costs) seems more like common sense than a principle: lower operating expenses, lower turnover resulting in lower taxes, and lower trading costs.

Principle Three—Lower Costs

All things being equal, lower cost leads to higher rates of return because you have saved more money to invest. It sounds simple, but here is what you don't always see in your statements.

Most no-load funds are loaded and the index fund is one of the only true no-load mutual funds. A true no-load fund has no sales commission when you purchase or redeem shares. It has no back-end loads, redemption fees, or 12b-1 marketing fees. However, all mutual funds have operational expenses that include management fees and administrative expenses. The average retail equity fund today has a total expense ratio of 1.64 percent. The *expense ratio* is the operating expenses expressed as a percentage of average net assets. Operating expenses include management, administrative, and custody fees. The average retail mutual fund operating expenses are almost three times greater than those available to institutions. It's the difference between buying retail versus buying wholesale. I'd like to show you how to buy wholesale. But first you need to understand what you are dealing with.

Lower Turnover Resulting in Lower Taxes

The average retail mutual fund had an approximately 86 percent turnover rate in 2005. If you had invested $100,000 in an average growth-oriented mutual fund, approximately $86,000 would have been bought and sold in the underlying securities for the year. This is important because each time you trade, there is a transaction cost involved—whether it's a commission and/or the "bid/ask" spread—which can easily amount to much more than the total operating expenses that are disclosed in the prospectus.

Why do retail mutual funds have such high turnover? For a few reasons, the first of which is that the fund managers are under tremendous pressure to perform. The second reason is that the only way a mutual fund manager can add value "perceived in the market" is to attempt to guess market turning points or the individual securities that are going to outperform the market. Just attempting these two feats creates substantial turnover. And by the laws of probability, a few of them will succeed, but most will not. In addition, a portion of the retail public is chasing performance. They tend to move in and out of retail mutual funds, forcing the manager to buy and sell more often than he or she would like.

When mutual fund managers succeed, they are highlighted in the financial press and money comes racing in. Imagine that you are a mutual fund manager and you were just written up in *Money* magazine as the top-performing mutual fund manager of the year. When fund managers win these public awards they are likely to receive a significant increase of new monies once the public reads about their success. But who do you think pays the cost of investing these funds? The existing shareholders bear the burden of investing new money, not the new investors. If you have a mutual fund with $500 million, and $100 million in new money comes in, that's a 20 percent increase in assets. The new shareholders are going to buy at today's net asset values (NAVs). The fund manager now has to buy securities for the new investors with their $100 million. The trading costs of investing that amount of money will be significant. There may be some market impact that will drive up the prices of the very stock the manager placed with the new monies.

The shareholders bear the cost of this "hot money," as the academics call it. But what happens when the fund performs poorly? The mutual fund may be featured in *Money* magazine's Ten Worst Funds section. And that hot money leaves. Who pays that cost? The exiting shareholders are able to redeem at NAV, so the cost of selling out that portfolio is borne by the shareholders who stay in the fund. That's why institutional investors do not invest in publicly available funds. They understand what is going on and separate themselves from the public—and you should, too.

Here's another problem. You are most likely subject to tax. You need to determine how effective index or asset class mutual funds are in a taxable environment. Each time the mutual fund manager sells a security, assuming that you have a profit, the client has a capital gains distribution. Mutual funds are required to distribute 98 percent of their taxable income each year, including realized capital gains, to stay tax-exempt at the mutual fund level. Since no mutual fund manager wants to have his or her performance reduced by paying corporate income taxes, they distribute all income. Unless you are investing inside a qualified plan, you will receive dividends for both ordinary income, composed of interest and stock dividends, and capital gains distributions from profitable sales by your mutual fund. If your mutual fund has a turnover of 80 percent per year, on average you will realize 80 percent of the capital gain, and these gains will be taxable each year. On the other hand, for index funds and asset class funds, the average turnover is approximately 16 percent—on average, 84 percent of the taxable gains are deferred until you want to recognize them.

Two academic studies indicate that mutual fund capital gains and dividends will reduce after-tax returns for shareholders, and that asset class mutual funds can protect against those tax losses.

These two studies, one from Stanford University[3] and the other published in the *Journal of Portfolio Management*[4], demonstrate that tax efficiency is an important factor to consider in equity mutual fund selection. Numerous mutual funds, in their quest for top performance, may reduce their shareholders' potential after-tax returns by producing high taxable distributions, such as capital gains resulting from frequent buying and selling of appreciated securities in a fund. Dividends, taxed as ordinary income, may also reduce potential after-tax returns.

Passive indexing is a very difficult strategy to beat on an after-tax basis and, therefore, active taxable strategies should always be benchmarked against the after-tax performance of an indexed alternative.

Lower Trading Costs

Trading costs can be much more significant than operating expenses and harder to determine. Let's just examine one trade that a mutual fund might execute over the counter on Nasdaq. If the stock was currently at $10 ask and $9.50 bid, what would be the cost of buying and selling the stock, assuming no price change? The mutual fund would buy it for the clients at the ask price of $10 and sell it at the bid for $9.50—a $0.50 cost. This represents a 5 percent cost of trading on the purchase price of $10. If the clients' portfolio turned over 80 percent during the year, they would have a cost of 80 percent of 5 percent, or a total hidden cost due to turnover of 4 percent—a hidden cost that can derail anyone's investment program.

What most investors don't realize is that trading costs can exceed management fees. Trading costs are composed of agency cost (commissions and/or bid/ask spread) and market impact.

---

3 John B. Shoven, professor of Economics at Stanford University, and Joel M. Dickson, a Stanford Ph.D. candidate, found that taxable distributions have an impact on the rates of return of many well-known retail equity mutual funds. The study measured the performance of 62 equity funds for the 30-year period. It found that the high-tax investor who reinvested only after-tax distributions would end up with accumulated wealth per dollar invested equal to less than half (45 percent) of the funds' published performances.

4 Robert H. Jeffrey and Robert D. Arnott, "Is Your Alpha Big Enough to Cover Its Taxes?" *Journal of Portfolio Management*, 1993, pp. 15–25, concluded that extremely low portfolio turnover can be a factor in improving a fund's potential after-tax performance. The study found that only 5 (5 of the 72 funds) outperformed an index fund after factoring in taxes.

What this all means is that you end up with less money working for you. What you want is more money working for you in order to compound faster.

Compounding is the process of earning a rate of return on your money that is invested, and then reinvesting those earnings at the same rate. For example, a $100 investment earning compound interest at 10 percent a year would accumulate to $110 at the end of the first year, and $121 at the end of the second year, and so on. The actual formula is:

Compound sum = (principal) (1 + interest rate), to the Nth power, where N is the number of years

The essence of the formula is that at the end of each year, interest is earned not only on the original amount, but also on all the previously accumulated interest amounts—you are earning interest on interest!

The typical compounding table (Table 5.3) shows you how a single investment of $100,000 will grow at various rates of return. Five percent is what you might get from a Certificate of Deposit (CD) or with a government bond; 10 percent is about the historical average stock market return; and 15 percent would have been possible over the last 20 years. But historically, you should average around 11 percent.

A simple way to figure how long it takes your money to double is the *Rule of 72*. Divide the number 72 by the interest rate or rate of return you are earning, and the result is the number of years it takes your money to double. For example, if you are earning 10 percent, your money will double in 7.2 years. If you are earning 12 percent, it only takes 6 years for your money to double.

Your goal is to maximize the rate of return you are earning, but to minimize the risk you are taking. If you can earn just 10 percent in 20 years, because of compounding your money will have grown by almost 800 percent.

Principle Four—Invest along the Efficient Frontier

When different asset classes are combined in a portfolio, they determine an optimum combination of investments that will give you the highest possible rates of return based on a certain level of

TABLE 5.3

Compound Growth

Year	5%	10%	15%
1	$100,000	$ 100,000	$ 100,000
5	$128,000	$ 161,000	$ 201,000
10	$163,000	$ 259,000	$ 405,000
15	$208,000	$ 418,000	$ 814,000
25	$339,000	$1,083,000	$3,292,000

risk. These combinations of portfolios exhibiting this optimal risk/ reward trade-off form what we call the *efficient frontier curve.*

This curve is depicted on a two-dimensional graph by calculating the expected rate of return, standard deviation, and correlation coefficient for each institutional asset-class mutual fund. This information can be used to identify the portfolio at the highest expected return for each incremental level of risk. By plotting each combination or portfolio representing a given level of risk and expected return, we are able to describe mathematically a series of points or *efficient portfolios.* (It is important to note that while a portfolio may be efficient, it is not necessarily prudent.) You can then determine the point at which the maximum amount of risk an investor is willing to tolerate intersects with the maximum amount of reward that can potentially be generated.

All portfolios or assets lie somewhere along the curve, as illustrated in Figure 5.6, which shows the efficient frontier relative to the "market" and demonstrates the potential trade-offs between equities, bonds, and cash. You have low risk in owning a money market fund, but you also get a low expected return.

Most investor portfolios fall significantly below the efficient frontier. Portfolios such as the S&P 500 (that is often used as a proxy for the market) fall below the line when several asset classes are compared. Investors can have the same rates of return with an asset-class portfolio with much less risk or higher rates of return for the same level of risk.

Rational and prudent investors will restrict their choice of portfolios to those that appear on the efficient frontier and to the specific portfolios that represent their own risk tolerance level.

FIGURE 5.6

The Efficient Frontier Curve

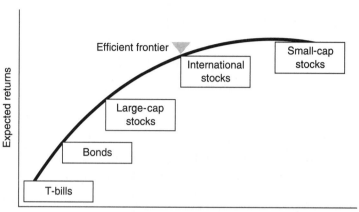

Volatility or standard deviation

Principle Five—Diversify in Non-Dollar-Based Assets

To be effectively diversified you should have some of your money out of the U.S. dollar. The U.S. dollar to most Americans is like water to fish—and like the fish, we can't see the paradigm we live in. But the dollar is just another currency. And currencies, just like any other commodity that can be bought or sold, are subject to the laws of supply and demand. When more people want a particular currency, the cost of the currency in terms of other currencies will go up. When demand decreases, the value goes down.

Our dollars are actively traded just as a stock is traded on the stock market. Over a trillion dollars worth of foreign exchange is traded globally every day. One of the purposes of currency markets—called *spot, forward,* or *futures* markets—is to help offset the risk of adverse price movements when one country trades with another. When one country buys another's products, those imports usually need to be paid for in the currency of the country from which they originate. Foreign exchanges exist to simplify the process: exchanging one country's currency for an equivalent amount of another's. As you can imagine, foreign exchange rates are not static; they are very dynamic and can change many times within a single minute.

Here is the challenge. The whole purpose of investing is to accumulate and store value that you can use at some time in the future. Hopefully, that value will grow to offset higher prices, which we call *inflation*. Most people define inflation simply as the rising price of things, but prices can also rise because the value of your dollar falls relative to other currencies. When this happens, it causes a reduction in purchasing power.

What this means is that you could get everything right: you could listen to the best advisors, follow all the principles of successful investing, and still lose if all your assets are tied to the U.S. dollar. That is why this last principle is critical. That's also why in 2003, for the first time in his life, Warren Buffett began buying foreign currencies—to the tune of $12 billion by year-end. He cited continuing weakness in the U.S. dollar as the reason.[5]

By the beginning of 2005, Buffett's foreign currency holdings were increased to $20 billion. At the time he began buying up overseas currency, the euro was worth 86 cents to the U.S. dollar. By January 2005, the euro traded at $1.33, an improvement of over 50 percent. In the first three quarters of 2004, Buffett's company, Berkshire Hathaway, netted $207 million on currency speculation. Looking back at the fall of the dollar against the euro—33 percent between 2002 and 2005—it would seem that Buffett's timing was great. In his famous plain-speaking way, he explained his concerns about the value of the U.S. dollar: "If we have the same policies, the dollar will go down."[6]

Buffett's switch to foreign currencies is significant and worth noting. You must have some of your money in non-dollar-based assets. There are many events that could cause our dollar to drop. As employees retire, obligatory payments have to be made out of operating profits and—while few corporate types want to talk about this—those very pension obligations and depressed returns on invested assets may be a leading factor in the high number of corporate bankruptcies. What happens when corporations cannot meet their pension obligations? We have a personal savings rate

---

5 William Meyer, "Warren Buffett's Economic and Political Influence Grows Each Year," *Personal Finance*, May 29, 2004, at www.persfin.co.za.
6 Warren Buffett was quoted in "Economic and Political Influence Grows Each Year," *Personal Finance*, May 29, 2004, at www.persfin.co.za.

of less than 1 percent (2004)—low relative to the nearly 7 percent rates averaged over the previous three decades.[7]

Then there is the issue of our debt. Our national debt is growing exponentially with no end in sight—with massive increases in military spending for wars in Iraq and Afghanistan and monies for Hurricane Katrina cleanup and other natural disasters. Most people just accept the fact that the national debt is so high. They don't realize, though, that the exponential expansion of debt cannot continue without a catastrophic economic outcome.

There is also growing credit card and mortgage debt. The consumer-based credit problem mirrors the national debt (and longer-term national obligation) problem.

Our modern variety of inflation is seen not in prices and wages but in stock and bond prices. The 1990's asset bubble had a huge impact on the economy of the time, and consumers in the new decade are going to pay the price. The equivalent of this type of growth for a nation involves investment in economic expansion—business inventories, plants, and equipment; competitive trade imports and exports; and sound monetary policies.

The only way to prevent a big correction in stocks and bonds, continuing loss of purchasing power, and losses in competitiveness in world markets is to correct the imbalances. But do you really think that is going to happen?

Then there are those huge trade imbalances—a dangerous trend because this relates directly to the loss of purchasing power. Think about how the United States grew in the past. We dominated the world manufacturing markets, and our dollar was king. But that was then. Economics is based on cause and effect. Just as a strong dollar strengthens a market, a weak dollar weakens it. And if the dollar falls, you should have some of your money in other currencies—currencies that have a negative correlation to the dollar, so if the dollar falls, they rise, and vice versa, offsetting the effects of each.

If you believe we are going to continue having trade and budget deficits, that oil prices will increase catastrophically,

---

7 Alan Greenspan, testimony before the Committee on Banking, Housing and Urban Affairs, February 17, 2005.

and/or that the dollar may decline, then you should hedge a portion of your portfolio in non-dollar-dominated investments.

Principle Six—Rebalancing

The principle of rebalancing is to maintain the same percentages in the various asset classes you have chosen in order to maintain proper diversification in all market environments. By rebalancing, you may give up some short-term gains if you reduce your holdings of winning stocks prematurely, but you'll also miss the big losses when and if they collapse.

Although the mechanics of rebalancing are fairly straightforward, there are a variety of methods that could be used to reach that optimal portfolio goal of maximizing returns while minimizing risk.

Many investment advisors rebalanced their equity positions down to their allocation targets as the bull market pushed equity values upward. Then, last year, they increased equity positions as the declining markets dropped those positions below targets. As a result, they have been selling high, then buying low. See the logic?

When the price is down, you are able to buy more shares. Plus, you're reinvesting the money you've made along with your principal and compounding your growth.

An investment advisor or consultant should be knowledgeable about the various issues surrounding rebalancing and, ideally, should be able to explain them in a way that makes the desired method acceptable and practical to apply.

Some studies show that more frequent rebalancing improves results, which would indicate that a style that is outperforming the broad market does not stay in favor for long periods of time. But rebalancing generally incurs transactions fees and it may have tax implications. Therefore, rebalance only when you add new money or when your asset allocation has shifted substantially out of alignment. I suggest a 25 percent rule. Rebalance if your allocation is greater than 25 percent of the original percentage allocated.

Rebalancing an investment portfolio seems simple on the surface, but as you start to think through the method, frequency, tolerance limits, fees, and commissions, the subject reveals itself to be quite complex and without easy answers. This is probably not an exercise that an average first-time investor would pursue on his or her own. This is where a qualified advisor can help.

Principle Seven—Asset-Class Investing

Asset-class investing is easy to understand. First, determine what proportion of your money is going to be invested in which asset classes, and then leave it alone!

Asset-class funds are passively managed, which means there is no "active" decision making occurring about buying and selling—the issues that are contained within the mutual fund. The funds' sole purpose is to mimic the markets while experiencing very low turnover and significantly below-average costs.

The best way to do asset-class investing is by investing in either index funds or academically defined asset-class mutual funds because they represent a specific asset class. Index funds represent a target index. The most popular index mutual funds are those that track the S&P 500, but there are also special index funds, such as those based on the Russell 1000 or the Wilshire 5000. These funds are a relatively new hybrid created by Dimensional Fund Advisors, an institutional money manager. Although not available to the general public, institutional asset-class mutual funds can be purchased by individuals through selected groups of investment advisors who are required to educate their clients on the benefits of passive asset-class investing.

Advisors have predefined asset-class portfolios representing various levels of risk; these portfolios vary only by the percentage allotted to bonds. For example, a conservative portfolio may have 40 percent stock mutual funds and 60 percent bond mutual funds, while an aggressive one may have 80 percent stock and 20 percent bond funds.

Many financial advisors who understand these portfolio categories still attempt to use traditional retail mutual (actively managed) funds to implement them. Let me explain why retail funds handicap your investing. Actively managed mutual funds tend to do what advisors call "style drift." Active managers are under tremendous pressure to deliver returns, even though that may not be the function of a particular fund. They will drift out of their asset class into another asset class in an effort to, hopefully, boost their returns.

It is very difficult to maintain a balanced portfolio with actively managed funds because of this style drift. Let's say you wanted a portfolio that is a 50-50 mix of large growth companies and small value companies. If the manager of the fund of large growth companies starts buying small value companies because large growth isn't doing well, or vice versa, that messes up your 50-50 allocation.

And, if every fund went to large growth when growth was doing well, then when growth plummeted, your whole portfolio would plummet. That's why many investors today are down 70 percent. They may have tried to remain diversified, but the managers of those funds drifted. If each one "fudged" just a little in the direction of whatever was up at the time, it would be enough to cause big trouble to a portfolio.

Investors without any knowledge or advice naturally pick the funds with the best returns for the last period, and that's how they end up with everything in one asset class. Then if the fund doesn't deliver performance, investors take their money out of that mutual fund and go elsewhere. And the fund manager gets fired.

Your advisor should search for managers who have been consistent and will not chase returns in a neighboring asset class to prop up returns. They should monitor the managers, and if they start drifting, they should be replaced.

Asset-class funds and index funds are not under pressure to perform like actively managed funds. If asset-class funds are not available, the next best alternative is to build a portfolio of index funds. Even though they are only numerical commercial benchmarks and not academically defined, as asset-class funds are, it is still possible to build a superior portfolio with index funds. For example, the S&P 500 is a good one to utilize, and, frankly, the large growth managers have trouble beating it. Each year, the S&P 500 index outperforms 82 to 95 percent of the actively managed funds whose stated goal is to beat the S&P 500.

GLOBAL INVESTING

You may have noticed that I didn't list investing globally as a principle. By investing in international large and small equity asset-class funds, you *are* diversifying globally. The purpose is not to get a higher return on international companies, but most international market prices move opposite to U.S. funds.

The next chapter will give you a more complete understanding of the asset classes and enable you to effectively diversify and allocate your assets for the amount of risk you're willing to take.

CHAPTER 6

Understand Your Asset-Class Choices

*A*sset class is a term frequently used in the investment world to refer to a category of investment. For the purpose of our discussion, we are going to divide them into the following classes (see Figure 6.1):

- Cash (cash, money market, certificate of deposit)
- Fixed income (fixed annuity, bonds)
- U.S. annuities
- U.S. large growth companies
- S&P 500
- U.S. large value funds
- U.S. small growth companies
- U.S. small value companies
- International equities
- International large companies
- International small companies

CASH

The first asset class, *cash,* includes money market funds, which are made up of T-bills, certificates of deposit, and commercial paper. These are called cash because the NAV (net asset value)

FIGURE 6.1

Understand Asset-Class Choices

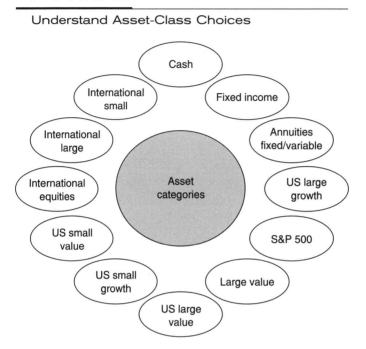

is always one dollar; in other words, the price doesn't fluctuate. Few people understand that when their holdings are in cash, they're invested in an asset class—the U.S. dollar.

FIXED INCOME

Bonds are divided into two main groups: stable bonds such as U.S. government and AAA corporate bonds, and higher-yield bonds such as BB corporate bonds and "junk bonds."

Short-term bonds, meaning five years or less to maturity, will give you 94 percent of the return without the long-term bond volatility. If you are in a long-term bond fund and interest rates move up, your fund can drop 25 percent in a day. Junk bonds or bb corporate bonds add volatility without gaining the expected returns of a stock and are actually unsecured loans of a company.

An *annuity* is a contract between an insurer and recipient (annuitant) whereby the insurer guarantees to pay the recipient a stream of payments in exchange for an amount of money paid to the insurer.

A *fixed return annuity* is one where the insurance company guarantees to make payments of a fixed amount for an agreed-upon term of years or for the lifetime of the annuitant or joint annuitants. In order to make any profit from such an arrangement, the company offers to pay a rate of interest that is less than it expects to be able to earn by investing the funds it receives for the contract.

Sometimes people confuse an annuity with a mutual fund. There is an important difference. An annuity can offer investment growth similar to a mutual fund, but can also offer potential tax advantages that a mutual fund cannot. The annuity plans, of which there are many, can be structured so that, once the investor begins to draw on the funds, they make regular payments for life.

One of the most important benefits of annuities is that they may permit the investor to defer taxes on his or her savings, thereby building assets faster than can be done in other investments. While annuities can be used to put money aside for various purposes, most often they are associated with retirement accounts. This is not a coincidence. Several features of annuities make them especially attractive for a retirement plan, including:

- *Security for the Investor's Family.* If the annuity owner dies before the earnings of the annuity are distributed, his or her beneficiaries can receive the full value of the annuity. In most instances, by naming a beneficiary the annuity may be able to bypass probate and avoid the resultant costs.
- *Ease of the Investment Process.* Record keeping is little more than monitoring the statements you can periodically receive.

Although the investor doesn't own the investments the annuity makes, he or she benefits from the investment. Since the insurance company owns the investment, the investor's savings can grow, with all the gains being tax deferred. This is an advantage that owners of most mutual funds are prevented from taking. When an investor buys a mutual fund, he or she pays a capital gains distribution tax at the end of the year. Even if the investor reinvests the gains, this is a taxable event. With an annuity, however, any profit made that is left in the annuity continues to grow in a tax-deferred state.

Since annuities are products of insurance companies, the fees paid by the investor are different from the fees paid for mutual funds. For most annuities, there are no front-end load fees or commissions. Instead, in an American annuity, there are "surrender" charges for investors who withdraw funds early. Surrender charges apply usually during the first 5 to 10 years. It should be noted that this is not the case in Swiss annuities, which will be discussed in Part Three.

When annuities are compared to other investment alternatives, especially when one is looking for an investment through which to accumulate savings for retirement, annuities clearly become the product of choice. Annuities, without question, are safe, solid investments.

Warning: Some American annuity companies advertise a bonus rate, in which insurers add on as much as 8 to 10 percent to their current interest rates. But many of these alluring bonuses can be illusory. In most cases, the bonus rate is only paid if the annuity is held for many years and then taken out in monthly installments instead of a lump sum. If an investor asks for the cash in a lump sum, the insurer will retroactively subtract the bonus, plus the interest that compounded on the bonus, plus a penalty on the original investment. Even more insidious are tiered-rate annuities, so named because they have two levels of interest rates. They highlight an above-average interest rate, but, as with their bonus-rate cousins, the accrued earnings in the account reflect this so-called accumulation value rate only when the payout is made over a long time. A straight withdrawal, by contrast, will knock the annuity down to a low "surrender value" rate for every year invested. Other insurers simply resort to the time-dishonored practice of luring customers with lofty initial rates that are lowered substantially at renewal time. All of this nonsense has given the American annuity business a bad name.

Variable annuities, often called "mutual funds with an insurance wrapper," combine the best aspects of a traditional domestic fixed annuity (tax deferral, insurance protection for beneficiaries, tax-timing controlled-income options) with the benefits of traditional mutual fund portfolios (flexibility in selecting how to invest funds, the potential for higher investment returns).

Unique to variable annuities are several forms of investment alternatives that vary in their potential for both reward and risk.

Domestic variable annuity investors control their contract options. They dictate the amount, frequency, and regularity of their contributions, how their contributions are invested, and when the money is disbursed. The investor pays a premium to the insurance company, which then buys accumulation units, similar to mutual fund shares, in an investment fund. The IRS imposes no limits on the annual nonsheltered amount an individual may contribute to a variable annuity funded with after-tax dollars.

Unlike a fixed-rate annuity, where the insurance company determines how to invest funds, the investor can choose his or her own investments. A domestic variable annuity offers a number of different investment options that are much like mutual fund categories, including stocks, bonds, and balanced funds. These investments may be managed by a mutual fund company or by the insurance company.

Unlike a mutual fund, an annuity does not pay out earnings or distribute any capital gains, so these are compounded on a tax-deferred basis. And, like a fund, as the value of the stocks in the portfolio varies, each unit in your variable annuity varies.

Variable annuities provide similar payment options:

- *Lifetime Income.* The entire account value is converted to a monthly income stream guaranteed for as long as the annuitant lives.
- *Lifetime Income with Period Certain.* The income stream is guaranteed for a specified number of years or for as long as the annuitant lives, whichever is longer.
- *Refund Life Annuity.* The entire account value is converted to a monthly income stream guaranteed for as long as the annuitant lives. If the annuitant dies prior to the principal amount being annuitized, the balance is paid to the beneficiary.
- *Joint and Survivor.* The income stream is guaranteed for as long as either annuitant lives (for example, you or your spouse).
- *Fixed Period Certain.* The entire account value is fully paid out during a specified period of time.

Because of their insurance benefits, variable annuities generally cost more than traditional taxable investments, such as mutual funds, including front-end charges (loads), management fees, and sometimes back-end surrender charges for early withdrawals from the policy.

Variable annuities offer more protection than fixed annuities because the variable annuity is kept in a "trust fund" separate from the other assets of the insurance company.

In the United States, 23 states provide some protection for annuity contracts. It appears that only 9 states offer any substantial exemption protection for annuity contracts, and most of those require that the proceeds be payable to someone other than the contract owner. Because an annuity contract is simply a contract between an individual and an insurance company, it's not recorded in any public database, like the register of deeds or the records of corporations. No reports are filed with the IRS until the contract owner requests a distribution.

U.S. EQUITIES

Equity is investment jargon for a *stock*. The equity asset classes are often categorized according to the size of their market capitalization ("cap"). *Capitalization* is the number of outstanding shares multiplied by the current stock price. They are divided into asset classes called large value and small value. The same applies to growth and international equity asset classes.

U.S. Large-Cap Growth

These are very large companies that are doing very well. (They have an average capitalization of approximately $7 billion or greater.) This type of company usually has good sales, good prospects for the future, and good earnings.

S&P 500 (Standard & Poor's Index of the 500 Largest U.S. Stocks)

It seems there is a lot of confusion between asset classes and indexes, but there is a distinction. *Asset classes* are academically defined, whereas an *index* is simply a numerical group of stocks. Indexes are commercial benchmarks. The S&P 500 is an index of 500 stocks. We also call it an *equity asset class*, even though it contains both large growth and large value stocks. It's well known and it gives people something to compare to.

Asset classes for stocks are further refined into value and growth stock categories according to their potential total return over time.

U.S. Large-Cap Value

These are large U.S. publicly traded companies that may be temporarily out of favor. The companies are distressed economically and aren't doing well by any measurement.

U.S. Small-Cap Growth

These are publicly traded U.S. smaller companies with an average capitalization of less than $2 billion. They have good sales and good prospects for the future.

U.S. Small-Cap Value

These are U.S. publicly traded smaller companies (with an average capitalization of less than $2 billion) that aren't doing very well.

International Large

The last two equity asset classes are international. This group generally is comprised of stocks of companies based outside the United States from any part of the world with established free markets. The international large equity asset class includes both growth and value stocks, and everything in between that is doing well.

International Small

This asset class is the same as international large, except that these companies aren't doing so well.

Table 6.1 shows how these seven equity subclasses have done individually compared to an entire diversified portfolio over the last 30 years.

The first five asset classes across the top are U.S.; the next two are international. And the last is a combination of all. Each

TABLE 6.1

Rates of Return by Asset Class

Year	Small Value	Small Growth	Large Value	S&P 500	Large Growth	Int'l. Small	Int'l. Large	Diversified Portfolio*
1970	0.31	(18.61)	11.90	4.03	(5.23)	0.90	(9.65)	(2.09)
1971	14.40	23.49	9.44	14.32	23.60	68.25	59.87	26.45
1972	6.96	3.75	15.97	18.98	21.65	64.22	53.25	22.52
1973	(26.01)	(39.10)	(2.75)	(14.67)	(20.34)	(13.68)	(22.34)	(20.06)
1974	(18.11)	(33.40)	(22.38)	(26.46)	(29.96)	(28.61)	(33.68)	(27.08)
1975	54.45	63.17	51.92	37.21	35.66	49.86	65.26	50.30
1976	53.55	43.51	44.98	23.85	18.38	11.46	5.55	31.18
1977	21.81	20.32	.75	(7.18)	(9.13)	74.08	40.61	15.72
1978	21.82	18.63	6.63	6.57	7.01	65.53	33.22	19.58
1979	37.95	47.26	23.779	18.42	20.69	(0.78)	2.11	23.83
1980	29.09	46.07	16.54	32.41	33.87	35.46	38.48	32.67
1981	10.54	(4.09)	11.23	(4.91)	(7.90)	(4.65)	0.86	0.40
1982	37.66	25.99	27.35	21.41	17.60	0.82	5.22	21.41
1983	44.22	26.92	26.77	22.51	16.23	32.40	22.23	27.33
1984	5.08	(8.87)	14.07	6.27	(1.07)	10.08	11.39	4.62
1985	34.73	28.51	29.46	32.17	31.45	60.11	48.28	35.85
1986	16.86	5.82	20.36	18.47	13.70	50.10	59.95	23.04
1987	(6.30)	(10.00)	2.32	5.23	6.40	70.55	41.43	10.82
1988	28.84	20.46	24.64	16.81	12.82	26.01	24.81	2.165
1989	19.69	19.09	28.35	31.49	31.52	29.34	14.67	25.22
1990	(20.81)	(18.13)	(13.94)	(3.17)	1.43	(16.77)	(18.38)	(12.25)
1991	39.37	52.11	29.82	30.55	41.14	7.05	13.95	32.98
1992	29.86	11.23	21.16	7.67	7.14	(18.37)	(9.44)	9.55
1993	22.56	14.04	21.16	9.99	2.01	33.49	36.44	18.15
1994	(0.95)	(2.88)	(4.57)	1.31	1.47	12.42	7.63	1.11
1995	29.24	31.28	37.19	37.43	37.92	0.48	13.72	29.11
1996	21.36	12.92	15.69	23.07	21.20	2.26	7.49	16.05
1997	34.40	16.27	31.70	33.37	30.28	(25.11)	(4.37)	20.41
1998	(7.03)	0.38	14.93	28.58	33.61	8.04	15.46	13.63
1999	10.76	47.73	1.89	21.03	28.16	20.15	32.87	22.83
2000	1.03	(18.42)	8.20	(9.10)	(13.53)	(5.69)	(16.08)	(7.27)
2001	35.43	6.00	(0.47)	(11.88)	(15.17)	(10.69)	(22.03)	(1.05)
2002	(10.20)	(28.07)	(27.71)	(22.11)	(21.95)	1.78	(13.76)	(18.80)
Annualized Returns %	15.42	9.19	13.04	10.81	9.50	14.88	12.28	12.72
Standard Deviation	20.96	25.67	17.59	17.52	19.29	30.19	26.57	17.72
Years Best	9	3	4	1	4	8	4	0
Years Worst	2	9	4	1	6	7	4	0

*Diversified Portfolio = 16% in each U.S. Asset Class, 10% in each International Asset Class.

Source: Returns Program, Dimensional Fund Advisors. Past performance is not an indicator of future expected returns.

column of assets represents every stock in its respective category. They are more precisely defined as follows:

First Column: Small Value Stocks. This is the smallest 8 percent of the market universe[1] based on total capitalization. From that range, a value screen is given in which all issues' Book-to-Market values (BTMs) are calculated. In other words, small value companies are very small in size, temporarily distressed, and there are a huge number of them, over 2,000.

Book-to-Market value is a ratio comparing the book value of a share of common stock with its market price. High BTM companies are companies in distress (and investors demand to be compensated for the perceived higher risk). Low BTM companies (like Microsoft and Wal-Mart) on average will do well and, because they are so popular, investors are not compensated as well. Their cost of acquiring capital is less than other companies not in this group.

Second Column: Small Growth Stocks. The smallest 8 percent of the market universe,[2] using the lowest BTM ratio. These are small companies, but they are doing very well compared to small value companies. Their sales are good, price to earnings is good—everything is going great—they are just small. Because they are doing so well, they don't have to pay as much for capital as other companies.

Third Column: Large Value Stocks. From the largest 90 percent of the market universe,[3] these have the highest BTM ratios. They are large companies that are distressed because they are not doing so well.

Fourth Column: S&P 500. An index of stocks composed of the 500 largest companies in the United States. The index is market weighted, which means the larger the company, the larger the weight in the index. The index is widely used as a

---

1 *Market universe* is defined as all stocks in the NYSE, AMEX, and Nasdaq. Source: Dimensional Fund Advisors Firm Profile & Returns Program.
2 Ibid.
3 Ibid.

stock benchmark for account performance measurement. This index includes 400 industrial stocks, 20 transportation stocks, 40 financial stocks, and 40 public utilities, whether they are growth, value, or those stocks in between.

Fifth Column: Large Growth Stocks. The largest 90 percent of the market universe with the lowest BTMs in the top tenth percentile are chosen. These companies are doing very well, and they just happen to be very big also.

Sixth Column: International Small Stocks. The smallest 8 percent of companies in the following regions: Japan, United Kingdom, Austria, Belgium, Denmark, Finland, France, Germany, Greece, Ireland, Italy, the Netherlands, Norway, Spain, Sweden, Switzerland, Australia, Hong Kong, New Zealand, and Singapore.

Seventh Column: International Large Stocks. The largest 60 to 75 percent by market cap ranking in Australia, Austria, Belgium, Denmark, Sweden, Finland, France, Germany, Greece, Hong Kong, Ireland, Italy, Japan, the Netherlands, New Zealand, Norway, Portugal, Singapore, Spain, Switzerland, and the United Kingdom.

Eighth Column: Diversified Portfolio Composed of All Asset Classes. We wanted this diversified portfolio to be structured without bias, so it is a ratio of 80 percent U.S. stocks and 20 percent international. We divided 80 by 5, which gave us 16 percent in each of the 5 U.S. asset classes; and put 10 percent in each of the international asset classes. This portfolio is for the person who says, "Since I don't know what to do, I'll just divide my money equally among the asset classes."

The light gray boxes depict the worst-performing asset class for that year. The dark gray boxes depict the best-performing asset class for that year. The black boxes represent years when the diversified portfolio outperformed the S&P 500.

Do you see any pattern in the chart? Does it appear that one asset class is superior? No—if you look closely, it's totally random. The people who are trying to time the dark and light gray chart will always fail miserably. The down years of 1973 and 1974 are intentionally included in the chart. Look at the best asset classes during those years. If we had started the chart in 1975, overall returns would have been a lot higher.

Now, cover up the top row containing the names of the asset classes. Look at the data near the bottom of the chart, showing the annualized return, standard deviation, and the number of years that the asset class was best or worst. If you had only this information and you could invest in just one asset class, which would you pick? You would most likely choose small value because of its annualized return of 15.42 percent.

Next, look at the year 1998. You'll see that small value returned a negative 7.03 percent, while large growth for that year was up 33.61 percent. That's a 40 percent difference. If someone had advised you in 1998 to invest in the "best" asset class of small value, you would have underperformed by 40 percent. And you probably would have sold out after it did so poorly, especially because the financial media were telling people that value would never be good again.

What this tells you is not to invest all of your money in any one asset class. The sea of light and dark areas in this chart shows that every asset class behaves differently and without predictability at any given time. This is why all of them are nec- essary to build a successful portfolio.

But in 2001, the chart shows that small value was up 35.43 and large growth did a negative 15 percent, more than a 50 per- cent difference.

Let's compare small growth and small value over the 33-year period from 1970 through 2002. Small value outperforms small growth. Over 2,057 stocks make up the small value asset class. You could buy any one of the small value stocks and it might or might not perform like the asset class, but if you bought them all, you would get the return indicated. There is safety in numbers.

During that same period, large value outperforms large growth. Why did value outperform growth? Value companies are the poorest companies and are therefore riskier. Their cost of capital is greater. It's the same principle that the person who can least afford the loan pays the highest interest rates. During the years 1995 to 1998, there were hundreds of media articles proclaiming that value was dead. But look at 1995 on the chart— large value was up 38 percent.

On the other hand, large growth companies, such as GE or Microsoft, are highly successful companies, but look at their returns. If asset classes all earned the same rate of return, we would all buy large growth because it's the safest. Small outperforms large because large is safer.

Academic studies have shown that international investing is no different when it comes to the risk factors—international value beats international growth; international small value beats international small growth. In other words, small has always beaten large over long periods of time. This is exactly the same for value versus growth.

A typical investment plan invests in either individual stocks and bonds or mutual funds. Maybe it will have a daily money market fund (this simply means cash), a bond fund, a balanced fund, two or three equity funds, and an international or overseas fund. You allocate your investment by percentages to your choice(s) of the funds being offered. You can pick as few or as many as you want. This will depend on your investment strategy.

MUTUAL FUNDS

A *mutual fund* is an investment company that makes investments on behalf of its participants, who share common financial goals. Mutual funds continually issue new shares of the funds for sale to the public. The number of shares and the price are directly related to the value of the securities the mutual fund holds. A fund's share price can change from day to day, depending on the daily value of its underlying securities.

Think of a mutual fund as a financial intermediary that pools all its investors' funds together and buys stocks, bonds, or other assets on behalf of the group as a whole. Each investor receives a certificate of ownership and a regular statement of his or her account indicating the value of the shares of the total investment pool. But there are over 8,000 of funds—don't you have to find the best mutual fund to invest in? No! In fact, sometimes the worst fund one year may end up to be the best fund the next year. It really doesn't matter which fund you choose once you've found the appropriate asset class that fund represents.

The main reasons people invest in mutual funds are convenience, accessing professional knowledge, and the opportunity to earn higher returns through a combination of growth and reinvestment of dividends. To understand why mutual funds are so popular, let's examine just how they work.

How Mutual Funds Work

The manager of the mutual fund uses the pool of capital to buy a variety of individual stocks, bonds, or money market instruments based on the advertised financial objectives of the fund. Mutual funds are directly regulated by the Securities and Exchange Commission (SEC), and management fees are taken out at the daily net asset value (NAV). This is the value of the fund's total investment, minus any debt, divided by the number of outstanding shares. For example, if the fund's investment value is $26,000,000 with no debt and 1,000,000 shares outstanding, the NAV would be $26 per share. The NAV is not a fixed figure because it must reflect the daily change in the price of the securities within the fund's portfolio.

In a mutual fund that includes thousands, and often millions, of shares, the NAV is calculated on a daily basis without commissions, in full and fractional units, with values moving up or down along with the stock and bond markets.

The two basic kinds of costs are management fees and sales charges.

Management Fees

Because of the large amounts of assets under management, investment companies are able to offer economies of scale, or competitive fee schedules, to their customers. Fund costs are an equally important factor in the return that you earn from a mutual fund. Fees are deducted from your investment. All other things being equal, high fees and other charges depress your returns.

The management fees charged depend on the complexity of the asset-management demands. Foreign equity management requires substantially more research, specialized implementation, and transaction costs than the management of a U.S. government bond fund. Asset-management fees reflect those differences. Equity mutual fund fees are higher than bond mutual fund fees. Actively managed funds typically have higher fees than index funds, since they seek to outperform the indexes and must, therefore, invest substantially in research and typically be more active in trading.

Fee comparisons are particularly important. Remember to compare the proverbial apples to apples—in this case, similar equities to equity mutual funds and similar bonds to bond mutual funds. (See Table 6.2.)

Sales Charges

Sales charges (or loads) are commissions paid on the sale of mutual funds. In the past, all commissions were simply charged up front, but that has changed. There are now several ways that mutual fund companies charge fees. The sales charge is subtracted from the initial mutual fund investment. A no-load fund does not have this charge, although other fees or service charges may be buried in its cost structure. Don't be misled: Nearly all mutual funds have a sales charge. Some are hidden; some are not. Let's talk about the ones that you can see.

A front-end load mutual fund charges a fee when an investor buys it. Loaded mutual funds can also be back-end loaded—

TABLE 6.2

Fee Comparisons of Various Mutual Funds

Mutual fund	Annual Performance	Management Fees	Net Performance
Foreign Equities	12.50%	1.25%	11.25%
US Large Cap	12.50%	1.00%	11.50%
US Small Cap	13.00%	1.20%	11.8%
Investment-Grade Bonds	7.80%	0.65%	7.15%
High-Yield Bonds	9.25%	0.75%	8.50%
Foreign Bonds	9.25%	0.90%	8.35%

having a deferred sales charge—and are sometimes known as B-shares. This option has higher, internal costs. If you decide to redeem your shares early, usually within the first five years, you pay a surrender charge.

- *A-shares*: You pay the commission all at once.
- *B-shares*: You have a contingent deferred sales charge. They are more popular with brokers because you don't pay any up-front load, but every year they take out the equivalent of 1 percent to pay the broker.
- *C-shares:* You typically have even higher internal expenses, and pay the selling broker up to 1 percent per year based on the amount of the assets. This fee comes directly from your investment performance. C-shares may have no up-front fee, but a possible 1 percent deferred sales charge in the first year (sometimes longer), and higher annual expenses (up to 1 percent extra per year).
- *No-load mutual funds*: This does not mean no cost. Some no-load funds charge a redemption fee of 1 to 2 percent of the net asset value of the shares to cover expenses mainly incurred by advertising.

Funds generally fall into one of the following asset-class subcategories:

Stock

Balanced

Income

Fixed Income

Cash

Money Market

Tax-free

Specialized

This can get confusing. The terms most funds use are elementary descriptions of the actions of various types of asset classes: U.S. large or U.S. small would simply be called Growth.

Equity Funds

A stock mutual fund is called an *equity fund*, which is usually a higher growth vehicle that stresses capital appreciation. The rule of thumb is that the volatility (or a better word is *variance*) will be twice the expected return. Variance measures the degree to which the period-by-period values of an individual stock or bond is expected to deviate from the statistically expected mean value of the stock (or bond) for a given period of time. The more the values are expected to deviate from the expected mean value, the greater the variance of the stock, hence the greater the risk.

The statistically expected variance of an individual stock (or bond) is expressed as a "range" estimate; that is, the most likely degree by which the possible outcomes in value deviate from the expected mean value (i.e., expected return). The range estimate of variance thus describes the degree of uncertainty of a point estimate (i.e., expected mean value).

What this means is an equity mutual fund is not an appropriate investment for someone with a short-term time horizon. Nor is it a good place for your intermediate money. When the time frame is five years or more, an equity mutual fund is a good choice.

Bond Funds

The key advantage of a bond fund is that, unlike individual issues, the fund managers can switch bonds from time to time within a fund. A bond fund is always replacing bonds in its portfolio to maintain its average maturity objective. A bond mutual fund's value is determined by what the open market will pay for the individual bonds in its portfolio. If interest rates are heading higher, there is a good chance the fund's share price will go down, and vice versa.

SEPARATELY MANAGED ACCOUNTS

These differ from mutual funds because the portfolio manager buys securities specifically for the *individual* investor and the securities are held in the name of the account holder. No assets are shared with other institutions or retail clients. Separately managed accounts generally have lower fees and allow you to build in performance-based fees.

The term *separately managed account* is synonymous with and used interchangeably with the term *individually managed account* or *managed account,* but for the purposes of this book and to avoid confusion, we're going to refer to these simply as *separate accounts.*

There is nothing magical about separate accounts. They provide the same opportunity as other investment choices for investors to grow capital, but with certain unique capabilities. Chief among these capabilities are the ability to customize portfolios with individual securities, better manage tax liabilities, and better control and manage cash flows. These accounts bill similarly to collective investment funds. A majority of separate account managers have a minimum of dollars they will manage, ranging from several hundred thousand to millions, based on the type of fund and manager.

However, advances in technology have expanded the availability of separately managed accounts to more investors. While individual customization may be somewhat diminished, the fact that thousands of accounts can be administered and reported on with ease has enhanced the marketability of separate accounts.

Separate accounts are not without controversy. Pundits question whether they provide adequate diversification when only one or two managers are employed, whether they are as cost efficient as more traditional investment products such as mutual funds, and whether they actually deliver the degree of tax control advertised. In the end, it must be recognized that separate accounts are just another investment alternative—an opportunity that will be suitable for some but not for all.

These accounts ultimately provide the same benefits as other investment packages—growing capital in a systematic process using professional investment managers to help people achieve their financial objectives—but they may do so with greater satisfaction. The real issue is not whether they provide benefits (they do), but how and for whom they should be employed. For example, say in 1995, you hired Nicholas Applegate, a mid-cap growth separate account manager whose standard deviation back then was around 20 percent. The S&P 500 at that time had a standard deviation of around 10.1. Today, the S&P 500's standard deviation is around 15.24, or 50 percent more volatile than 11 years ago. That means the market is twice as risky as it used to be in terms of volatility.

But, unlike the S&P 500, Nicholas Applegate's standard deviation isn't 5 percentage points higher; its standard deviation is closer to 44 percent. And, while it's true that they were one of the top fund managers from 1995 to 2000, they are also one of the fund managers with the largest decline from 2000 to 2002.

OTHER DEFINITIONS

Lifestyle or *asset-allocation funds* are starting to catch on as a supplement to the traditional funds. Companies generally offer three asset classes: moderate, conservative, and aggressive. Some managers use a fund of funds (multiple mutual funds within each category); others manage these in a non-mutual-fund environment. These funds are popular for investors who do not have time to understand the markets, but can fill out a simple questionnaire in order to find out which risk category they should be in.

A multi-discipline account (MDA) is very popular right now, specifically within Smith Barney. Acronyms are used to describe packaging together investment disciplines in predetermined percentages—often with lower investment minimums. The MDA manager is really a sponsor. A program sponsor is the investment advisor, the entity responsible for establishing and maintaining the program.

Multi-style account (MSA) is Cerulli Associates' umbrella term for the growing list of acronyms used to describe the packaging together of investment styles in predetermined percentages—often with lower investment minimums.

Unified managed account (UMA) is a centralized platform for brokerages to support a service of their financial consultants' fee-based businesses.

Client-directed, fee-based account is when the client directs the investments on a discretionary basis and can trade as much as he or she wants, but is only charged one fee. These accounts are rising in popularity and usually contain trading restrictions to control the frequency of trading.

Broker-directed account or *personally advised account* is when the stockbroker directs the investments on a discretionary basis. There is no independent money manager. Pioneered at EF Hutton, these programs are usually only available through a limited number of experienced, prequalified brokers.

Guided managed account programs are brokerage accounts that use their research departments to put together "buy" lists and give broker-advisors a choice of one or two securities in each category for the clients. These programs are some of the fastest growing products at many firms.

Fee-based brokerage account is used interchangeably with *guided portfolio account*, where the broker manages on a discretionary basis.

Wrap fee account was originally an individually managed account run by a professional money manager on a discretionary basis for the client. *Mutual fund wraps*, also known as *mutual fund managed accounts*, consist of a portfolio of mutual funds with an advisory fee overlay. This was the hottest product in the 1990s, but cooled down because diversified asset allocation did not perform well in the technology-heavy bull market.

The next goal is to combine what you have learned in Chapters 5 and 6 and put all this knowledge to work to build an effectively diversified portfolio that delivers consistent and specific results—results that can be replicated.

CHAPTER 7

Building Your Investment Portfolio

Structuring an investment portfolio is like painting a picture: you combine different factors to create an overall effect. You put together specific investment vehicles for the consistent way they deliver their styles.

The starting point for implementing the winning strategy is to buy passively managed funds, such as index or asset-class funds so that you will receive a market rate of return in a tax-efficient manner. Markets compensate investors with returns commensurate with the degree of risk they take. But always remember your assets are based in the U.S. dollar, and if you believe that the dollar may decline, you should hedge a portion of your portfolio in non-dollar-dominated investments.

The term *hedging* means strategically using instruments in the market to offset the risk of any adverse price movements. Technically, to hedge, you would invest in two securities with negative correlations such as the euro and the U.S. dollar. (This is Principle 1—Effective Diversification.)

When you've hedged a portion of your portfolio, the impact of an event like the fall of the dollar could be significantly reduced. An everyday example is, if you own your own home and buy home insurance, you are hedging yourself against fires, break-ins, or other unforeseen disasters.

To further illustrate the impact of hedging, let's look at the research of Steven Holt Abernathy from an article that appeared in the March/April 2006 *Journal of Retirement Planning*, entitled "Avoiding Portfolio Losses: Key to Effective Estate Planning." Mr. Abernathy is a principal and portfolio manager in a New York-based wealth management company. His graph (see Figure 7.1) depicts three variables of a $1,000 investment in the S&P 500 index since 1980.

The acronym CAGR stands for *compound annual growth rate.* When analyzing a company's results over a multiyear period, it is handy to have a single number that expresses the growth rate for the entire period. Suppose a company generates the following revenue from 2000 to 2003.

	2000	2001	2002	2003
Revenue	$100.00	$103.00	$108.00	$116.00
Growth		3.0%	4.9%	7.4%

If the company grew its revenues at an annual rate of 5.07 percent each year, it would also arrive at sales of $116 three

FIGURE 7.1

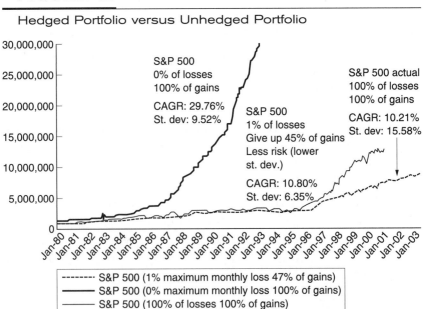

Hedged Portfolio versus Unhedged Portfolio

years later. Notice that $\$100 \times (1 + 5.07\%)^3 = \$116$. Solving for the growth rate we can represent the formula for a CAGR as:

$$CAGR = (C_t/C_0)^{(1/t)} - 1$$

In other words, for a three-year CAGR, take the value in year three and divide it by the value in year zero. Then take that result and raise it to the $1/3$ power. Then subtract one.

The bold top line is a projection of the S&P 500 gains since 1980 without any of the losing months. Of course, that is a purely hypothetical assumption since the S&P 500 had many losing months over the past 25 years, but this helps benchmark how return is given up to losses. The dotted line depicts the actual S&P 500 performance, including both gains and losses. The thin center line represents a hedged portfolio that mimics the S&P 500 index—but with two important differences. First, when the S&P has a down month, the hedged portfolio might also be down, but not more than 1 percent because of the protection provided by hedging. In exchange for avoiding large losses, the hedged portfolio gives up 45 percent of the gains! That seems like a staggering amount to surrender to protect the core assets. Now look at the hedged portfolio's low 6.35 percent standard deviation and average annual returns. Despite giving back almost half the gains, it actually outperforms the S&P slightly while reducing the standard deviation by some 60 percent. In other words, the strategy of avoiding monthly losses above 1 percent not only outperforms the S&P 500, it does so while reducing risk by 60 percent. The conclusion is that you can give away almost half of the index up-side and still outperform by hedging against big losses!

It's apparent why hedging techniques have become a significant strategy for protecting wealth for individual investors, and this supports the concept that you need some percentage of your portfolio in non-dollar-dominated investments to hedge your bets.

What is a *reasonable* growth rate of return? The general rule of thumb is that you take the percentage of decline level (how much money you could stand to lose) with which you are comfortable in a given quarter, divide that percentage in half, and add a money market rate (typically 3 to 4 percent). The result is a reasonable rate of growth over a three- to five-year period. Again, how little or how much risk you take directly affects how much growth you can expect. For instance, if you are willing to take a 10 percent decline quarterly, divide that number in half (5 percent) and add 3 to 4 percent. A reasonable rate of growth that you can expect to capture is 8 to 9 percent annually over a three- to five-year period.

It is important to know that there will sometimes be periods when you will experience declines in excess of this amount, and at other times your returns might be superior.

Table 7.1 shows what a reasonable expected return is, based upon your decline level (column one) over different time periods. The further the risk-ometer needle is to the right, the more risky the investment and the higher the potential rewards. For simplification purposes we are using a five-point scale.

Figure 7.2 illustrates how the optimal portfolio works. The optimal portfolio is usually located somewhere in the middle of the curve, because as you go higher up the curve, you take on proportionately more risk for a lower incremental return. On the other end, low-risk/low-return portfolios are pointless because

TABLE 7.1

What Is a Reasonable Expected Return?

Level of decline	Target growth rate	Time frame	Portfolio strategy	Asset risk-ometer
8%	6–8%	6 mos –2 yrs	Conservative portfolio 1	
10%	8–9%	18 mos –3 yrs	Balanced fund portfolio 2	
15%	10–13%	5–7 yrs	Conservative portfolio 3	
35%	11–14%	5–10 yrs	Aggressive portfolio 4	

FIGURE 7.2

Identifying Efficient Portfolios

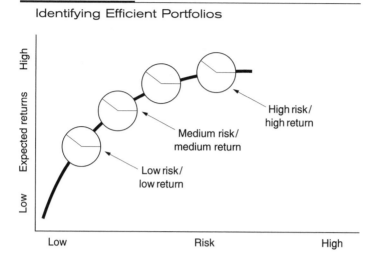

you can achieve a similar return by investing in risk-free assets, like government securities.

You can choose how much volatility you are willing to bear in your portfolio by picking any other point that falls on the efficient frontier. The efficient frontier is the curved line where return intersects volatility. It was first defined by Harry Markowitz in 1952. Markowitz found for any portfolio of assets there exists an efficient frontier, which represents variously weighted combinations of the portfolio's assets that yield the maximum possible expected return at any given level of portfolio risk.

In other words, this will give you the maximum return for the amount of risk you wish to accept. Optimizing your portfolio is not something you can calculate in your head. There are computer programs that are dedicated to determining optimal portfolios by estimating hundreds (and sometimes thousands) of different expected returns for each given amount of risk. It is similar to the way a printing process works. When a copy editor wants to print a photograph of a face for a magazine, he or she has photographic equipment that scans the face and breaks the picture into three component colors. The photograph might be 50 percent blue, 30 percent red, and 20 percent yellow. Next the camera assigns a percentage to each color throughout the face. Then it breaks the results into a pointillistic system with a filter that makes little dots in those proportions. When the dots are

F I G U R E 7.3

Selecting a Suitable Portfolio

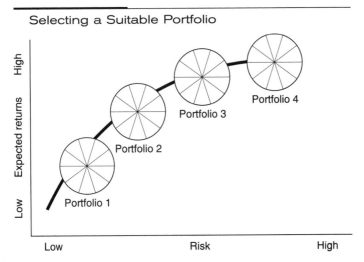

F I G U R E 7.4(A)

Hypothetical Portfolio 1: 20 Percent Equities/80 Percent Fixed

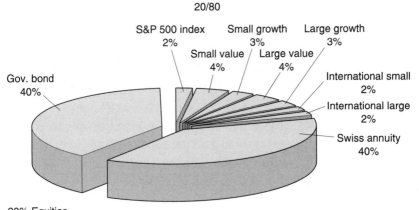

20/80

Gov. bond 40%

S&P 500 index 2%

Small value 4%

Small growth 3%

Large value 4%

Large growth 3%

International small 2%

International large 2%

Swiss annuity 40%

20% Equities
80% Swiss annuity/bonds

Swiss annuity	40%
Gov. bond	40%
S&P 500 index	2%
Small value	4%
Small growth	3%
Large value	4%
Large growth	3%
International small co.	2%
International large co.	2%

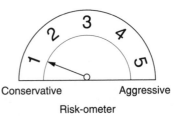

Conservative   Aggressive

Risk-ometer

printed onto the paper, it makes a model of the face, based on those colors specified. Building an efficient portfolio is a similar process. (See Figure 7.3.)

The list that follows shows four established examples of how you could build an efficient investment portfolio.

- Defensive (20 percent equities/80 percent fixed)
- Conservative (40 percent equities/60 percent fixed)
- Normal (60 percent equities/40 percent fixed)
- Aggressive (80 percent equities/20 percent fixed)

INVESTMENT VEHICLES

For our four hypothetical model portfolios [see Figures 7.4(a), 7.4(b), 7.4(c), and 7.4(d)], we use asset-class funds that were defined earlier.

FIGURE 7.4(B)

Hypothetical Portfolio 2: 40 Percent Equities/60 Percent Fixed

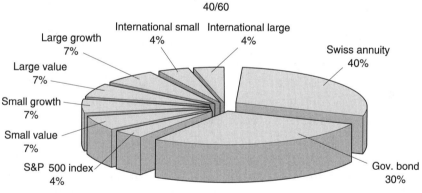

40% Equities
60% Swiss annuity/bonds

Swiss annuity	30%
Gov. bond	30%
S&P 500 index	4%
Small value	7%
Small growth	7%
Large value	7%
Large growth	7%
International small co.	4%
International large co.	4%

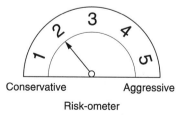

Conservative   Aggressive

Risk-ometer

FIGURE 7.4(C)

Hypothetical Portfolio 3: 60 Percent Equities/40 Percent Fixed

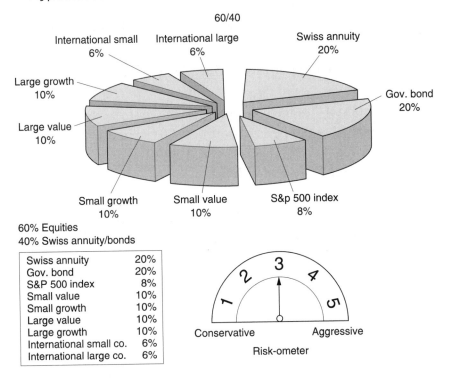

60/40

International small 6% — International large 6% — Swiss annuity 20%

Large growth 10%

Large value 10%

Gov. bond 20%

Small growth 10% — Small value 10% — S&p 500 index 8%

60% Equities
40% Swiss annuity/bonds

Swiss annuity	20%
Gov. bond	20%
S&P 500 index	8%
Small value	10%
Small growth	10%
Large value	10%
Large growth	10%
International small co.	6%
International large co.	6%

Conservative   Aggressive
Risk-ometer

No-load (no commission) low-cost funds buy and hold a representation of a very specific segment of the market (e.g., U.S.-based large company value stocks).

We substitute the Swiss annuity for the bond portion of the portfolio because of the risk of inherent greater volatility with long-term U.S. bonds without the reward for that risk. The Swiss annuity also acts as a hedge since it is held in Swiss francs.

Strategy Tips

- It's still up to you to do your homework. Take your time.
- Put assets inside protective legal structures.
- Follow the seven principles of successful investing.
- Hedge a portion of your portfolio in non-dollar-dominated investments.

FIGURE 7.4(D)

Hypothetical Portfolio 4: 80 Percent Equities/20 Percent Fixed

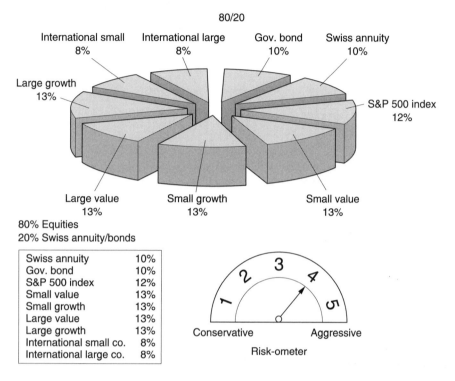

80/20

| International small 8% | International large 8% | Gov. bond 10% | Swiss annuity 10% |

Large growth 13%

S&P 500 index 12%

| Large value 13% | Small growth 13% | Small value 13% |

80% Equities
20% Swiss annuity/bonds

Swiss annuity	10%
Gov. bond	10%
S&P 500 index	12%
Small value	13%
Small growth	13%
Large value	13%
Large growth	13%
International small co.	8%
International large co.	8%

Conservative   Aggressive

Risk-ometer

- Know your appropriate return.
- Understand the different investment asset classes.
- Follow a strategy that works.

Now let's look at what investment vehicles are ready-made with the built-in wealth protection features of the right entity with the right structure in the right jurisdiction.

DOUGLAS COLLEGE LIBRARY

DOUGLAS COLLEGE LIBRARY

PART THREE

Debtor-Friendly Jurisdictions

Once you've utilized the protection precautions of entities and learned the most tax-advantaged risk management structures, it is important to consider as well how jurisdictions can enhance asset-protection and risk-management strategies. The characteristics of a favorable jurisdiction should include indisputable financial safety through a strong currency and a stable, conservative government that practices fiscal restraint, as well as an absolute right to financial privacy.

While a number of foreign countries are currently attractive for one reason or another, my research shows that there is only one I would recommend that has proved to provide consistent and tested safety through currency, privacy, and government. Switzerland is the most desirable jurisdiction for offshore investing. It stands out from all others. With Switzerland's world-class banking system and fabled political stability, investors can expect high degrees of privacy and security.

When implemented properly, the wealth-protection strategy presented here can preserve your privacy, protect your assets, and reduce taxes both legally and safely in Switzerland, the world's third largest financial center and the private banking capital of the world.

The Perfect Jurisdiction— Switzerland

Switzerland is the "Gold Standard" of the asset-protection countries. It stands out from all others in terms of desirability for investing internationally. With Switzerland's world-class banking system and fabled political stability, investors can expect high degrees of privacy and security.

According to the International Country Risk Guide,[1] Switzerland (which scored 91.5 out of 100 possible points) is the safest nation of the 129 countries surveyed for political, financial, and other risks of investment. (See Table 8.1.)

WHY SWITZERLAND?

A Brief History of Switzerland

How has Switzerland maintained financial privacy and independence while other nations have not? The answer lies in Switzerland's history and its people. The country of Switzerland has been at peace with its neighbors for many centuries. Investors who have had the foresight to place their wealth in Switzerland have never been affected by war, strife, or tyrannical governments.

---

1 Christian H. Kalin, *Switzerland Business and Investment Handbook* (New York: John Wiley & Sons, 2006), p. 67.

TABLE 8.1

Criteria Test—Switzerland

	Yes	No
Safety	x	
Enhanced return	x	
Income stream	x	
Currency risk and strength	x	
Asset protection: seizure and judgment	x	
Privacy and confidentiality	x	
Ability to liquidate quickly	x	
Diversified	x	
Low expenses	x	
Guaranteed yield	x	
Ownership rights	x	
Tax benefits	x	
Simple and uncomplicated	x	

Founded in 1291, Switzerland is the world's oldest surviving democracy. Switzerland's mountainous territory is quite small, about half the size of Maine, but approximately 7.5 million people live there, including some 1.5 million foreign nationals, who reside or work in the country.

Author John McFee, in his book *The Swiss Army*, records this account of the Swiss defense system provided by Adrien Tschumy, the commanding officer of the Swiss Tenth Mountain Division: "You must understand that there is no difference between the Swiss people and the Swiss Army. There is no difference in will; economic, military, it's the same thing. For 700 years freedom has been the fundamental story of Switzerland, and we are not prepared to give it up now. We want to defend ourselves, which is not the same as fighting abroad. We want peace, but not under someone else's conditions." The Swiss refer to their defense philosophy as the "porcupine principle"; roll yourself up and make your quills so hard and sharp that any predator will think twice about attacking you.

The Swiss have long had a strict policy of armed neutrality. As first drafted in 1515, the Swiss Code of Neutrality states: "We will attack no one, participate in no war, will make no alliance and will defend ourselves." This policy has produced the largest army in Western Europe. Switzerland's mostly civilian army has helped to save the country from involvement in two major twentieth-century wars. The Swiss believe that neutrality is best achieved by defensive strength. Within 48 hours the country can mobilize an army of 625,000 soldiers, 800 battle tanks, and 300 jet fighters, along with missiles and artillery all stored in hundreds of defense positions and underground fortresses. Highways are built to serve as emergency runways. Most of this defense structure is totally invisible by air. Arsenals, hospitals, and even fighter plane hangars are hewn into the mountainsides. An entire army division can fit inside some hidden mountain holes.

Underground fortresses are stocked with stores of gold and currency for the post-war reconstruction phase. While other nations provide such bunkers only for their political and military leaders, the Swiss provide this protection for every Swiss citizen.

All able-bodied men between the ages of 20 and 50 serve in the army and are trained for specific jobs. The private sector makes this Swiss defense system work because each male citizen is paid a full salary by his employer while he serves in the military two or three weeks a year. During war or other national emergencies, the Swiss can call upon 520,000 trained civil defense workers. And the civil defense program is intended to protect Swiss citizens against nuclear, biological, and chemical warfare.

Rather than having a traditional division between military and civilian roles, Swiss defense is a community effort. For instance, the Swiss are the only soldiers in the world who use their homes to store arms, ammunition, and other defense equipment. There is no difference between the Swiss people and the Swiss Army.

The Swiss Confederation was founded as a defensive alliance among three cantons. In succeeding years, other localities joined the original three. The Swiss Confederation secured its independence from the Holy Roman Empire in 1499. Switzerland's borders were fixed in 1815 by the Congress of Vienna, which also guaranteed Switzerland's neutrality. Several Catholic cantons tried to secede from the Swiss Confederation in 1847. But a new Swiss Constitution in 1848 gave each canton enough control over its local affairs to hold the nation together.

Switzerland's sovereignty and neutrality have long been honored by the major European powers, and the country was not involved in either of the two World Wars. The political and economic integration of Europe over the past half century, as well as Switzerland's role in many UN and international organizations, have strengthened Switzerland's ties with its neighbors. However, the country did not officially become a UN member until 2002. Switzerland remains active in many UN and international organizations, but retains a strong commitment to neutrality.

An often-overlooked point of history is that the Swiss confederations strongly influenced America's founding fathers and the structure of American government. It's not an accident that America's first governing document, The Articles of Confederation, closely resembles the governmental design of the Swiss Republic, then known as The Helvetian Confederation. Thomas Jefferson borrowed a defining phrase of the Declaration of Independence, "the pursuit of happiness," from a lesser-known Swiss thinker, Jean-Jacques Burlamachie, who lived from 1694 to 1748 and was a public official and professor from Geneva widely admired by the leaders of the American Revolution.

Demographics

Switzerland has a population of approximately 7,523,934. Bern, the capital, has a population of about 300,000 in its metropolitan area; Geneva has almost 400,000. Zurich is the largest city, with 840,000 in the metropolitan area.

In Switzerland, we find a culture that is very ethnocentric and circumspect toward outside influence, although the younger generation is becoming more open. The culture of Switzerland is made up of four subcultures: German, French, Italian, and 1 percent of the population that is indigenous.

Given these diversities, many might expect Switzerland to be a land torn apart by its differences. But, in fact, Switzerland is very stable. The reason for this is not hard to find: The Swiss elevate the rights of the individual above virtually all else. The democracy is based on this principle and is characterized by extreme decentralization of power.

Language

Switzerland has four official languages: French, Italian, German, and Romansch, a language descended from Latin. In addition to one or more of these languages, most businesspeople in the cities speak English as well, particularly those who work in financial institutions. Approximately 65 percent of the population speak Swiss-German dialects, many of which are not understood by other Germans. The Swiss learn to write in conventional German. About 18 percent of the people speak French, 10 percent speak Italian, and 1 percent speak Romansch.

Government

The Swiss Confederation is a federal state of 26 sovereign cantons. The president is head of both the state and the government. There are two legislative houses: the 46-seat Council of States and the 200-seat National Council.

The legislature, called the Federal Assemblies, is composed of a popularly elected National Assembly, which is also known as the lower house, and an Assembly of States, which is much like the Senate of the United States and has one or two members representing each canton. (Present-day cantons are much like states in the United States.)

Members of the Federal Assemblies meet four times a year for two- to three-week sessions. They elect a Federal Council composed of seven members that acts as the national executive branch. The Council then elects one of its members to serve a one-year term as president.

The Swiss put great stock in the people's right to referendum. Any bill enacted into law by the Federal Assemblies is subject to a general referendum by the country's electorate if the opposition to the law gathers a minimum of 50,000 signatures in a petition. In the referendum, if more than 50 percent of the votes cast oppose the law, it is rescinded. This is a marvelous way of making sure that the power of governing resides with the people.

Knowing the power of the referendum, politicians are reluctant to pass laws that are unpopular with the general public.

They make great effort to know what the people want and govern accordingly.

All of the major political parties are represented in the Federal Council, which also represents Switzerland's cultural, religious, and linguistic diversity. Imbued throughout the political system and interwoven throughout the fabric of life is a belief in working toward consensus rather than confrontation.

As in the United States, power that is not delegated to the federal government resides with the cantons. Since most of the citizens of Switzerland identify more strongly with their cantons in terms of politics and culture, the cantons, historically, have enjoyed a good measure of independence within the federal framework. Much of Swiss political power in fact is wielded by the 26 cantons, which are autonomous and possess far more power than states in the United States do.

Because of their special brand of democracy, where power resides mostly in cantons and communes and federal authority is largely limited by popular referendum, the Swiss are able to play an active role in their government. Over the years they have evolved as a people who are moderate in temperament and conservative in their traditions. This is especially true regarding economic and financial concerns.

The rights of Swiss citizens are protected by three political safeguards designed to make sure that the people rule the government, and not the other way around. A weak chief executive, the practice of voter referendums, and the right of voter initiative all severely limit the power of the central government in Bern.

The Swiss president (currently Moritz Leuenberger) has little power and no effect on the daily lives of most Swiss citizens. Unlike many other nations' chief executives who are constantly surrounded by secret police protection, the president of Switzerland can often be found riding to work on the public streetcars in Bern.

The Swiss do not make a profession out of politics. Only the seven-member federal council consists of professional politicians, and all others serve briefly by avocation, not as a primary profession. The presidency is a rotating office among the seven-member federal council, changing each year like clockwork. Members of this executive branch are equals who consider themselves colleagues rather than subordinates to a president. This system prevents the rise of a strong chief executive and it seeks political consensus rather than confrontation. The Swiss federal government is weak by design, and the Swiss want to keep it that way.

The Swiss philosophy of government by the people delicately balances the rights of the individual with the interests of the communes, villages, the city, the canton, the state, and the federal government. Parliament is comprised of two chambers with representatives from each of the 26 cantons representing a dozen different political parties.

Switzerland's concept of the right of initiative is unique in the world today. It allows Swiss citizens actually to create legislation. One hundred thousand petition signatures result in a national election to approve or reject the proposed law, so long as the law meets certain legal standards. Swiss citizens also vote for their own teachers, judges, and priests.

These political practices have a great effect on Swiss banking for one central reason: Swiss voters almost always reject any measure that increases government power or government spending. Swiss voters also rejected a graduated income tax, which would have increased tax rates on those with higher incomes; instead the Swiss maintained their flat rate income tax.

Swiss Banking Industry

For centuries the Swiss have been investment bankers to both the kings and commoners of Europe. Those who seek safety and security for their money have found a haven in the rugged Swiss Alps and in the values, traditions, and character of the Swiss people.

Today, banking is Switzerland's largest industry and Switzerland has become the world's premiere private banking center. The *London Financial Times* has estimated that Swiss banks manage some 40 percent of the world's private wealth.

At present, there are over 600 banks of various types operating in the country, including The Big Two, other big banks, cantonal banks, and private banks. Including branches, there are over 5,000 locations where banking can be performed.

Switzerland's private banks play an important and unique role in providing banking services. They are the oldest banks in the country and are unlike any banking institution found in the United States. Most private banks in Switzerland operate in the form of a partnership, and the deposits in private banks are backed by the personal fortunes of the partners.

The comprehensive Bank Act of 1934 provides the legal basis for the so-called Secrecy Laws and provides severe criminal penalties for past and present bank employees who violate the laws. The law states that a violation of banking secrecy is punishable by a prison term of up to six months and a fine of CHF 50,000. It is interesting to note that not a single banker in Switzerland has *ever* been convicted of violating this law!

Within the array of services that Swiss banks offer is a broad selection of bank accounts. Some types of accounts are very similar to those customarily offered by American banks; other types are nonexistent in the American banking system and might be considered unusual or even outrageous to American bankers.

If normal Swiss bank accounts are not secret enough, the Swiss have allowed an added layer of secrecy with the so-called *numbered account*. No other element of Swiss banking has given rise to so much folklore. All bank accounts in Switzerland, like everywhere else, are assigned account numbers. By special request, some banks will agree to replace an account name on bank records with a special code number. The number (or a series of letters and digits) is the only way a bank clerk can identify the account. There is no doubt that customers do enjoy the added confidence that numbered accounts provide. A numbered Swiss account is considered the ultimate secret available to the owners of wealth. Bank accounts are easily opened by mail, but those banks that do offer numbered accounts will most likely require a personal visit by the prospective customer.

Swiss bank accounts can include Current Accounts, Private Accounts, Savings Accounts, and even Managed Accounts that provide instant access to investment opportunities. Investors use them to buy stocks, bonds, currencies, and precious metals traded anywhere in the world. Their fees are competitive, and they offer expert investment advice.

Swiss Real Estate

Switzerland is a postcard-pretty paradise located at the top of Europe and draws tourists from around the world. Because of this, the Swiss have constructed bureaucratic barriers to protect their land from overdevelopment. For this and many other reasons, Swiss real estate is considered the most highly valued in Europe.

It is extremely difficult to obtain permanent residency in Switzerland. As a foreigner, you generally need permission from the government to buy real estate. It's possible but difficult for foreigners to buy land, a free-standing home, or an estate in rural areas; it's almost impossible to obtain permission to purchase property in cities such as Zurich and Geneva. In recreational regions, condominiums are the only properties readily available.

However, the laws are not nearly as limiting as they may seem because many areas considered rural are within a few miles of the ever-popular ski resorts and spas. And the condominiums are attractive and spacious, many with traditional Swiss architecture, mountain views, and privacy.

Unless you have a Swiss Residency permit, you cannot occupy your Swiss property for more than three months per calendar year. You can, however, arrive at the beginning of the last quarter of one year and depart at the end of the first quarter of the following year. This allows for a six-month stay.

Swiss Gold

Without question, gold is the most effective guard of purchasing power. Some investors have been disappointed with the performance of gold in the past several decades, but they are forgetting the primary purpose of gold as an inflation hedge.

Speculators have often lost badly with gold, but that is true of any speculation, and it is not because of some inherent characteristic of gold. This speculation is very different from what most investment advisors say is the proper use of gold in an

investment portfolio: as a means of achieving balance, diversification, and inflation insurance.

The Swiss know how to invest in gold the right way. Many
Swiss banks offer gold accumulation programs that allow an
investor to enjoy all the benefits of investing in gold without the
responsibilities and costs of handling and storage. Buying gold
through accumulation programs can provide you with a number
of advantages. You can make purchases at any time and benefit
from the bank's being able to buy at wholesale prices normally
available only to large purchasers. Your order can be combined
with other orders so that you do not pay an extra fee on small
unit amounts or the regular spread charged when buying or selling gold. These savings can be as much as 3 percent because of
the wholesale price and another 8 percent from not having to
pay small order surcharges. Naturally, such accounts are treated
with the same secrecy as any other Swiss bank account. Each
investor's account is held separately by the bank in a fiduciary
(trustee) relationship.

Swiss Insurance Industry

Few people realize that the relatively unglamorous Switzerland
is actually the most important insurance center in the world. For
example, Swiss life insurance companies are among the safest in
the world. In the past 150 years, not a single insurance company
has failed; this is a record that even Swiss banks envy. Not one
single company has ever failed to fulfill its obligations to its
clients. This perfect record is due to the strict code of practice
with which the companies have to comply and a very prudent
investment policy.

What Makes the Swiss Insurance Industry Solid?

What makes the Swiss insurance industry solid are the rigid regulations of the Swiss Federal Office of Private Insurance (FOPI).
It strictly supervises and governs the activities of Swiss insurance companies to a degree that surpasses all other countries.
Conservative, century-old laws determine asset values in insurance companies' balance sheets. Behind the times? It may seem so,

but you are the one to profit from the Swiss insurance industry's conservative stance. Safety and security are top priority—by law.

The Swiss government has extensively regulated all Swiss insurance companies since 1885. The Swiss federal constitution forbids Swiss life insurance companies from making the kinds of risky or speculative investments that have landed U.S. life insurance companies in so much trouble. The bulk of funds are invested in blue chip bonds and preferred stocks, first mortgages, and Swiss real estate. In addition, each insurance company creates and maintains a guarantee fund following the strict regulations of the Swiss Federal Act on the Guarantee of Life Insurance Policies.

According to this law, a separate reserve must be set aside by each company in order to cover all policy liabilities owed to shareholders. In other words, if everyone who held a policy with a Swiss insurance company wanted to or was eligible to collect all their policy benefits at once, that company could use its guarantee fund to pay off each and every policyholder in full! It is this special feature of Swiss life insurance companies that makes them safer and more conservative than even the biggest and safest Swiss banks.

U.S. insurance companies have neither the stringent reserve requirements nor the legal responsibility to keep their policyholders' money from being commingled with other assets. In fact, assets from certain types of insurance policies, including fixed annuities, are considered part of a U.S. insurance company's "general account." As such, they are not segregated into a separate account for the protection of the policyholders.

The insurance industry in Switzerland benefits from unique tax advantages and knowledgeable and conservative management. The combination leads to solid and surprisingly productive investment opportunities. Some people equate a conservative approach to investments with low or marginal returns, but this is not the case with Swiss insurance companies.

The returns from these companies are quite high, because the companies seldom have to deduct losses on bad investments that decrease the yield. Without losses in their investment portfolios, it is possible to maintain a conservative approach to investment with high returns.

Switzerland has only about 20 life insurance companies. All of them are very solid and well managed. Swiss insurance companies do not engage in rate competition. Instead, they focus their energies on maintaining their strength. Because the insurance industry is somewhat concentrated, it is, on the whole, stronger and easier to supervise than the insurance industry in the United States where there are thousands of companies to regulate, all on a state-by-state basis.

As stated earlier, the Swiss Federal Office of Private Insurance (FOPI) regulates the insurance industry in Switzerland. It has a reputation of being a strict regulator. Because the Swiss government regulates the insurance industry tightly, investments in any of the products offered by Swiss insurance companies carry an extremely low risk. Indeed, the risk level has been described by some as being nil.

For example, liquidity and valuation of investments are ultra-conservative. A maximum of 30 percent of investable funds may be put in real estate. This is a very low percentage, especially considering that, on average, Swiss real estate is the most highly valued in Europe. Consequently, exposure to any downturn in real estate prices is limited.

Many American banks and insurance companies undoubtedly are sorry that they did not follow a real estate investment policy similar to that of their Swiss counterparts during the 1980s and into the early 1990s. And if the banks and insurance companies aren't wishing it, certainly their policyholders are, because when the value of real estate dropped virtually throughout America, the values of many investments dropped accordingly. Some portfolios that were overextended in real estate were ruined.

The Swiss insurance companies go a step further in the effort to protect their investors. Often they carry their real estate holdings at less than half of the holdings' present market value. This wide margin allows for a significant downward spiral in prices and value in real estate before the safety of investments is affected.

The Swiss also handle their accounting in a conservative manner. Unlike many American companies that tend to overvalue assets in order to achieve high prices in the stock market, Swiss insurance companies frequently have hidden reserves of millions of dollars. This means a major depression or deflation could strike all the world markets and the Swiss insurance firms would have room to lose up to half the book value of their assets and still be solvent and able to meet all their financial obligations.

When Swiss insurance companies openly claim that their "sobriety, prudence, and conservatism make Swiss insurance institutions the safest and most respected in the world," it cannot be dismissed as commercial boasting. These qualities are powerfully present in daily management decisions, within the insurance industry itself and within the insurance industry's watchdog—FOPI. These qualities are also the guidelines for the insurance companies' portfolio allocations. This conservative attitude, along with the historically secure Swiss financial system, has given utmost financial stability to the Swiss insurance industry.

Policyholders in Switzerland enjoy a degree of security and protection that is maintained more strictly than in any other country, thanks to the long existence of stringent insurance legislation and rigorous supervision of the acquisition, business, and premium policies of the insurance companies by the Swiss Federal Office of Private Insurance.

The controls and regulations made by FOPI are exceedingly strict. No other sector is so rigorously supervised, and probably no other branch of the Swiss economy accepts this supervision with as good grace as private insurance companies, which go as far as paying the full cost of the supervision. Together with the strict authorization conditions for the insurance company, the supervisory authority has prevented any disreputable companies from gaining a foothold in the Swiss insurance market.

All Swiss insurance companies must fulfill the high standards set forth by the FOPI. Failures as experienced in other sectors in recent years, or in insurance businesses in the United States and in Great Britain, have not occurred in Switzerland. The Swiss system of strict insurance supervision has proved its worth for the benefit of policyholders and the entire economy.

How Strict Is Strict?

The primary aim of the state supervisory board is to protect premium payers from being overcharged and to ensure the ability of the insurance company to pay, so that if the insured event or damage occurs, the person insured can be sure of receiving payment. The latter would not be guaranteed if the insurance company—for competitive reasons—were to offer premiums set too low. The result: Swiss insurance companies must have their rates examined and approved, a function performed by FOPI. It only approves premiums that lie within the premium maximum (protection from overcharging) and minimum (guarantee of payment capability); competition among insurance companies can then take place within these limits, which is in the policyholders' best interest.

Supervision and approval of insurance companies' premium policies are not the end of the course. It would be conceivable that despite a good premium policy, an insurance company would one day no longer be capable of meeting its obligations toward policyholders (e.g., by investing money entrusted in them in risky ventures). FOPI therefore also checks that the companies do indeed invest their funds as profitably as possible, but broadly based, in order to protect them against risk of losses or variations in earnings from the different investment categories. In addition, FOPI supervises the observance of the strict regulations concerning the assurances to be given and the guarantee fund, as stipulated under the guarantee and security laws.

For example, escalating real estate values of recent years resulted in market price excesses. As a result, the Swiss legislature was concerned about the large amount of funds being poured into Swiss real estate and, in late 1989, voted to limit the percentage of new capital to be invested in Swiss real estate to a maximum of 30 percent of new funds not yet invested. Not a single Swiss insurance company was endangered by the real estate slump that followed. (See Figure 8.1.)

Figure 8.1 is from one of Switzerland's leading insurance companies and is representative of the industry. It reveals that Swiss real-estate-related investments (real estate and mortgages) amount to approximately 34 percent of the entire investment portfolio and another 56 percent is allocated to fixed-interest instruments and equities. What this chart does not show, however, is that the real estate holdings are held at the initial purchase price and

FIGURE 8.1

Profitable Asset Allocation

Typical investment portfolio

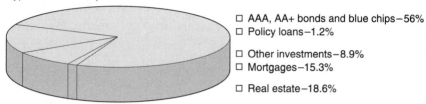

- ☐ AAA, AA+ bonds and blue chips–56%
- ☐ Policy loans–1.2%

- ☐ Other investments–8.9%
- ☐ Mortgages–15.3%

- ☐ Real estate–18.6%

TABLE 8.2

No Debt!

Liabilities	1998
	Sfr
Technical reserves	5,067,201,544
Actuarial reserves	4,886,397,458
Premiums brought forward	32,444,381
Reserves for outstanding claims	34,911,518
Profit-sharing fund	113,301,660
Other technical reserves	146,527

not at the (sometimes inflated) market value. Bond portfolios are carried in the books at actual market values. Consequently, a major protective price cushion is factored into the insurance company's portfolio.

The largest liability shown in Table 8.2 is "Technical Reserves." This table represents the "guarantee fund," which is the sum of all cash obligations the insurance company has undertaken to pay. It includes all annuity payments due now and into the future and, adding all future premiums due, includes all insurance claims that eventually will become due.

New European Accounting Standards
Reveal Hidden Reserves

After the start of the European Union's (EU) common market, Swiss insurance companies dealing throughout Europe restated their balance sheets in order to comply with prevailing European accounting standards.

As an example, a renowned Swiss insurance company showed shareholders' equity amounting to 2.66 billion Swiss francs. Under the new prevailing European accounting standards, the same company's shareholders' equity was restated as 3.70 billion Swiss francs. As reported by the *Financial Times* of London, "Under the new reporting principles, the figure should actually be adjusted to 4.64 billion Swiss francs."—proof that assets have been enormously underestimated all along! Nearly all major Swiss insurance companies have understated their true net worth in their balance sheets for dozens of years. Even if a deep financial crisis were to engulf the future and assets were subject to a major deflation, these companies will have enough assets and liquidity to honor all due payments! It is no exaggeration that Swiss insurance companies are indeed the safest in the world.

Insurance Supervision in Switzerland

The supervision of private insurance, existing since 1885, reposes on Article 34 Paragraph 2 of the Federal Constitution and aims primarily to protect the insured party. The laws that define the range of this supervision and determine the competencies of the Supervision Authority are the following:

> Federal Law of June 23, 1978 on the supervision of private insurance institutions (Law on Insurance Supervision, LIS) has replaced the supervision law of June 25, 1885
>
> Federal Law of February 4, 1919 on the guarantee deposit of the insurance Institutions (Deposit Law, DL)
>
> Federal Law of June 25, 1930 on the security of the claims of insurance policies of domestic life insurance institutions (Security Law, SL)

The dispositions for the execution of these laws are contained in various decrees of the Federal Council. In its supervisory role, the Swiss Federal Office of Private Insurance (FOPI) has, in addition, to pay attention to a certain number of instructions of the Federal Department of Justice and Police (FDJP) to which it is attached. The insurance contracts signed by Swiss insurers subject to supervision are regulated by the Federal Law of April 2, 1908 on Insurance Contracts (LIC).

Supervision Authorities. The supervision authorities are the FDJP and the FOPI. The supervision as well as the power to make decisions are incumbent upon the FOPI if the LIS does not explicitly reserve the competence to the FDJP. The FOPI is part of the FDJP and consists at present of 30 collaborators, divided into executive management, a management staff, an administrative office, and three specialized sections:

- A section for accident, illness, and material damage insurances (including reinsurance companies)
- A section for life assurance
- A legal section

Supervision System. Every insurance company doing business in Switzerland must be licensed by the FDJP. To receive the license the insurance company has to fulfill conditions as to firm type, capital, organization, etc. If the conditions are fulfilled, the insurance company receives the license. There are neither "numerous clauses" nor other local obstacles to insurance business.

The LIS reposes on the principle that only the real control of the insurers subject to supervision secures the effective protection of the assured against the consequences of operations involving losses. The LIS requires therefore a permanent and detailed supervision of the whole business of the insurance companies. The law grants the Supervision Authority the necessary competences.

The principle of an effective real insurance protection encompasses as well the obligation imposed upon the life assurance companies to set apart a portion of their assets for the guarantee of the claims of the assured. For the Swiss life assurance institutions, this is attained by the establishment of a Security Fund. It is a legally prescribed fund to guarantee the obligations of the life assurance companies toward their clients. The amount of the "guarantee fund" is principally determined by the mathematical or actuarial reserves. Assets equal to this amount are separated from the remainder of the assets and allocated as security for the rights of the life assurance policyholders.

Competence of the FOPI.   The supervisory duty of the FOPI applies to all of the activities of the private insurance institutions subjected to supervision. The business bases, especially the technical, financial, and juridical aspects, are routinely examined.

The examination by specialists of the business bases of a private insurance institution is carried out by the FOPI first of all, during the treatment of the requests for the authorization to do business, which have to be directed to the FDJP (the authorization is only granted if the insurance institution meets the legal exigencies and in particular offers the necessary guarantees concerning solvency, organization, and management).

The examination of the report that the insurers have to present every year to the FOPI constitutes a considerable part of its activities. The report has to be established on forms prepared by the FOPI and gives detailed information on all aspects of the business activities. It constitutes the most important document for the critical examination of the situation (solvency) of the companies. Moreover, these reports are used to establish the "Report on the Private Insurance Institutions in Switzerland" published annually by the FOPI. Thanks to the balances, the annual accounts, the tables, and the commentaries contained in it, this report gives detailed information on the state of the supervised insurance institutions and on other important aspects of private insurance.

Another duty of the FOPI for the protection of the assured consists of the examination of the elements of the operating plan submitted by the insurers, namely the principals, for calculating mathematical reserves; bonus schemes as well as the General Policy Conditions; and the tariffs that are allowed to be utilized only after approval by the Supervision Authority. The Policy Conditions have to conform to legislation and must not contain misconceptions or contradictions. For the tariffs, established on the basis of calculations and statistics submitted to it, the FOPI takes care that the premiums stay within certain limits that guarantee the solvency of the individual insurer on one side and, on the other side, secure the protection of the assured against abuse. The policies issued are regulated by the Federal Law on Insurance Contracts.

The control of the legally required guarantee for the insurance claims constitutes for the FOPI an important aspect of its work. The Security Law (SL) obliges the FOPI to verify once every year at the domicile of each insurance company the amount of the security fund and the correspondence with its cover, as well as the presence of the assets allocated to it. The FOPI participates in the administration of the deposits at the Swiss National Bank of all insurance institutions subject to supervision insofar as the choice of the assets requires its approval.

Numerous requests for information on various questions concerning private insurance are directed to the FOPI. The office supplies this information when this seems compatible with the secrecy of office, with its position as a neutral supervision authority, and with the principle of the separation of powers.

Investment Prescriptions

Every insurance company (life and nonlife) must respect the following principles:

Security

Asset yield

Appropriate diversification in respect to the different categories of investments and their proportion

Foreseeable liquidity requirements

The assets allocated to the guarantee fund serving as cover for the life assurances accepted by assurance institutions are subjected to the private assurance institutions' supervision[2]. Owing to the revision on December 1, 1986 of this decree, the Swiss life assurance institutions are within certain limits allowed to invest their money in assets of foreign debtors and in foreign currency to cover the liabilities of the Swiss insurance portfolio.

As to the assets not allocated to the guarantee fund (or the guarantee deposit) there exist no legal prescriptions concerning the composition of these investments. But the Supervisory Authority in practice pays attention to the maintenance of similar principles as for the assets of the guarantee fund.

---

2 September 11, 1931 (AVO, SR 961.05).

THE SWISS FRANC

Investing in Switzerland gives you the chance to diversify into a strong and safe currency, the Swiss franc, or, if you wish, into the two reserve currencies of the new millennium, the euro and the dollar. Swiss francs provide a safe haven from most of the major forms of financial risk in today's world: political risk, tax risk, currency risk, and litigation risk. And all this protection begins with the laws and traditions of Switzerland, a centuries-old bastion of democracy.

Switzerland's currency, the Swiss franc, has an enviable record. The franc has maintained its value better than any other major currency in the world. No other currency comes close to the total performance of the Swiss franc. The Swiss franc was worth 23 cents when the United States stopped backing its currency with gold in 1971. As of the beginning of 2004, the Swiss franc was worth 81 cents.

In other words, the Swiss franc has appreciated 252 percent against the U.S. dollar during the past 33 years. If someone had invested in a Swiss annuity earning just 4.5 percent instead of leaving it in U.S. dollars, today that investor would be ahead by over 400 percent, or an average of a nearly 9 percent compounded annual return over the past three decades. Figure 8.2 shows the increase in value of the Swiss franc against the U.S. dollar from the point in 1971 when the dollar was stripped of its backing in gold to 2003.

There are many sound reasons behind the strength of the Swiss franc:

1. *Gold Backing.* The Swiss National Bank is mandated under the Swiss Constitution to accumulate reserves, a portion of which may be in gold. Applying current market prices, the Swiss gold reserves significantly exceed currency in circulation. Gold reserves add stability to a nation's economy by minimizing both inflation and deflation and, thus, gold will likely continue to play a crucial role in the Swiss central bank's portfolio.

F I G U R E   8.2

Swiss Franc versus U.S. Dollar, 1971 to 2003

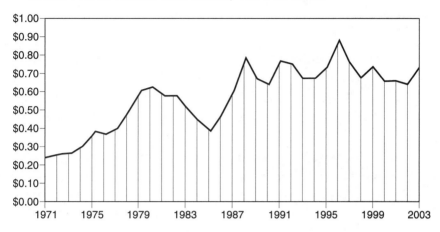

2. *No Exchange Controls.*   Switzerland is the only country in the eastern hemisphere that has never imposed
   external exchange controls on the outflow of funds. The
   knowledge that one's money will never be held hostage
   makes more investors buy that currency, thus bidding
   up its price.

3. *Political Neutrality.*   Switzerland's policy of strict neutrality protects the wealth of all investors.

4. *Strong Democracy, Weak Central Government.*   The
   Swiss control their government—not the other way
   around—through the national referendum and
   initiatives.

5. *Frugal Traditions.*   The Swiss enjoy the highest per
   capita wealth and income in the Western world, with
   a long-established tradition of financial privacy and
   fiscal responsibility.

6. *Low Money Growth.*   Swiss money supply growth is
   low and stable, which is the best indicator that the
   Swiss franc will enjoy low inflation rates over the long
   term, maintaining its strong purchasing power in the
   future.

These fundamental reasons point to a lower dollar and a higher Swiss franc in the years to come.

SUMMARY

1. Switzerland is the international banking capital of the world.

2. Switzerland is known as the life insurance capital of the world, and it offers the finest policies available. (See Table 8.3.)

3. In the past 150 years, not a single insurance company has failed; this is a record that even Swiss banks envy. Not one single company has ever failed to fulfill its obligations to its clients. This track record is unique in the world. In the United States, for example, several major life insurance companies have failed or gone bankrupt. And in 2000, even Equitable Life, Britain's oldest life insurer and once one of the proudest names in the industry, had to close its doors to new business. This case actually raised some fundamental questions about the provision and regulation of private pension insurance in the United Kingdom. In Switzerland, things are quite different. The Swiss Federal Office of Private Insurance regulates all Swiss insurance business by enforcing the strictest regulations known in the industry. Life insurance companies are required to maintain a security fund that covers all their obligations plus an additional security margin. This fund is segregated from the company's operating assets. The investment parameters for the security funds are very conservative, the only priority being their safety and liquidity.

4. Switzerland's sophisticated banking and insurance industries are built on three rock-solid premises: (a) your right to financial safety through the world's strongest currency; (b) a conservative government that practices fiscal restraint; (c) your absolute right to financial privacy.

TABLE 8.3

International Insurance Ratios

Amount spent on insurance premiums per capita and country (without Social Security, in US$, 2004)		
	Per capita premiums	Life insurance
Switzerland	**5,660**	**3,431**
United Kingdom	4,059	2,617
Japan	3,771	3,003
Ireland	3,670	2,313
USA	3,638	1,658
Denmark	3,116	2,038
Netherlands	3,094	1,562
Belgium	2,876	2,005
Finland	2,714	2,127
France	2,698	1,768
Sweden	2,358	1,602
Norway	2,321	1,323
Germany	2,051	0,930
Australia	2,041	1,129
Italy	1,913	1,238
Canada	1,872	0,723
Austria	1,847	0,811
Hong Kong	1,833	1,484
Singapore	1,621	1,300
South Korea	1,243	874
New Zealand	1,215	272
Spain	1,146	489
Israel	1,041	461
Russia	98	34
China	36	25

Source: sigma/Swiss Re.

5. Switzerland is the oldest democracy in the world—now over 700 years old—and certainly won't change its course overnight.

6. Switzerland is a free-enterprise country with minimal government regulation and economic control.

7. When you send your money to Switzerland, it is immediately governed under some of the most consumer-oriented laws of asset protection in the world.

8. When you invest in a Swiss annuity, you have no stock market or bond market risk to worry about. Instead, you have an ironclad set of guarantees from the best insurance companies in the world.

9. For some, Swiss interest rates seem low, yet viewed historically; the long-term return has run nearly 9 percent when measured in U.S. dollars.

CHAPTER 9

The Swiss Annuity

Many conservative financial planners believe that the Swiss annuity is the single most effective way to diversify some of your capital out of the U.S. dollar and into Swiss francs. Americans investing in a Swiss annuity are acquiring protection by purchasing what may be the safest and most straightforward overseas investment available today.

Most international investors establish their Swiss annuities with a single premium deposit. On the other hand, other investors choose to dollar-cost-average these investments by making periodic deposits, and many make arrangements for these payments through a Swiss bank account.

However, you don't have to have a Swiss bank account to make your premium deposits. In fact, such an account would be reportable under U.S. law, thus removing one of the advantages of Swiss annuities. Instead, there is another way to make your premium deposits—through a *premium deposit account.*

This method has so many advantages it is surprising that so few people know about it. In effect, a *premium deposit account* is an interest-bearing "bank" account opened at your insurance company. It has two distinct advantages over a regular Swiss bank account.

First, it is not reportable to the tax authorities because you are making payments to an insurance company, not a bank. Second, it pays interest rates about 1 percent higher than bank deposit (savings) accounts. Moreover, there is no withholding tax on the interest; all payments are tax-free. Remember, when you send your money to Switzerland, it is immediately governed under some of the most consumer-oriented laws of asset protection and privacy in the world.

The policy owner may choose to receive annuity payments immediately or may arrange for the payments to be deferred for a number of years. Deferred contracts are usually for five years or longer. The most popular type of Swiss annuity is the deferred annuity. The appreciation of the Swiss franc, combined with the annual interest and profit sharing make this a true wealth builder.

Payment from the annuity can be received as a one-time, lump-sum payment or by installments—either for life or for a fixed number of years. The payments are typically made by check or bank transfer and are a combination of accrued interest, profit dividends, and a portion of the capital invested. Upon the death of the person insured, the proceeds are paid to the designated beneficiaries.

It is common to set up a Swiss annuity so that it passes to the surviving spouse at the death of one spouse, and then to the children when the surviving spouse dies. This gives complete control over the annuity during the life of the policy owner, and when both spouses are gone, control will be transferred directly to the children.

During the accumulation period, the program can be denominated in Swiss francs, euros, or U.S. dollars, and you can switch from one currency to another. Payments can be converted at the investor's bank in Switzerland, or the investor may instruct the insurance company to make the conversion. Payments can be received annually, every six months, or quarterly. Although a monthly option is available, it is restricted to Swiss residents. Payments can be sent anywhere in the world or sent to the bank of the investor's choice. Most North Americans prefer to receive their annuity payments by check in U.S. dollars.

In addition, Swiss life insurance companies will "custom make" an annuity if desired. The off-the-shelf Swiss annuity products are truly outstanding, but if a customized annuity is needed, one can be tailored for you at no additional expense.

Last but not least: a Swiss annuity is completely worry-free. There is no need for supervision—a definite advantage when you invest overseas.

VERSATILE OPTIONS

Most people buy annuities so that they will have a constant source of income during retirement. The Swiss realize that the needs of people differ and so they have developed a variety of options for both single and joint annuities.

When you consider the various options Swiss annuities offer, there are several factors you should examine. First, you should consider your age and the age of your spouse when the income from your annuity is likely to begin. You must also consider the amount of the investment you are willing to make. Such factors will play a crucial role in the type of annuity you select.

Of all the factors you should examine, it is age that probably will have the greatest impact. The older an investor is, for example, the more income difference there will be between an annuity without refund and one with any of the beneficiary options. For example, should you purchase an annuity when you are 55, the difference in life income created under each option is not that much, because the life expectancy for both men and women at 55 exceeds 25 years. Based on life expectancy and payment rates, the insurance company will likely have to pay out the entire amount of the plan no matter what option the contract contains. Options will have different effects, based on age.

There are many options from which you may choose. Assessing your financial goals and situation is important. Asking yourself questions similar to the ones that follow can prove helpful:

- Who is dependent on my financial support?
- What is the purpose of my buying an annuity?
- How much money can I open the account with?
- How much money can I invest monthly? Yearly?

- When (based on current considerations and factors) do I plan to take funds out?
- How (based on current considerations and factors) do I plan to take funds out?

Your answers to such questions can lead you to your best options with an annuity. For example, if you wish to use the annuity to provide income for your spouse someday, then you would consider a plan that does in fact provide for that person. You might consider a joint annuity, a plan called "10 years certain, with refund," or you might decide on taking out single annuities, one for you and one for your spouse.

On the other hand, if you have no dependents, and are over 65, you may decide on a straight-life annuity that pays you the highest income for as long as you live. In this case, there would be no need to leave any funds behind. After your death the insurance company would stop all payments. You would receive the highest income possible for the rest of your life, but there would be nothing for beneficiaries.

If you wish to provide for beneficiaries, you should consider annuities "with refund," or "10, 15 (or any number) years certain." Each plan has special features. *With refund* is a plan in which, at the death of the policy holder, the unused portion of the premium paid is refunded to the beneficiary in a lump sum. The amount of the payment is calculated by subtracting the amount of income that was paid out from the original premium. After the final payout, the account is closed.

Ten years certain is a plan in which income is paid for a minimum of 10 years. If the annuity owner dies after receiving payments for only 3 years, his or her beneficiary would receive the income for another 7 years. The number of years is written into the contract at the time the annuity is bought. Thus, the purchaser can buy an annuity with an option of 10 years certain, 15 years certain, 25 years certain, or whatever he or she wishes.

Joint annuities work in the same way regarding payments. Assuming a 10 year certain contract, if one of the owners dies after receiving payments for three years, the other owner, or beneficiary, will receive payments for the remainder of the contract. (See Table 9.1.)

TABLE 9.1

Swiss Annuity Programs Available

Deferred Life Annuity	Annuity payments start after the end of a deferral period, predefined by the owner (provided the insured person is alive at that date), and continue throughout the lifetime of the insured person.
Immediate Income Life Annuity	Annuity payments start immediately and continue throughout the lifetime of the insured person.
Immediate Fixed-Term Annuity	Annuity payments begin immediately and end after a specified period, but not later than the death of the insured person.
Deferred Fixed-Term Annuity	Annuity payments begin after a deferral period predefined by the owner if the insured person is alive at that date. Payments end with the death of the insured person or, at the latest, at the time fixed by the owner.
Single Life Annuity (with* or without refund**)	An annuity is paid for life.
Fixed-Term Annuity (with* or without refund**)	Annuity payments are made for a fixed number of years determined by the owner (5 years minimum). With a Joint and Survivor Life Annuity (with* or without refund**) two lives are insured and annuity payments are made until the death of the second person.
Life Annuity, "X" Years Certain	Annuity payments are made as long as the insured person is alive. Annuity payments are made for a guaranteed minimum number of years, determined by the owner. If the insured person dies during this period, payments continue to the beneficiary for the rest of the period. If the insured person survives this period, payments continue for life.

* Annuities "with refund" return any capital sum left after the death of the insured person to the beneficiary.

** Annuities "without refund" give higher annuity payments but any capital sum remaining after the death of the insured person is retained by the insurance company and there is no cash value after the accumulation period.

HOW HAS THE SWISS ANNUITY PERFORMED?

How much profit can be made with a Swiss annuity? Over the past decade, the increasing value of the Swiss franc *alone* puts you ahead of the U.S. inflation rate. When you add in the 4 to 5 percent annual return you earn each year in interest and profit sharing, you see that the Swiss franc is a super-conservative investment with a strong potential for delivering a higher yield due to the historical strength of the Swiss franc.

As noted, the best method for growing Swiss francs during the past 30 years was to place them in a Swiss annuity. Inside the annuity, money grows without any stock or bond market risk in a guaranteed, tax-advantaged account. This is entirely legal and is fully approved by the U.S. government.

A Swiss annuity gives you a twofold return: (1) the interest and dividends ("profit sharing," as the Swiss put it) paid into the annuity and (2) the appreciation of the Swiss franc. (Note: There is no guarantee, of course, that the Swiss franc will continue to grow in value against the dollar. Americans who want to invest in Swiss annuities without taking the currency risk can make and keep their investment in U.S. dollars.)

Keep these factors in mind:

- Declining interest rates come with decreased inflation. Decreased Swiss inflation means the Swiss franc will appreciate, which means a greater return convertible in your own national currency.
- Rising interest rates produce a higher investment yield for the insurance company and this can mean higher dividend payments to the policyowner.

This combination of annuity interest, profit sharing, and the appreciation of the Swiss franc would have provided an average annual return of nearly 9 percent since 1971. Almost one-half of that growth came from the appreciation of the Swiss franc against the U.S. paper dollar. Albert Einstein once said that the greatest mathematical principle in the universe was the power of compound interest. (See Table 9.2.)

To illustrate, a $100,000 U.S. investment in a Swiss annuity in 1971 would have been worth over $1.5 million in 2004!

TAX CONSIDERATIONS

Swiss Taxes

Although Swiss residents face a 2.5 percent stamp tax when purchasing a Swiss annuity, nonresidents (e.g., U.S. persons) will pay no Swiss tax on purchase or liquidation of the annuity. Swiss annuities are completely exempt from Swiss taxes for everyone

TABLE 9.2

Appreciation of the Swiss Annuity
Performance in Terms of U.S. Dollars of a Swiss
Franc Annuity Yielding 4.5 Percent P.A.

Year	Exchange	SFR 432,000 Earning 4.5 Percent Interest per Year	When Converted into $ in Resp. Years	Compounded Yield P.A. in U.S. $
Jan. 1, …	$1-SFR…	SFR	U.S. $	%
1971	4.32	432,000	100,000	0.0
1972	3.92	451,440	115,163	15.2
1973	3.77	471,754	125,133	11.9
1974	3.25	492,983	151,687	14.9
1975	2.54	515,168	202,822	19.3
1976	2.62	538,350	205,477	15.5
1977	2.44	562,576	230,563	14.9
1978	2.00	587,892	293,946	16.7
1979	1.63	614,347	376,900	18.0
1980	1.58	641,993	406,324	16.9
1981	1.76	670,882	381,182	14.3
1982	1.81	701,072	387,332	13.1
1983	1.99	732,620	368,150	11.5
1984	2.18	765,588	351,187	10.1
1985	2.60	800,040	307,707	8.4
1986	2.06	836,041	405,845	9.8
1987	1.62	873,663	539,298	11.1
1988	1.28	912,978	713,264	12.3
1989	1.50	954,062	636,041	10.8
1990	1.55	996,995	643,222	10.3
1991	1.28	1,041,860	813,953	11.1
1992	1.35	1,088,744	806,477	10.5
1993	1.47	1,137,737	773,970	9.8
1994	1.47	1,188,935	808,799	9.5
1995	1.32	1,242,437	941,240	9.8
1996	1.16	1,298,346	1,119,240	10.1
1997	1.35	1,356,772	1,005,016	9.3
1998	1.46	1,417,827	971,114	8.8
1999	1.38	1,481,629	1,073,644	8.9
2000	1.59	1,548,302	973,775	8.2
2001	1.59	1,617,975	1,017,594	8.0
2002	1.65	1,690,784	1,024,717	7.8
2003	1.38	1,766,869	1,280,340	8.3
2004	1.23	1,846,378	1,501,120	8.6

Source: SwissGuard.

residing outside Switzerland. This applies to income tax, as well as inheritance and estate taxes.

Moreover, unlike other authentic Swiss franc investments (bonds, stocks, Swiss bank accounts, etc.), they are not subject to the 35 percent Swiss withholding tax—a definite advantage over other sound Swiss franc investments.

No Excise Tax

Unlike many other foreign annuities, Swiss annuities are not subject to the 1 percent U.S. excise tax on the purchase of foreign annuity and insurance premiums. This is a by-product of the adoption in 1998 of a new Swiss-U.S. Double Tax Treaty and applies to premiums paid by a U.S. citizen to an insurance company domiciled in Switzerland.

U.S. Tax Issues

Swiss and foreign fixed annuity contracts issued since January 12, 2001 are no longer tax deferred in the United States (see Internal Revenue Service Regulations, Tax Treatment of Certain Annuity Contracts).[1]

A Swiss fixed annuity is a debt instrument,[2] that is, a "promise to pay a sum certain," in addition to being an insurance contract. Accordingly, the owner of a Swiss fixed annuity (as well as other foreign annuities that are seen as debt instruments) pays tax on the income that accrues, including currency gains if the annuity is denominated in a foreign currency.

Tax experts agree that as a result of the loss of tax deferral, distributions prior to age 59½, including loans against the policy, are not subject to the 10 percent penalty for early withdrawals. Thus, it is possible to take tax-free withdrawals from a Swiss fixed annuity whenever the policyholder chooses.

This different tax treatment for foreign annuities on the whole provides substantially more flexibility for Americans purchasing Swiss fixed annuities. Interest and dividends on U.S. annuities are tax-deferred until withdrawn while those on Swiss annuities are taxable each year as ordinary income. For U.S. annuities, all

---

1 U.S. Internal Revenue Code Sections 163(e) and 1271 through 1275.
2 IRS Code Section 1275.x.

previously untaxed amounts on withdrawals, liquidations, and loan proceeds are taxed as ordinary income, with premature distributions (before age 59½) assessed a 10 percent penalty. No such taxes or penalties apply for Swiss fixed annuities. You can decide when or how to draw money from your annuity. Loan interest is never tax-deductible for U.S. annuities and tax-deductible for Swiss annuities when the loan proceeds are used to purchase other investments (such as stocks in a Swiss bank account).

Swiss annuities can be placed in various U.S. tax-sheltered plans, including IRAs, Keoghs, or corporate plans. Such plans can also be rolled over into a Swiss annuity. If you wish to put a Swiss annuity in a U.S. pension plan, the only thing required is a U.S. trustee—a bank or similar institution—and that the annuity contract be held in the United States by that trustee. For a minimal administration fee, many banks offer "self-directed" pension plans, which can easily be used for this purpose.

The inside buildup of an annuity contract is generally deferred from U.S. income taxation until withdrawn, at which time it is taxed under the provisions of Internal Revenue Code (IRC) section 72, including possible penalties for early withdrawal.

IRS Tax Treatment

In the United States, a Swiss annuity is not even considered to be a "foreign investment account." IRS regulations clearly exclude overseas insurance and annuities from ownership declaration on an annual 1040 tax form or on Treasury form 90-22.1. (See Table 9.3.)

It should be noted that Swiss insurance companies do not report annuity payments to the IRS or any other government agency; this is the policyholder's responsibility.

Income on Foreign Variable Annuities Can Be Tax Deferred

Death benefits in a policy do not make it a debt instrument. The inside buildup of a foreign variable annuity continues to be tax free. The death benefits included in the policies do not make the annuities debt instruments (promises to pay a sum certain) and, therefore, are not tax deferred under Code Section 1275. They do not constitute debt instruments because they promise to pay

TABLE 9.3

Tax Treatment of a U.S. Annuity versus a Swiss Annuity

	U.S. Annuities	Swiss Annuities
Earnings during accumulation phase	Tax-deferred	Usually taxable
Partial withdrawals	Taxable	**Tax-free**
Full liquidations	Taxable	**Tax-free**
Annuity payments	Taxable	**Tax-free**
Premature withdrawals (pre-age 59½)	Taxable, with penalties	**Tax-free, no penalties**
Loans	Taxable, with penalties	**Tax-free, no penalties**
Loan interest	Never tax-deductible	**Can be tax-deductible**

a designated sum only if the owner dies. There is no guarantee of a particular sum if the owner cashes in the policy while he or she is alive.

In addition to the above criteria for determining whether a variable annuity is a debt instrument, two further conditions need to be met for tax deferral:

1. *The Variable Annuity Must Not Be Self-Directed.* The income from a variable annuity is tax free if the owner (or his or her advisor) is not managing the investments himself or herself (a so-called self-directed annuity). Owners are permitted to choose investment categories, but under the self-directed annuity rules they may not choose the actual investments. If they do, they are treated as the owners of the underlying assets and the income generated by those assets is taxable.

2. *The Variable Annuity Must Be Adequately Diversified.* The inside buildup of variable annuities is tax free if the underlying portfolio is adequately diversified as defined in the U.S. Tax Code. An account meets the "diversification rule" if

    a. No more than 55 percent of the value of the total assets of the account is represented by any one fund;

b. No more than 70 percent of the value of the total assets of the account is represented by any two funds;

c. No more than 80 percent of the value of the total assets of the account is represented by any three funds; and

d. No more than 90 percent of the value of the total assets of the account is represented by any four funds.

To make certain that variable annuities comply with the diversification rule at all times, portfolio rebalancing is required on at least a quarterly basis.

The tax-deferred status of Swiss variable annuities has consequences for early withdrawal just as U.S. contracts do. Swiss variable annuities, however, offer a combination of asset protection, a choice of asset-allocation strategies based on an investor's risk profile and other needs, and tax deferral for U.S. investors. This makes them ideal long-term investments that can harness the power of compound growth for a retirement portfolio.

One of the concerns many practitioners have had concerning the use of Swiss annuities was that in cases of large annuities and/or annuities purchased by large estates, the designation of the spouse and/or children as beneficiaries of the annuity usually would not be consistent with a sound estate plan. Therefore, although the asset protection aspect of the annuity was attractive, the estate planning limitations were a hindrance.

Now that it is clear that an entity can be named as irrevocable beneficiary of a Swiss annuity on the annuitant's death, the estate planning concerns could be eliminated by naming the individual's estate planning trust as the beneficiary. Note, however, that if a nongrantor trust is named as the lifetime owner, the tax deferral (for variable annuities) will be lost because of the application of Code Section 72(u).

Tax-Free Exchange

The IRS allows a 1035 tax-free exchange from one annuity to another—including to a Swiss annuity. This is a direct transfer of money from a U.S. annuity into a Swiss annuity contract. Properly done, a 1035 exchange does not trigger any taxes.

In addition, certain retirement annuities can be transferred to Swiss insurance companies. Hundreds of thousands of school-teachers, nurses, doctors, and others who work in the nonprofit sector are allowed to have what is known as a 403(b) annuity. Tax-sheltered annuities (TSAs) are eligible to be transferred to a Swiss annuity.

Neither the United States nor Switzerland has any foreign exchange controls. So, any amount of money can be transferred legally. However, if you take cash or negotiable papers in excess of $10,000 over the U.S. border, you must report it.

There may be particular situations where a U.S. individual already owns deferred annuities issued by a U.S. insurance company, but the individual resides in a state that does not offer any creditor protection for such annuities. Generally, it would be undesirable to liquidate them, since liquidation would typically result in payment of an income tax on the appreciation, and further, the proceeds would be immediately available to creditors. Instead, the individual could make a tax-free exchange of the U.S. annuities for a Swiss annuity under the U.S. Tax Code.[3] U.S. tax regulations provide that a U.S. annuity may be exchanged for a foreign annuity on a tax-free basis, provided that the exchange does not result in a non-U.S. person becoming the owner of the contract.[4]

This result was confirmed in IRS Private Letter Ruling 9319024, and the fact that a fixed annuity, if exchanged for a variable annuity (as is likely to be the case with the exchange for the Swiss contract), does not affect the tax-free exchange. Note again that the exchange should be for a Swiss variable annuity, since a foreign fixed annuity would not offer tax deferral.

SWISS PRIVACY

Few people truly understand the nature and extent of Swiss privacy laws and regulations. Some people associate the Swiss with banking secrecy. They believe that Swiss secrecy makes the country a haven for "dirty" money, and that the Swiss have constructed

---

3 IRS Code Section 1035(a)(3).
4 IRS Code Section 1035(c).

obstacles to hinder law enforcement agencies from obtaining the evidence needed to prosecute criminals effectively. Then there are those who have come to believe that Swiss secrecy has deteriorated and doesn't exist anymore. Neither of these positions is true.

In Switzerland, no one expects you to reveal your private financial matters. The Swiss consider open discussion of one's wealth to be in very poor taste. These standards of the people of Switzerland have led to the creation of a sophisticated banking and insurance industry built on three rock-solid premises:

1. The indisputable right to financial safety through a strong currency
2. A conservative government that practices fiscal restraint
3. An absolute right to financial privacy

Article 47 of Switzerland's Bank Secrecy Act of 1934 makes it a crime for a bank or insurance company employee to reveal information about a customer's account without the customer's written permission. Executives and employees alike are governed by these secrecy laws (and subject to criminal charges) even after they have left the banking or insurance business. The Swiss have stood firm in maintaining and protecting this right of confidentiality, even in the face of tremendous international pressures.

According to Swiss civil law, the information about a customer and his or her finances and investments is protected as a part of the individual's right to privacy. This has been made a part of Article 28 of the Swiss Civil Code. It not only protects the information, but places the burden of paying damages on any person who violates the privacy of another. Any bank employee who does give information about a customer faces fines or imprisonment. The employee and his or her bank can be subject to penalties should a violation of privacy occur.

Only when authorized under existing statutory provisions or by a Swiss court order can a bank legally disclose information about a customer. Indeed, privacy is interpreted in such a manner that it is illegal for a bank to confirm whether or not an individual is even a customer. Put bluntly, a bank can't say whether a person is a customer or not.

While banking personnel are prevented from making disclosures of the financial dealings of their customers, the customers, of course, can authorize the banks to make certain information available. For example, the customer can waive secrecy and ask the bank to provide a credit reference to a specific creditor. Such waivers, however, are valid only if the customer's request is voluntary and he or she has not acted under duress. No one but the customer can waive secrecy.

On the other hand, Swiss secrecy is not absolute. Some specific statutory provisions can take precedence over privacy. These statutes usually have a limited scope, however, and concern Swiss inheritance law, the enforcement of judgments from creditors, and cases of bankruptcy or divorce. Criminal investigations are another area where privacy can be overridden. If a Swiss citizen commits a crime, criminal investigators can ask through a court order that secrecy be lifted. Treaties that Switzerland has with other countries extend this possibility to foreign crimes committed by foreign citizens, but the degree to which privacy may be set aside is limited by the language of each treaty.

Certain conditions must be met before the Swiss will honor any request that affects privacy:

- In the case of criminal acts, the offense being prosecuted is considered to be a criminal offense in both the requesting country and in Switzerland.

- In cases regarding taxes, a disclosure of information is possible only if the investigation of the foreign tax law violation would also be considered to be a violation under Swiss law. There is a special provision between the Swiss and the United States (the Swiss–United States Treaty on Mutual Assistance in Criminal Matters) that provides for Swiss legal assistance to U.S. prosecutors in tax evasion cases when the investigation involves a suspected member of organized crime.

The information obtained in Switzerland through a legal assistance procedure, generally, may neither be used for investigative purposes, nor introduced as evidence in the requesting state in any matter other than the specific offense for which the assistance was originally granted.

Foreign authorities can't directly request financial information from a Swiss financial institution about any customer. The authorities must first obtain a Swiss court order. Although financial privacy is not absolute in Switzerland—for the obvious necessities regarding criminal matters—the rules and traditions governing it are solid and clearly defined.

In summary, Swiss insurance companies do not report purchasing information—not the purchase of the policy, not the payments into the policy, not the interest or dividends earned—to any government agency in Switzerland or the United States.

LIQUIDITY

Another important feature of Swiss annuities is instant liquidity. Most annuities don't offer this. In a Swiss annuity account, all capital plus all accumulated interest and dividends are accessible after the first year without penalty. Unlike most American annuities, if you need your funds for an emergency or wish to make another investment, you are not prevented from obtaining your money and you are not subjected to high penalties.

Most Swiss life insurance companies have a simple process for withdrawals, loans, or complete surrenders. This process requires minimal paperwork. You will have your funds wired directly to your bank within two to three weeks from the time they receive the paperwork.

Both Swiss annuities and American annuities have back-end deferred penalties when you withdraw more than a certain amount of money or when you withdraw the money too early in the contract period. However, Swiss annuities have a much lower penalty and much shorter penalty period than do American annuities. A typical American annuity might have 5 to 15 percent penalties for withdrawals over a period ranging from 5 to 15 years.

Many investors are excited about the low fees charged on Swiss annuities and Swiss life insurance policies. American annuities have much lower fees than American life insurance policies, but still they are usually more than twice as high as the expenses on a Swiss annuity.

In addition to saving investors money on fees, Swiss annuities offer more liquidity than American annuities in another important way. With a Swiss annuity, you can borrow a percentage of your money any time you want. Some Swiss life insurance companies will allow you to borrow up to 90 percent of the value of your annuity. If you have a Swiss annuity worth $1 million, you can get your hands on more than $900,000 of it almost instantly, *with no company penalty*, simply by taking out a loan.

Swiss annuities offer no load fees. They do offer low surrender fees on withdrawals, short surrender periods, loan privileges, and the option of taking lifetime income. Access to your money is truly a hallmark of the Swiss annuity.

ASSET PROTECTION THROUGH SWISS LIFE INSURANCE POLICIES

Beneficiaries Are All Important

When a person residing outside of Switzerland (hereinafter referred to as the "policy owner") purchases a life insurance policy from a Swiss insurance company and designates his or her spouse and/or descendants as beneficiaries of the policy, or irrevocably designates any other third party as beneficiary (e.g., a legal entity such as a trust), the insurance policy is protected by Swiss law against any debt collection procedures instituted by the creditors of the policy owner and also is not included in any Swiss bankruptcy procedure in this regard. Even when a foreign judgment or court order expressly decrees the seizure of the policy or its inclusion in the estate in bankruptcy, the policy may not be seized in Switzerland or included in the estate in bankruptcy.

Beware Fraudulent Conveyance

Creditors may only seize the policy or have it included in the estate in bankruptcy when the purchase of the policy or the designation of the beneficiaries is considered to be a fraudulent conveyance under Swiss law. This condition is fulfilled when the policy owner has designated the beneficiaries not more than one year before the initiation of debt collection proceedings that eventually lead to a bankruptcy decree against the policy owner or to the seizure of the policy owner's assets.

This condition is also met when the beneficiary has been designated with the clear intent to damage creditors or to treat some creditors more favorably than others and the designation was made within five years from the date debt collection proceedings resulting in a bankruptcy decree or in the seizure of assets were initiated against the policyholder. The creditors concerned, however, need to prove not only the policy owner's intent—and here we can see where the law stands—but also that the beneficiary had knowledge of the intent to defraud. Clearly such intent to defraud cannot be proved when the beneficiaries were designated at a time the policy owner was solvent and no creditors had yet asserted any claims against him or her that could have rendered him or her insolvent.

When the policy owner has designated his or her spouse and/or descendants as beneficiaries, the insurance policy will be protected from claims made by his or her creditors irrespective of whether the designation is revocable or irrevocable. The policy owner may therefore designate his or her spouse and/or descendants as beneficiaries on a revocable basis and later revoke this designation prior to the expiration of the policy if at such time there are no threats from any creditors. At the expiration of the insurance policy, the policy holder will be able to collect the proceeds pursuant to the policy, extend the existing policy, or roll the proceeds over into a new policy. It should be noted that if, at the time of expiration, a creditor appears or the owner becomes insolvent, a new policy would not be protected, whereas an extended policy would.

Protection Even under Duress

When an insurer receives a letter from the policy owner revoking the beneficiary designation (in connection with a foreign court order to revoke a past beneficiary designation in order to include the respective assets in a foreign bankruptcy estate), the insurer may come to the conclusion that the instruction received from the policy owner does not express the policy owner's true intent and was forced upon him or her by the foreign judge or court. The Swiss insurance company can only act upon orders of the owner if his or her actions are deemed not to have been made under duress. If there is any evidence that an order has been forced upon the owner, the insurance company cannot follow the instructions so issued. In such a case, the beneficiaries should inform the insurance company.

Automatic Protection in Case of Bankruptcy

In case of bankruptcy of the policy owner, protection is also guaranteed because ownership is transferred to the beneficiaries automatically. Any instructions from the original policy owner that are forced upon him or her can no longer be acted upon; only his or her beneficiaries, as the new owners, can give instructions to the insurance company.

ANALYSIS OF SWISS ASSET PROTECTION LAWS

Conditions for the Protection of Life Insurance Policies in Swiss Debt

Collection and Bankruptcy Proceedings

According to the Swiss Insurance Act, a life insurance policy is protected from the policy owner's creditors under the following conditions.

Irrevocable Designation of Third Party as Beneficiary. If the policy owner has irrevocably designated a third party as beneficiary of a life insurance policy,[5] the policy may not be seized by the policy owner's creditors. In the cited decision, the Federal Supreme Court held the following with regard to the effects of an irrevocable designation of a third-party beneficiary:

> In case of enforcement measures against the policy owner, if the designation of the beneficiary is irrevocable, there is in the estate of the

---

5 Article 79, paragraph 2 of the Swiss Insurance Act.

policy owner no insurance claim and the policy owner has no right to revoke the beneficiary's right as normally would be the case. The creditors of the policy owner may, therefore, not seize, have listed or auction off [an insurance policy]. If the policy owner has waived his or her right to revoke the designation, then the insurance policy may not be seized by the policy owner's creditors.[6]

The designation of a third party as beneficiary will only be considered to be irrevocable if the policy owner has waived his or her right to revoke the designation in writing and the policy is physically handed over to the beneficiary.[7] By signing the relevant declaration and handing the insurance policy over to the beneficiary, the policy owner will meet these requirements.

Designation of Spouse and/or Descendants as Beneficiaries. If the policy owner has designated his or her spouse and/or descendants as beneficiaries of the insurance policy in question, the policy may not be seized by his or her creditors unless the policy owner has explicitly granted a security interest in the policy to a creditor. The designation of the spouse and/or descendants as beneficiaries is not subject to specific formal requirements.

There is a special rule[8] when the spouse and the descendants of the policy owner are beneficiaries of an insurance policy that the designation as beneficiary may no longer be revoked when the policy owner is declared bankrupt as would normally be the case in accordance with the act. The claim against the insurer may not be subject to enforcement measures, and the beneficiaries at the time when bankruptcy is declared will enter into the rights and obligations of the insurance agreement replacing the policy owner[9] unless they expressly decline such transfer of the agreement.

In contrast to the designation of another third party as beneficiary, it is irrelevant in the case of the designation of a spouse and/or descendants whether the designation is irrevocable or revocable. The insurance policy will also be protected from the policy owner's creditors if the designation of the spouse and/or descendants is revocable. If the policy owner falls into bankruptcy

---

6 Ibid.
7 Article 77, paragraph 2 of the Swiss Insurance Act.
8 Articles 80 and 81 of the Swiss Insurance Act .
9 Ibid.

or if the debt collection office certifies to his or her creditors after a seizure that the assets seized do not cover the policy owner's debts, any spouse and/or descendants who are beneficiaries of the policy will be assigned all the rights and duties of the policy owner under the relevant insurance policy.[10]

Rules on Fraudulent Conveyance

According to the Swiss Insurance Act, creditors of a policy owner may seize the policy even in the above cases if they can prove that the irrevocable designation of a third party or the designation of the spouse and/or descendants as beneficiaries is to be viewed as a fraudulent conveyance.[11] The purchase of an insurance policy and the designation of beneficiaries are considered avoidable preference under the Swiss fraudulent conveyance rules in the following cases:

Designation Made within One Year Before Bankruptcy or Seizure. Gifts or gratuitous settlements made by a debtor are avoidable preference when the debtor is declared bankrupt or the debtor's assets are seized within one year after the initial transaction was made.[12] In calculating the one-year period, the duration of certain specific time periods will be added (the duration of preceding composition proceedings; the duration of a stay of opening a bankruptcy; in proceedings to liquidate an estate, the period between the date of decease and the liquidation order and the duration of preceding enforcement proceedings). Because the gratuitous designation of a third party as beneficiary under an insurance policy can be regarded as a gratuitous transfer to that third party, such a designation may be voided by the creditors if it was effected within this one-year period.

Designation Made with the Intent to Damage Creditors. All transactions are avoidable that the debtor carried out during the five years prior to the seizure of assets or the opening of bankruptcy proceedings with the intention, apparent to the other party, of putting his or her creditors

---

10 Article 81 of the Swiss Insurance Act.
11 Article 285 et seq. of the Swiss Debt Collection and Bankruptcy Act.
12 Article 286 of the Swiss Debt Collection and Bankruptcy Act.

at a disadvantage or of favoring certain of his or her creditors to the disadvantage of others.[13] The five-year period may be extended[14] if the designation of the spouse and/or the descendants or of a third party was made with the specific intent of the debtor to damage creditors and the beneficiaries knew of this intent, the designation is also avoidable. To void the transfer, the creditors concerned need to prove the intent as well as the beneficiary's knowledge. It is, however, not sufficient for the proof of such intent to demonstrate that the designation took place at a time at which the policy owner was—due to his or her professional activities or investments—aware of certain risks as long as the policy owner's assets still covered all his or her debts and he or she could not foresee an insolvency.

Protection of Foreigners Who Purchase Swiss Life Insurance Policies

The following rules regarding debt collection and bankruptcy procedures against foreigners in Switzerland apply only to assets located in Switzerland. It is important to note that the rights under an insurance contract between a foreigner and a Swiss insurance company are, according to Swiss law, deemed to be located at the domicile of the Swiss insurance company. If the policy owner's and the beneficiaries' rights are embodied in a policy that must be considered as a security, however, a creditor could claim that the security could be seized in accordance with the debt collection and bankruptcy rules of the country in which the security is deposited, because securities normally are subject to the debt collection and bankruptcy law of the country in which they are deposited. This problem, however, can be avoided if the insurance policy is deposited in Switzerland.

Debt Collection and Bankruptcy Procedures Against Foreign Debtors

According to these rules, only assets that a creditor can seize in a debt collection procedure can be attached.[15] Because this principle

---

13 Article 288 of the Swiss Debt Collection and Bankruptcy Act.
14 Article 288a of the Swiss Debt Collection and Bankruptcy Act.
15 Article 275 of the Swiss Debt Collection and Bankruptcy Act.

also applies to foreign debtors, a Swiss insurance policy purchased by a foreigner is protected under the conditions set forth above. Therefore, if creditors do not file for an attachment but rather for the recognition of a foreign bankruptcy decree, the insurance policy is nevertheless protected. The debtor's assets in Switzerland will be auctioned off for the benefit of his or her creditors[16] in accordance with Swiss bankruptcy rules.[17]

Because debt collection and bankruptcy procedures in Switzerland are always based on Swiss bankruptcy rules alone, and these rules[18] include life insurance policies, they are protected in accordance with Swiss law.

In particular, only the Swiss rules on fraudulent conveyance apply, so the designation of beneficiaries cannot be avoided by creditors unless they prove that the conditions for fraudulent conveyance described previously are met, even if the purchase or designation was avoidable under the fraudulent conveyance rules applicable in the debtor's domicile.[19]

The creditors of a person residing outside of Switzerland, therefore, may not in Switzerland seize or include in the estate in bankruptcy any life insurance policies that are protected under Swiss law even if they have a judgment or a bankruptcy decree that is enforceable in Switzerland, unless they can prove that the designation of the beneficiaries of the insurance policy is avoidable preference under Swiss fraudulent conveyance rules.

Revocation of Beneficiary Designation by Order of Foreign Judge

A foreign judge or court may order a policy owner to revoke a past beneficiary designation in order to include the respective assets in the foreign bankruptcy estate. To comply with such an order or judgment, the policy owner may inform the insurer that he or she revokes the prior beneficiary designation. The question arises whether under Swiss law the insurer has to comply with such an instruction by the policy owner, which was forced upon him or her by a foreign judge or court.

---

16 Article 170 IPRG.
17 Article 79 Section 2 and Article 80 VVG.
18 Article 79 Section 2 and Article 80 VVG.
19 Article 171 IPRG.

In the event of an irrevocable designation of a third party,[20] an insurer will not comply with the instruction by the policy owner because this would contradict the irrevocability of the beneficiary designation.

In the event of a revocable designation of the spouse or descendants, the spouse and descendants of a policy owner automatically succeed into the rights and obligations arising from the insurance contract at the moment when the policy owner is declared bankrupt, unless they expressly object to such succession. The spouse or descendants have to inform the insurer accordingly. Therefore, if the foreign policy owner has been declared bankrupt previously and later instructs the insurer that the beneficiary designation is revoked, the insurer will refuse to comply with such an instruction because at this time the rights and obligations arising from the insurance policy were already assigned to the beneficiary. In this context, it is important to make sure that the insurer in fact knows about the foreign bankruptcy decree and that the beneficiaries inform the insurer of their succession.[21] Moreover, if an insurer receives a letter from the policy owner revoking the beneficiary designation, the insurer may come to the conclusion that the instruction received does not express the policy owner's true intent and was forced upon him or her by the foreign judge or court.

In case of a discrepancy between the real intent and the intent expressed in writing, a person who receives such writing and knows that it does not express the real intent normally has to follow the real intent and ignore the writing.[22] Although there is no court precedent dealing specifically with this situation, it is a general principle of Swiss law that a person who receives a written declaration of another person has to give the declaration the meaning that complies with the real intent of that person, if he or she knows the real intent. In other words, if an insurer receives a letter from a policy owner that he or she knows does not reflect the real intent, the insurer can and has to ignore the letter.

Swiss law clearly protects the policy from creditors. Also, the policy owner can achieve asset protection for the beneficiaries of

---

20 Article 79 Section 2 VVG.
21 Article 81 Section 2 VVG.
22 Under Article 18 of the Swiss Code of Obligations (CO).

the policy by stating on the annuity application that annuity payments may not be assigned and are not subject to the rights of the beneficiaries' creditors.

For a higher level of protection, the policy owner could have a Swiss bank or trust company hold his or her annuity, or if the policy owner has an offshore asset protection trust, the policy could be placed inside the trust.

If asset protection is one of your primary financial concerns, we recommend you consider combining a Swiss annuity with one or more of the additional layers of protection listed in Table 9.4.

Whichever way you buy and hold a Swiss annuity, it will offer you a very high level of protection under Swiss law. If protection from lawsuits is of prime importance to you, before you buy your annuity carefully consider whether obtaining the extra protection of a domestic or an offshore trust may be a smart move.

Why do the Swiss offer this incredible level of asset protection for holders of Swiss annuities? Quite simply, it is because the

TABLE 9.4

Levels of Protection

Type of Asset Protection	Level of Protection	Protective Features
Swiss annuity bought by mail from Switzerland	Good	• Annuity governed under Swiss law
Swiss annuity bought in person by traveling to Switzerland	Better	• Annuity governed under Swiss law • Purchase made on foreign soil
Swiss annuity bought either by mail or in person and then placed in a U.S. irrevocable trust	Even Better	• Annuity governed under Swiss law • Ownership of the annuity by trust eliminating you as the owner who can "retrieve" the annuity to pay a judgment against you
Swiss annuity bought either by mail or in person and then placed in an offshore trust	Best	• Annuity governed under Swiss law • Ownership of the annuity by trust eliminating you as the owner • Trust governed by foreign laws that will not recognize a judgment against you

Swiss believe that annuities and insurance are ultimately for the benefit of one's spouse and children. Under Swiss law, the care and financial well-being of family members come above all else. In short, insurance is *for the family*, not for the benefit of creditors or other claimants.

ASSET PROTECTION

Swiss annuities are entirely protected from a host of creditors. If the annuity purchaser's wife or children are named as beneficiaries, no creditor, including the IRS, may seize or attach a Swiss annuity. Liens may not be attached to the annuity in any way. Thus, you are assured that the wealth contained in your annuity cannot be touched by any individual or government agency, and that the funds in your annuity will in fact go to your designated heirs.

Figure 9.1 demonstrates the steps a creditor would have to take to try to attack your Swiss annuity. As you can see, they would be unsuccessful.

Secrecy

The same criminal and civil penalties for violation of a client's privacy imposed on all Swiss bank officials and employees also apply to insurance company workers for life.

Instant Liquidity of Funds

You can liquidate up to 100 percent of your account without penalty after the first year. With many Swiss annuities, you may immediately borrow up to 90 percent of the cash value at a net interest rate of only 0.5 percent.

Safety

Switzerland is financially one of the soundest (if not the soundest) countries in the world. Its currency is considered to be the most solid among the world's industrialized nations. The Swiss insurance industry has not had a failure in 150 years.

FIGURE 9.1

The Obstacle Course

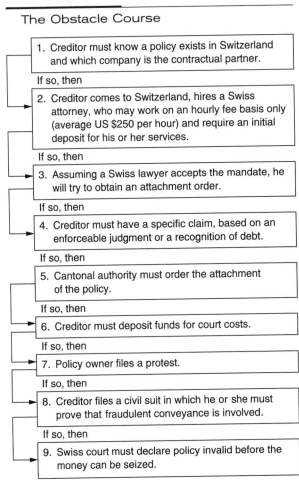

1. Creditor must know a policy exists in Switzerland and which company is the contractual partner.

If so, then

2. Creditor comes to Switzerland, hires a Swiss attorney, who may work on an hourly fee basis only (average US $250 per hour) and require an initial deposit for his or her services.

If so, then

3. Assuming a Swiss lawyer accepts the mandate, he will try to obtain an attachment order.

If so, then

4. Creditor must have a specific claim, based on an enforceable judgment or a recognition of debt.

If so, then

5. Cantonal authority must order the attachment of the policy.

If so, then

6. Creditor must deposit funds for court costs.

If so, then

7. Policy owner files a protest.

If so, then

8. Creditor files a civil suit in which he or she must prove that fraudulent conveyance is involved.

If so, then

9. Swiss court must declare policy invalid before the money can be seized.

Tax Advantages

Different tax treatment for foreign annuities on the whole provides substantially more flexibility for Americans purchasing Swiss annuities. You can decide when or how to draw money from your annuity

No Swiss Tax

Swiss franc annuities are free from Swiss taxes. If, however, you accumulate Swiss francs through other types of investments, you will be subject to the 35 percent withholding tax on interest or dividends earned in Switzerland.

No Tax Reporting Required

As with all their financial transactions, the Swiss elevate privacy to a priority. A Swiss franc annuity is not a "foreign bank account," and subject to the reporting requirements on the IRS Form 1040, or the special U.S. Treasury form for reporting foreign bank accounts. Furthermore, the transfer of funds by check or wire is not reportable under U.S. law by individuals. The reporting requirements apply only to cash and "cash equivalents," including items such as money orders, cashier's checks, and traveler's checks.

Immunity from Exchange Controls

Some investors pay little attention to exchange rates and controls, but those very rates and controls can exercise a major impact on the profitability of one's investments. Suppose that the U.S. government was to institute exchange controls that required overseas investments to be repatriated to the United States. This has happened in the past with other nations whenever governments have imposed exchange controls. Insurance policies would likely not be covered under any forced repatriation because they are considered to be a pending contract between the investor and the insurance company. (Note that Swiss bank accounts would probably not escape such controls.)

No Load Fees

Investment in Swiss annuities offers the advantage of no load fees, front-end or back-end. In addition, you can cancel at any time, without a loss of principal, and with all principal, interest, and dividends payable if canceled after one year. If you cancel during the first year, you are subject to a small penalty of about 500 Swiss francs, plus the loss of interest.

Pension Plan Rollover

Corporate or self-employed pension plans or Individual Retirement Accounts (IRAs) can legally invest in and hold title to Swiss annuities or be rolled over into Swiss annuities.

Estate Planning

The ownership of Swiss annuities can be changed easily by the policy owner by written notice at any time with no legal formalities. Swiss annuities also provide for integrated estate-planning capabilities through flexible beneficiary designations. They are also well suited for making distributions separate from the policy owner's estate.

Ease of Payment

You can make deposits on your Swiss annuity with the same ease as mailing insurance premiums at your local post office box. You can also establish your own premium deposit account with the insurance company itself, from which periodic payments can be made. Such insurance accounts are not considered "bank" accounts under Swiss law and there is no tax imposed or need to report under U.S. IRS rules.

CHAPTER 10

Swiss Private Insurance Portfolio

A private insurance portfolio (sometimes referred to as a *portfolio bond, private placement life insurance,* or *insurance wrapper*) combines a bank account, a brokerage account, and an insurance policy under one asset-protected umbrella. Specifically, the investor closes a contract in his or her name with an insurance company, usually domiciled in Switzerland. The insurance company opens an account with a private bank selected by the investor, who in turn receives a policy from the insurance company. Legally, the investor is the client of the insurance company and the insurance company is a client of the bank. The investor chooses to have the bank or designated investment advisor manage the account.

Legal entities and natural persons can be designated as beneficiaries. With certain insurance companies, the policy owner may be a legal entity. The person insured, however, must in all cases be a natural person.

A private insurance portfolio provides the important benefits of an offshore account with a private bank: confidentiality and privacy, professional and individualized asset management, and personal attention.

PORTFOLIO MANAGEMENT

The private insurance portfolio can be considered as a sophisticated holding structure through which the investor (through his or her advisor) can direct the insurance company to invest in a wide range of investment vehicles. A private insurance portfolio serves the overall portfolio for the investor's long-term needs. This long horizon establishes one of the private insurance portfolio's greatest privileges: to focus on wealth-creating (high-return) investments.

A private insurance portfolio, then, becomes the main repository for relatively high-return hedge funds, private equity, and venture capital. Without a private insurance portfolio, the value of a portfolio of high-return investments would be dampened because of the extremely large tax exposure that typically results from a focus on long-term wealth creation.

This combination of a very long-term investment horizon with the private insurance portfolio's extreme tax efficiency establishes a unique platform upon which to build a wealth-protected portfolio.

Various government and private-sector studies have shown that approximately 70 percent of an affluent investor's portfolio is devoted to supporting his or her working and retirement lifestyle needs, and 30 percent of the portfolio represents assets that are not targeted for any specific purpose. This latter asset pool represents the bulk of the assets backing a family's trust and estate plan. Beyond that, the portion of an investor's individual investment portfolio that's invested in highly taxed instruments is a logical source of funding for a private insurance portfolio. Moreover, as wealth increases, the greater this free-standing asset pool becomes, relative to the total portfolio.

A private insurance portfolio presents a simple question to wealth-protected investors: If such long-term assets are not backing any particular lifestyle need, why subject them to taxes as well as to potentially adverse situations?

A private insurance portfolio provides affluent investors with an investment solution that can change the course of productivity in an investor's portfolio, not only for the current generation but also for multiple generations thereafter.

To maximize the private insurance portfolio's productivity, the underlying portfolio must be constructed to take advantage of a private insurance portfolio's unique structure. Using a private insurance portfolio's long-term horizon to establish a portfolio of high-returning investments, the future wealth of individuals and families can be dramatically improved.

OVERVIEW OF BENEFITS

Separate and Simple Estate Planning Device

Although a legal entity such as an estate planning trust can be named as an irrevocable beneficiary of the private insurance portfolio, this type of investment is also well suited for making distributions separate from your estate. However, depending on your home jurisdiction, some compulsory portions for legal heirs may be reserved. Neither power-of-attorney, nor last will, nor certificate of inheritance is required for payments to be made upon the policy owner's death. Beneficiaries get immediate access to the funds according to the payment method chosen by the policy owner.

Confidentiality and Privacy

In addition to the confidentiality provided by a bank account in the name of the insurance company, a second layer of confidentiality is provided by the confidentiality of insurance. In certain jurisdictions, insurance companies treat client information as do their banking counterparts. No information can be provided to any third party (natural person or legal entity).

With the introduction of U.S. withholding taxes on U.S. assets held in foreign accounts, and with the tough reporting requirements for investments made through offshore trusts, offshore insurance vehicles, if correctly structured and from the right jurisdiction, can add strong privacy to your existing investments in a trust or a bank account.

Trust Compatibility

A private insurance portfolio is not necessarily a structure to replace offshore trusts; rather it can be used to complement a trust and to strengthen its protection. For example, assigning investments to an offshore trust is much cheaper and easier if they are grouped together under one private insurance portfolio. This greatly simplifies the tax treatment of the structure, and consequently, the reporting requirements, either through a reduction in the number of assets to be listed or through the fulfillment of the conditions for tax deferral. Assets held within a private insurance portfolio are considered to be held by the insurance company. This allows an investor or a trust to hold assets privately as well under the new regulations on U.S. withholding taxes on U.S. assets held in foreign accounts.

Insurance Coverage

The estate's wealth is preserved through the death benefit. In effect, until the policy's cash value reaches the death benefit, the insurance company bears the entire downside risk of the portfolio's performance.

Depending on the investor's own needs and requirements for heirs, additional insurance coverage can be provided in case of death. Coverage can also be adjusted during the term of the contract. This feature can be very important if a remaining spouse is forced to pay off a mortgage or if heirs need cash to buy out business partners.

Flexibility

Apart from being able to choose the amount of insurance coverage, you can choose to receive a payout over several premiums or a single payment. As the underlying investments can be freely selected from a global palette of investments not available to the general public, you or your investment advisor (the latter for tax deferral) can optimize performance through wide diversification or hedging strategies.

Tax-Efficiency

A private insurance portfolio offers tremendous tax benefits that are available from few other investment vehicles without the need for expensive and complex trust structures:

Tax-inefficient assets can grow tax-deferred.

Investment gains can be free of all income tax.

Tax obligations on reinvestment are eliminated.

Death benefit for the estate is income tax free.

There is the potential to exclude it from estate taxes.

A favorable tax treatment on loans and withdrawals is provided.

The tax efficiency obtained will depend on the tax laws of your domicile. In most jurisdictions, it is possible to achieve tax deferment, if not total tax elimination, regarding income taxes, capital gains taxes, as well as estate taxes.

Asset Protection

A private insurance portfolio's key goal in asset protection is to provide protection from creditors and/or litigants arising from unforeseen, adverse events. Swiss insurance companies are among the safest in the world and are domiciled in jurisdictions that provide the highest levels of protection from creditors, frivolous lawsuits, and government confiscation.

Additionally, unless otherwise required by law or directed by the policy owner, the relationship between an international insurance company and a policy owner is held in strict confidence under the laws governing the insurance company.

Life insurance is one of the very few forms of investment that's often inherently protected from creditor claims. Private insurance portfolios, in particular, lend themselves to asset-protection planning and, for many individuals, will be a principal motivation for the investment.

Properly structured and established in the right jurisdiction, private insurance portfolios enjoy legal protection from creditors.

Global Investment Flexibility

A private insurance portfolio is a holding structure through which you, in conjunction with a professional advisor, can request that the insurance company invest in nearly any investment vehicle.

Access to Investment Opportunities

You wouldn't know it from the mainstream financial press, but international investments have been huge winners in recent years. (See Table 10.1.) How can you gain access to these markets? You cannot do this through a U.S. broker. A private insurance portfolio supports an array of high-return, wealth-creating assets such as hedge funds, private equity, or venture capital, which are wholly unavailable through traditional insurance solutions. In addition, the portfolio may be denominated in your currency of choice. Underlying accounts and assets may be denominated in most world currencies.

Finally, some private insurance portfolios allow for the insertion of existing assets and portfolios rather than cash (*premium in-kind*). You needn't sell your assets in order to fund your strategy. This feature facilitates a variety of sophisticated planning techniques; for instance, those required for the transfer of highly appreciated assets.

Tax Planning

Unlike many offshore investments and structures, private insurance portfolios are, in certain jurisdictions, completely

TABLE 10.1

Comparative Stock Market
Performance, 2005
(U.S. Dollar Adjusted)

Canada	+26.8%
Japan	+24.1%
Austria	+23.0%
Denmark	+22.5%
Switzerland	+14.9%
U.S. (S&P 500)	+30.0%

Source: Morgan Stanley Capital International Inc.

free of taxes. As far as income, capital gains, estate, or withholding taxes are concerned, the law of the investor's tax domicile is decisive. In many countries, insurance policies enjoy substantial tax benefits if correctly structured (i.e., the private insurance portfolio can be tailor-made to fit the legal requirements for privileged tax treatment). For U.S. persons this includes:

Tax Deferral during the Insured's Life. The inside buildup of the private insurance portfolio is generally income and capital gains tax-free. For U.S. individuals and corporations with assets abroad, using a Private Insurance Portfolio as a holding structure for these assets provides an efficient mechanism for sidestepping the 31% withholding tax on income and gains from U.S. assets held in foreign accounts.

No Income Taxes on Insurance Proceeds. At the policy owner's death, the insurance proceeds are generally income tax exempt.

No Estate Taxes on Insurance Proceeds. With proper planning (such as through the use of an irrevocable life insurance trust) insurance proceeds can avoid estate taxation at the death of the insured.

No U.S. Excise Taxes under Certain Conditions. Unlike many other foreign insurance policies, Swiss policies are not subject to the 1% U.S. excise tax on the purchase of foreign insurance policies. The U.S. treaty with Switzerland, moreover, provides that the tax exemption applies "only to the extent that the risks covered by such premiums are not reinsured with a person not entitled to the benefits of this or any other Convention which provides exemption from these taxes." The proof required to overcome this limitation—of whether the premiums are re-insured and, if so, whether the re-insurer is entitled to the exemption—could possibly defeat the privacy aspects of the policy, assuming the insurance companies would be willing to provide the information.

The private insurance portfolio qualifies as a life insurance policy for U.S. income tax purposes if it is based on a segregated investment account and the segregated account is adequately diversified:

> No more than 55 percent of the value of the total assets of the account is represented by any one investment;
>
> No more than 70 percent of the value of the total assets of the account is represented by any two investments;
>
> No more than 80 percent of the value of the total assets of the account is represented by any three investments; and
>
> No more than 90 percent of the value of the total assets of the account is represented by any four investments.

To make certain that the segregated accounts comply with this "diversification rule," the portfolio needs to be rebalanced at the end of the first policy year and on a quarterly calendar basis thereafter. If it satisfies Internal Revenue Code rules on death benefits, these ensure that the insurance protection meets certain minimum requirements from the inception of the policy.

If it is not self-directed, the policy owner must be deemed to have surrendered ownership or control of the assets. The income from a private insurance portfolio is tax-free if the owner is not managing the investments himself or herself. Conversely, the insurance company is deemed to be the beneficial owner of the segregated account. You may designate an investment advisor to manage the account. The insurance company will then hire the designated advisor to manage the assets. Policy owners are permitted to choose investment categories, but they may not choose the actual investments. If they do, they are treated as the beneficial owners of the underlying assets, not the insurance company, and the income generated by those assets would be taxable.

Prohibited Investments

The following considerations must be part of the process of funding the policy:

- Assets such as collectibles cannot be included in the private insurance portfolio because of legal and regulatory limitations.
- Assets such as closely held or restricted stock under direct investor control are not permitted.
- Investments in limited partnerships cannot simply be converted to a private insurance portfolio.

SUMMARY

To summarize, when a policy owner not residing in Switzerland purchases an insurance policy from a Swiss insurance company and designates his or her spouse or descendants as beneficiaries of such insurance policy, or irrevocably designates any other third party as beneficiary (e.g., a legal entity such as a trust), this insurance policy will be protected by law against any debt collection procedures instituted by the creditors of the policy owner and will also not be included in any Swiss bankruptcy procedure in this regard.

Even where a foreign judgment or court order expressly decrees the seizure of such policy, or its inclusion in the estate in bankruptcy, such an insurance policy may not be seized or included in the estate in bankruptcy, except where it is considered a fraudulent conveyance.

In case of bankruptcy of the owner, protection is also guaranteed since the ownership is transferred to the beneficiaries automatically. Any instructions from the original policy owner that are forced upon him or her can no longer be acted upon; only the beneficiaries, as the new owners, can give instructions to the insurance company.

The insurance company can only act upon orders of the owner if his or her actions are deemed not to have been made under duress. If there is any evidence that an order has been forced upon the owner, such as in the case where the owner revokes in writing the beneficiary designation prior to a bankruptcy declaration, the insurance company cannot follow the instructions so issued. In such a case, it is important that the beneficiaries inform the insurance company.

You can use a private insurance portfolio either in combination with offshore or domestic planning structures or as a stand-alone vehicle as a cost-effective tool to upgrade an existing portfolio of investments. A portfolio's features can be added or improved with regard to asset protection, confidentiality, reporting burden, insurance coverage, flexibility, and reducing costs and taxes, including estate taxes as wealth passes from one generation to another.

CHAPTER 11

Liechtenstein

Liechtenstein is a tiny enclave of 34,000 people nestled in the European Alps, bordering Germany, Austria, and Switzerland. While Liechtenstein is part of the Swiss Customs Union and uses the Swiss franc as its local currency, it is independent and has its own constitution and a judicial system wholly separate from Switzerland.

The small country is one of only two doubly landlocked countries in the world. (Uzbekistan is the other.) Liechtenstein is highly desirable to offshore investors because of its strong privacy laws, low geopolitical risk, and attractive investment vehicles. With 32,000 residents, this European principality offers a no-tax environment and long-standing banking privacy laws.

BACKGROUND

The Principality of Liechtenstein was established within the Holy Roman Empire in 1719; it became a sovereign state in 1806. Until the end of World War I, it was closely tied to Austria, but the economic devastation caused by that conflict forced Liechtenstein to enter into a customs and monetary union with Switzerland. Since World War II (in which Liechtenstein remained neutral), the country's low taxes have spurred outstanding economic growth. Shortcomings in banking regulatory oversight have resulted in concerns about the use of the financial institutions for money laundering. Liechtenstein has, however, implemented new anti-money-laundering legislation and recently concluded a Mutual Legal Assistance Treaty with the United States.

Despite its small size and limited natural resources, Liechtenstein has developed into a prosperous, highly industrialized, free-enterprise economy with a vital financial service sector and living standards on a par with its large European neighbors. The Liechtenstein economy is widely diversified, with a large number of small businesses. Low business taxes—the maximum tax rate is 20 percent—and easy incorporation rules have induced many holding or so-called letter box companies to establish nominal offices in Liechtenstein, providing 30 percent of state revenues. The government is working to harmonize its economic policies with those of an integrated Europe.[1] The government of Liechtenstein is a hereditary constitutional monarchy on a democratic and parliamentary basis. German is the official language, and the Alemannic dialect is also spoken.

The national currency is the Swiss franc, one of the world's strongest currencies. The strength of the Swiss franc is based on a multitude of factors. It is gold-backed and has a high correlation to the U.S. dollar. In 2004, Swiss francs per U.S. dollar equaled 1.2435. Liechtenstein has some of the world's strictest bank privacy laws. Those laws extend even to insurance companies.

How the country's investments are regarded by U.S. tax law, tax benefits for U.S. individuals and corporations with assets abroad, using a Liechtenstein private insurance portfolio (PIP) as a holding structure for assets provides an efficient mechanism for sidestepping the new 31 percent withholding tax on income and gains from U.S. assets held in foreign accounts. Liechtenstein has no income taxes on insurance proceeds.

Unlike many offshore investments and structures, Liechtenstein private insurance portfolios (P.I.P.) are, in certain jurisdictions, completely free of local taxes. As far as income, capital gains, estate, or withholding taxes are concerned, the law of the investor's tax domicile is decisive.

---

1 CIA, The World Factbook—Liechtenstein, https://www.cia.gov/cia/publications/factbook/print/ls.html

In many countries, insurance policies enjoy substantial tax benefits if correctly structured. The private insurance portfolio can be tailor-made to fit the legal requirements for privileged tax treatment.

For U.S. persons this includes:

- The inside buildup of the P.I.P. is generally income and gains tax free.
- Tax deferral is present during the insured's life.
- At the policy owner's death, the insurance proceeds are generally income tax exempt.
- There are no estate taxes on insurance proceeds. With proper planning (such as through the use of an irrevocable trust under which the insured has no control or benefits) estate taxation on insurance proceeds can be avoided at the death of the insured.

Like many other foreign insurance companies, Liechtenstein insurance companies are not "favored" by a similar tax treaty; Liechtenstein annuities are therefore subject to the excise tax. On the other hand, they are not subject to provisions with respect to disclosure of tax information, even where crimes have been committed under Liechtenstein law.

LEGAL PROTECTIONS

In addition to the confidentiality provided by a bank account in the name of the insurance company, a second layer of confidentiality is provided by insurance confidentiality. In certain jurisdictions insurance companies treat client information as would their banking counterparts. No information can be provided to any third party (natural person or legal entity). In Liechtenstein, for example, a separate insurance secrecy law protects the privacy of policy owners. This law subjects not only persons affiliated with or acting on behalf of insurance undertakings to professional secrecy, but also representatives of public agencies.

Properly structured and established in the right jurisdiction, Liechtenstein P.I.P.s receive legal protection from creditors. Liechtenstein's laws on the protection accorded life insurance policies and annuities are directly taken from the relevant Swiss laws.

If you do not reside in Switzerland or Liechtenstein and purchase an insurance policy from a Swiss or Liechtenstein insurance company and designate your spouse or descendants as beneficiaries of such insurance policy, or irrevocably designate any other third party as beneficiary (e.g., a legal entity such as a trust), this insurance policy will be protected by law against any debt collection procedures instituted by the creditors of the policy owner and will also not be included in any Swiss or Liechtenstein bankruptcy procedure in this regard. Even where a foreign judgment or court order expressly decrees the seizure of such policy, or its inclusion in the estate in bankruptcy, such an insurance policy may not be seized in Switzerland or Liechtenstein or included in the estate in bankruptcy, except where it is considered a fraudulent conveyance.

In case of bankruptcy of the policy owner, protection is also guaranteed since the ownership is transferred to the beneficiaries automatically. Any instructions from the original policy owner that are forced upon him or her can no longer be acted upon; only the beneficiaries, as the new owners, can give instructions to the insurance company.

The insurance company can only act upon orders of the policy owner if his or her actions are deemed not to have been made under duress. If there is any evidence that an order has been forced upon the owner, such as in the case in which the owner revokes in writing the beneficiary designation prior to a bankruptcy declaration, the insurance company cannot follow the instructions so issued. In such a case, it is important that the beneficiaries inform the insurance company.

While there are a number of civil law entities that could be utilized for asset-protection purposes, the most popular structures for U.S. planners are two trust-like entities, the *stiftung* and the *anstalt*, created under the law of Lichtenstein and foundations created in Panama. We will examine these entities and how they might fit into an overall asset-protection plan.

THE *STIFTUNG*

The *stiftung* is basically a fund for a particular purpose that has by statute been given the status as a legal entity. The *stiftung* is created by a "Founder" and has a separate legal identity from the Founder. The assets of the *stiftung* must be segregated from any personal assets and are typically not available to creditors of the Founder.

The *stiftung* can have some commercial activities, but it cannot be utilized solely for commercial purposes. Instead, the *stiftung* is designed to act basically as a private foundation, and it may be formed purely as a family foundation. For asset-protection purposes, however, it is better if the *stiftung* is formed for the promotion of some important interest (such as to further education or medical research) because there may be less chance that the *stiftung* will be considered an "insider" for purposes of evaluating whether the contributions to the *stiftung* were fraudulent.

A *stiftung* has no shareholders. However, a *stiftung* may be drafted to have beneficiaries, including the Founder as a beneficiary. Neither of these features is suggested, as the *stiftung* then starts looking like a foreign asset-protection trust. Instead, the *stiftung* should be limited by its terms to supporting the purpose for which it was created and used in that fashion. This does not mean, however, that there are not methods to utilize assets of the *stiftung* to endow private scholarships, etc.

The *stiftung* is managed by a Council of Members, which most often is originally appointed by the Founder. At least one person on the Council must be resident in Liechtenstein. Assuming that none of the persons on the Council are named as beneficiaries of the *stiftung*, it likely will be very difficult for a creditor to pierce the *stiftung*. Similarly, since the *stiftung* has no "owner," neither the *stiftung* itself nor its assets should be available to any creditors of the persons sitting on the Council. (See Figure 11.1.)

It is very difficult to get information about a *stiftung* in Liechtenstein. The by-laws of the entity, which control to whom and under what conditions distributions can be made, are typically not filed in any public registry. If they are kept in Liechtenstein, this means that a litigant seeking the information may have to bring legal action in Liechtenstein.

The Liechtenstein *anstalt* is an entity that has no members, participants, or shareholders and is a sort of hybrid between a corporation and a *stiftung*. An *anstalt* can have beneficiaries. The

FIGURE   11.1

Stiftung

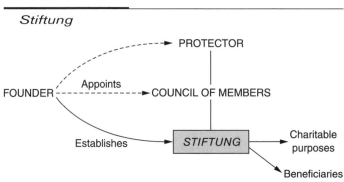

principal practical difference between an *anstalt* and a *stiftung* is that an *anstalt* can conduct all kinds of business activities. Liechtenstein also recognizes a form of registered trust, called an *eingetragenes treuunternehmen*, and an unregistered trust that simply may be filed confidentially with the Public Register Office, called a *treuhander-schaft*. The former operates as a separate entity, somewhat similar to a U.K. unit trust, while the latter is very similar to a common law trust, having no legal identity separate from its components. Neither, however, carries the legal background (and baggage) of restrictive common law interpretations, meaning that they offer somewhat better flexibility than common-law trusts.

Where these entities and the *stiftung* probably have their greatest use is not in holding significant assets, but rather as acting as the holder of stock in traditional domestic or offshore entities that are used as management companies. The civil law basis of these entities, and the fact that they usually do not have identifiable beneficiaries, make them very difficult for creditors' attorneys to conceptualize and thus attack. But note that a U.S. judge could also miss the subtle differences, and simply treat them as foreign asset protection trusts and order that their assets be repatriated. Also, Liechtenstein law may not protect the set-tlor from a U.S. court's finding of contempt.

Either in combination with domestic planning structures or alone, a Liechtenstein private insurance portfolio can be a useful and cost-effective tool to upgrade an existing portfolio of invest-ments. A portfolio's features can be added or improved with regard to asset protection, confidentiality, reporting burden, insurance coverage and flexibility, reducing costs and taxes, including transfer taxes as wealth passes from one generation to another. Whether they are concerned with taxes or the threat of litigation or are looking to diversify assets globally, with the portfolio bond, wealthy individuals can address those concerns as well as have access to leading investment managers and to investments otherwise not available to the public.

Getting Started

It may seem odd to end this book with "getting started." But now that you have a basic understanding of the different entities (i.e., umbrella insurance, life insurance, spousal/family transfers, incorporation of businesses, the use of trusts, both domestic and foreign, and all-in-one jurisdictions, such as Switzerland) that comprise a multi-pronged creditor protection strategy, it is time for you to implement a personal asset-protection strategy. It is important to put your assets out of reach of judgments before the need arises.

You have learned the basic tenets of investment risk management and how to structure your wealth for protection from losses due to volatility and taxation. But most important, you now have awareness of a "gold-plated" investment product that embodies all the criteria of entity, structure, and jurisdiction—and at the same time, enhances investment risk management through effective diversification. You must begin to utilize this knowledge for your own benefit!

Here is a quick checklist to the seven steps you should follow to protect and grow your wealth.

ONE—ESTATE PLANNING

Asset protection is increasingly becoming a key element in the typical estate plan, so it is incumbent upon advisors as well as high net worth individuals to become familiar with the numerous entities employed in asset-protection planning. It begins with asset recognition and valuation, the purpose of the asset, and the best way to protect it from creditors.

By learning the basic principles of asset protection, you will become more comfortable about how to protect your rights and where to go to ask questions. Don't put off getting the protection that is readily available to you to insulate your wealth because you don't understand or don't have time to learn. Get help now from a professional. The expense of financial planners, CPAs, and tax specialists will be much less than the regret and cost you may suffer later.

TWO—USE PRINCIPLES TAUGHT IN MODERN INVESTMENT THEORY

If you believe the dollar will continue to fall, if you believe that oil prices are going to increase over time, if you believe that foreign countries are going to drop their reserves, and people are going to lose faith in the U.S. dollar, you need to understand what to do.

When you comprehend the basic investing concepts employed by financial professionals, you tame your fear of risk (volatility) and learn how to use it to your advantage to create your highest possible probability for achieving your financial goals. By combining assets, such as non-dollar-denominated investments having low correlation, volatility can be lowered for portfolios while enhancing risk-adjusted rates of return.

The principles found in modern portfolio theory offer security to the investor because they have been tested and proven and are not investment sales hype. Armed with this knowledge, you can conquer one of the biggest challengers to your wealth protection—emotional behavior and decisions—and thus avoid the temptations of timing and speculation. The buy-and-hold strategy is the most favorable for any product—on or offshore.

THREE—FIND THE RIGHT STRUCTURE

The right structure, ideally, protects an investment while it continues to grow in a fertile environment to return the greatest amount of money at the end of a preset term, with a level of financial risk acceptable to you. What I have found is most investors and even their advisors start in the reverse order—that is, choosing a jurisdiction, then an investment vehicle, lastly the structure. As a result, the transfer of assets often is not the best one for the circumstances and, under challenge, is the weak link that leads to the failure of the plan or the process.

Consider advanced measures to make your assets litigation resistant and tax advantaged. Using an offshore annuity in combination with other protective techniques, such as offshore trusts, can raise the level of asset protection.

FOUR—UNDERSTAND YOUR INVESTMENT VEHICLE CHOICES

Choosing investment vehicles begins with understanding how asset classes respond differently to changes in the economy or the investment marketplace. Armed with this knowledge, you can readily recognize whether your portfolio is "effectively diversified."

To the extent you take advantage of effective diversification, you will increase the expected rate of returns of your portfolio over time. This is further enhanced by your asset allocation. (See Figure E.1.)

Just like the old familiar basic food groups pyramid, the base comprises the most reliable group of investments you should utilize. The riskier structures should be used sparingly and in proportion to their contribution to risk/return of the overall portfolio. As you see, the Swiss annuity is included in the foundation of the pyramid structure and should be viewed as one of your most secure assets in contrast with the futures strategies involving currency (Swiss franc) at the top of the pyramid.

FIVE—SELECT A BENEFICIAL JURISDICTION

It's not enough to simply put a veil over your assets to shelter them from prying eyes. Your assets should remain accessible to you and continue to work for you, safely and legally. Use only those countries (jurisdictions) that offer investment type products that return your money, not just hide it.

FIGURE E.1

The Investment Pyramid

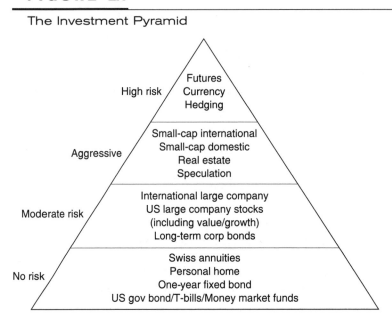

Source: Chambers and Associates

To date, only two countries, Switzerland and Liechenstein, have been time-tested and proven to not only meet the criteria but actually to set the ultimate standard for asset protection and risk management through the offshore element.

SIX—HOW TO BUY A SWISS ANNUITY

According to Swiss insurance company requirements, a foreign investor must use the services of a Swiss insurance broker (a Swiss representative) who can assist in the selection, purchase, and ongoing monitoring of the performance of the Swiss annuity.

A Swiss insurance broker is compensated directly by the insurance companies. This means that the premium(s) paid and the benefits received are exactly the same regardless of whether you deal directly with an insurance company or take advantage of a broker's services.

Many conservative financial planners believe that the Swiss annuity is the single most effective way to diversify capital out of the U.S. dollar and into Swiss francs. Americans investing in

Swiss annuities are acquiring protection by purchasing what may be the safest and most straightforward overseas investment available today.

SEVEN—KNOW WHERE TO GET HELP

It is crucial to understand all the aspects, both the beneficial ones and the vulnerabilities, of offshore products before you invest. While an off-the-shelf product may suit your needs, don't overlook the added protections that may come from customization that creatively combines products and structures.

Help is out there and there's no excuse for not asking for it when you need it. Work with established asset-protection attorneys and accountants; use large, reputable banks, insurance companies, and financial service firms. You should expect professionals to be knowledgeable in the entities, structures, and jurisdictions and review, update, and manage your assets for cutting-edge wealth protection.

Protect your assets *before* the need for protection arises. Best of luck!

Frequently Asked Questions

What are the typical fees and costs of setting up an offshore trust?

The legal fees for setting up an offshore trust generally range from $5,500 to $8,000, depending on the specific circumstances of each case. Certain more complex plans may be more expensive.

What types of assets may be transferred to an offshore trust?

While any asset may be transferred to an offshore trust, only truly foreign assets will be effectively shielded by the trust from claims of U.S. creditors. These assets include foreign bank accounts, foreign real estate, foreign brokerage accounts, and foreign securities or foreign depository receipts of U.S. securities held offshore.

I have heard a lot about Nevada corporations. How do they work?

Nevada corporations offer two possible advantages. First, there is no corporate income tax or franchise tax in Nevada. Second, Nevada has strict privacy rules protecting the identity of shareholders. However, if a Nevada corporation is conducting business in any other state, then that state may tax the Nevada corporation, even if Nevada does not. For example, a Nevada corporation that engages in real estate rentals, professional services, or manufacturing in California will have to register with the California Secretary of State and pay California corporate taxes. Additionally, Nevada's secrecy laws will not prevent a court and many creditors from being able to penetrate the secrecy shroud and ascertain the identity of shareholders.

My business is organized as a corporation. Is that sufficient asset protection?

Organizing your business as a corporation does only half of the job. A creditor suing the corporation will generally be unable to collect against the individual shareholders. However, a creditor suing a shareholder will be able to get the shareholder's stock of the corporation and then sell the stock and, possibly, corporate assets. The only way to protect the owner from business lawsuits and to protect the business from the individual lawsuits against the owner is to structure the business as either a limited liability company or a limited partnership.

Is it legal to acquire a Swiss annuity and send money abroad?

There is no law that prevents a U.S. citizen from acquiring a Swiss annuity issued under Swiss law in Switzerland.

How are annuity payments scheduled?

Annuity payments are available quarterly, semiannually, and annually. You can choose how you want the annuities paid out (e.g., by check to your home address or directly to a bank account anywhere in the world).

Once I choose to receive an annuity income, is there any charge for having my annuity payments transferred abroad?

Any standard banking expenses (e.g., transfer costs or costs for issuing a check) will be debited from your account.

What are the up-front fees, charges, or redemption fees?

There are no up-front fees. All of your invested capital will immediately go to work for you and begin to accumulate earnings. Also, there are no redemption fees when you cash in your Swiss annuity after the first year.

Is there a minimum investment required?

To make a Swiss annuity investment, you will need at least $20,000, or the equivalent in another currency to start, depending on the insurance company.

How much can I invest in a Swiss annuity?

There is no upper limit.

Can I increase my investment at a later date?

Certainly. For most programs you may increase your investment whenever you wish. After sending additional funds to the insurance company, it will automatically issue a supplementary addendum or new annuity certificate. Technically, this means you purchase a new certificate in the currency of your existing certificate or, if you so choose, in another currency.

How liquid is my investment?

It is 100 percent liquid after the first year. You can then withdraw any or all of your money including interest and dividends. If you need to redeem your certificate within the first 12 months, you will be charged a handling fee of 500 Swiss francs and you forfeit any first-year interest and dividend earnings.

How does the plan work?

Your investment money is placed with one of Switzerland's premier insurance companies for a given term (referred to as the *accumulation period*). Your principal earns interest and dividends until you redeem your plan in a lump sum or start drawing an income as an annuity. After income payments have begun, the unpaid balance of your capital still collects interest and dividend earnings, which are paid out with your life income.

When does my investment mature?

You determine the duration of your contract at the time of purchase, but you are free to change it at any time during the contract term. That is, you may extend or shorten your chosen term (effective on the next anniversary date of your certificate) or withdraw the cash value of your investment at any time.

What happens at the end of the accumulation period?

If you choose to extend the accumulation period you should do this two months prior to expiration at the latest. Otherwise you have two options at the end of the accumulation period: you may receive a lump sum payment of the full certificate value including all accumulated interest or choose to receive an income for either a specified period or for as long as you live.

What is the procedure I have to follow if I want to surrender my Swiss annuity certificate?

To surrender your certificate you must return the original policy along with a letter containing your payment instruction letter to your insurance company. You are then sent a cash-value statement. You sign and return this statement. Then the insurance company can proceed to make the payment as per your instructions. You may request either a check or a bank transfer to a designated bank account. (Generally, bank transfers will contain lower banking charges than a check does.)

How long does this procedure take?

The entire procedure takes approximately two to three weeks depending on the insurance company you have your policy with.

Can I borrow against my annuity?

You may borrow up to 80 or 90 percent of your account value at any time. There are some tax consequences, and they should be considered when borrowing against your annuity. Loans can only be granted during the accumulation period and must be repaid prior to the redemption period.

Procedure to apply for a loan: Mail the insurance company your loan request and your original certificate. Please use registered mail to do this. You will then receive a loan agreement that must be signed by you and returned. Included with the loan agreement you must provide the payment instructions. Upon receipt of these documents by the insurance company, your loan will be processed.

Please note that interest and profit sharing dividends will continue to accrue and are added to your account. Regular prevailing lending rates are applied to your loan. Considering that your benefits continue to accrue, you should have a very reasonable loan.

Can I make changes to my certificate at a later date?

Of course. You can make changes to your certificate relating to, for example, currency denominations, beneficiary clauses, and payment instructions. The only exceptions are the person insured and, of course, an irrevocable beneficiary. These may not be changed at any time. No special forms are required; simply send your instructions in writing.

What if I am the owner of the certificate but not the person insured?

The ownership of the certificate goes to your legal or designated heirs according to your last will and testament.

Can a legal entity be the owner of the certificate?

Any legal entity such as a trust, corporation, pension plan, foundation, or establishment can be the owner as well as beneficiary of the annuity certificate.

Does my choice of owner affect the value of my investment?

No. Whether the owner of the certificate is a person or legal entity (pension plan, trust, corporation, etc.), the certificate value remains the same.

In the Application for an Annuity Certificate, what does it mean to be the beneficial owner?

As both owner and beneficial owner, you are not acting on behalf of another person to invest his or her funds. In case you are doing so, by law insurance companies and banks are required to ask you who the beneficial owner is.

Does my choice of the person insured affect the value of my investment?

It depends. The investment's value remains virtually identical during the accumulation period. If you choose to annuitize, however, the annual income that is then paid for life will obviously vary according to the age of the person insured (because of different life expectancies).

Can I have the life income payments from my annuity certificate paid into a bank account outside my home country?

Yes, you can. Simply send your instructions in writing to the insurance company.

Can I change the beneficiary clause?

The beneficiary clause can be revoked or changed at any time as long as the beneficiary clause has not been designated as irrevocable. The clause cannot be designated as irrevocable if the beneficiary is a trust or some other legal entity. (The beneficiary must be a person if designated as irrevocable.)

What happens upon my death?

If, as in most cases, you are both the person insured and the owner of the certificate, the certificate value goes in a lump sum to the beneficiary(ies) you have named. Your beneficiaries are required to mail in a certified copy of the death certificate, the policy certificate, a copy of their ID, and payment instructions.

What happens if I die before recovering my investment?

If you are the insured person, the surrender value of the contract is paid immediately to your designated beneficiary. If you have named someone else as the insured, Swiss law limits the period of tax deferral after your death and requires the insurer to pay the surrender value to the designated beneficiary, in a lump sum, within five years of death. (It can be paid sooner, if the beneficiary desires.) However, if annuity payments have already begun when you die, these payments may continue at the same rate.

What about the owner and the insured person? Can they be changed, too?

While it would be possible to cede the ownership to another party, you cannot change the insured person. You would have to cancel the policy and take out a new one with the new insured person.

What about Swiss taxes?

Your earnings are never taxed in Switzerland. They accumulate tax free and, at maturity, are not subject to any Swiss tax. (Interest earned in a Swiss bank account is subject to a 35 percent withholding tax.) As a nonresident of Switzerland, you are not liable for any Swiss tax. There is no tax reporting and all transactions are held in strict confidence.

What about exchange controls?

Although exchange controls have existed in various countries and may recur one day for people who hold overseas bank accounts, these have never been applied to foreign annuities. It seems unlikely that a country would force repatriation of insurance products in the future.

In which currencies is a Swiss annuity offered?

Recognizing the international investor's interest in broad currency diversification, a Swiss annuity is offered in Swiss francs, euros, and U.S. dollars. With a Swiss annuity's currency convertible feature, you always have the option to switch currencies whenever you desire. Although a Swiss annuity is not designed as a short-term currency-trading instrument, it does allow you to hedge your currency or further diversify currency positions. A handling fee of 300 Swiss francs will be charged per switch and per certificate.

Can I invest in more than one currency simultaneously?

Yes. You would then receive a separate certificate for each currency investment. For a 50/50 Swiss franc and U.S. dollar investment, for example, you would receive two certificates, one in Swiss francs and another with the equivalent in dollars. (Minimum investment per currency: $20,000 or equivalent.)

Should I not just choose the currency that offers the highest interest rates?

Not necessarily. In the long run, the development of exchange rates could be a more decisive factor than interest rates. Such factors as inflation rates, savings rates, fiscal balances, current account balances, and economic growth greatly affect the value of a currency in the long run. A Swiss franc investment with a return of, say, 3 percent, could turn out to be substantially better than a U.S. dollar investment at 4 percent.

When converting from my home currency or switching between currencies, how is the exchange rate set?

Foreign exchange rates published in newspapers are on "round lots" of 5 million U.S. dollars traded among banks. These interbank rates are only "indicators" of what an individual investor might expect. Your deposits are always converted to the selected currency according to the prevailing exchange rate at the Swiss bank handling your payment.

Can I have my own bank convert my home currency into the investment currency(ies)?

Yes, your home bank can convert your home currency and make a Swiss franc or other currency transfer to Switzerland. However, experience has shown that this method is more costly (because of fees and less attractive exchange rates) than if you send your home currency funds directly to the insurance company and have it execute the currency exchange for you.

How private is my investment?

Swiss law forbids the disclosure of assets held by an individual in a Swiss bank or insurance company to any person or government authorities. Swiss insurance companies do not create or distribute mailing lists, and all information you send is held in strict confidence.

Is a Swiss annuity judgment proof?

According to Swiss law, insurance polices, including Swiss annuities, when properly structured, cannot be attached or seized and cannot be included in any bankruptcy proceedings. This applies even if a judgment or court order specifically orders the seizure of your annuity or its inclusion in the estate in a bankruptcy settlement. This advantage would be of particular interest to professionals, or anyone who is exposed to possible lawsuits, malpractice cases, nervous creditors, vengeful ex-spouses, etc.

Is an independent, general rating of Swiss insurance companies available?

No. The well-known rating companies do not analyze Swiss insurance companies. In any case, only five insurance companies have special policies for international investors, and all of these are either old, established blue-chip companies or are owned by one. All of the Swiss insurance companies (about 23 of them) would be rated AAA by U.S. standards.

How can I be sure my investment is safe?

In the more than 150-year history of the Swiss insurance industry, there has never been a single failure of a Swiss insurance company. Policyholders in Switzerland enjoy a level of security and protection greater than in any other country.

Are Swiss insurance companies regulated?

Yes. The lack of ratings is more than compensated for by the industry's long history of financial stability, the result of stringent insurance laws and rigorous supervision of the policies and activities of insurance companies by the Federal Office of Private Insurance. Federal regulators require that insurance companies fully cover their obligations with secure investments, adequate reserves, and sufficient cash flow.

Is it possible to transfer IRA funds into a Swiss annuity?

Yes, under certain conditions, a Swiss annuity can be held within an IRA. Also, it may be possible that funds may be transferred from a qualified corporate plan, a Keogh plan, a 401(k) plan, a 403(b) tax deferred retirement plan, a deceased spouse's IRA, or another IRA maintained by you.

If you wish to put a Swiss annuity in a U.S. pension plan, the only thing required is a U.S. trustee—a bank or similar institution—and that the annuity contract be held in the United States by that trustee. For a minimal administration fee many banks offer "self-directed" pension plans, which can easily be used for this purpose.

Are Swiss annuities subject to expensive and delayed probates?

Swiss annuities are not subjected to probate when beneficiaries are named as preferred class.

When do I receive my account statements?

You will receive a full account statement at the beginning of each year.

Estate Planning with Offshore Defensive Grantor

An intentionally defective trust with an offshore status has two advantages.

First, many offshore asset protection jurisdictions have repealed the law against perpetuities, making it possible to set up the trust as a dynasty trust. A dynasty trust can be set up to benefit multiple generations while being subject to the estate tax and Government Sales Tax (GST) only on the initial funding.

Second, a foreign trust may make it easier to change the trust's status as grantor or non-grantor. In a defective grantor trust, the grantor transfers most of his or her assets to the trust, but continues to pay taxes on the trust's income. While that is usually very advantageous, it is possible that the grantor will eventually exhaust his or her non-trust assets and will be unable to pay taxes. In that case, it may be beneficial to change the trust's status to non-grantor. While that may be accomplished by having the grantor relinquish certain powers, it is even easier to accomplish by changing the trust's classification as foreign or domestic for tax purposes.

If a trust is foreign for tax purposes and has a U.S. beneficiary, it is always a grantor trust. It is relatively simple to reclassify a foreign trust as domestic for tax purposes. Simply switching to a

U.S. trustee and subjecting the trust to the concurrent jurisdiction of a U.S. court should be sufficient. If the trust is not otherwise drafted as a grantor trust under Code Section 671, it will switch to non-grantor status.

An installment sale to a defective trust[1] in exchange for the trust's promissory note has become an increasingly popular estate transfer strategy with many significant benefits.[2] Generally, this technique is used to sell non-controlling interests in entities to the trust, while taking advantage of the valuation discounts and freezing the value of the estate.

The trust is drafted as an irrevocable dynasty trust, but intentionally violates one or more of the grantor trust rules under Code Section 671. Most frequently, the trust is made defective for income tax purposes by appointing the grantor as the trustee of the trust.[3] With respect to the appointment of the trustee in this setting, there is an often exploited distinction between the attribution rules for estate tax and income tax purposes. For example, if the grantor's spouse is appointed as a trustee with the power to sprinkle income among beneficiaries, that power is not attributed to the grantor (but the trust must be funded with the grantor's separate property, not community property of the spouses). However, the powers held by the grantor's spouse are attributed to the grantor for income tax purposes.

The note is typically structured as interest-only, with a balloon payment at the end. The note should bear an adequate rate of interest, determined under Code Section 7872. In Revenue Ruling 85-13, 1985-1 C. B. 184 and several private letter rulings, the Service ruled that the sale of property by the grantor to

---

1 These defective grantor trusts are sometimes referred to as "intentionally" defective grantor trusts. The author believes the word *intentionally* to be redundant, because a trust would not be drafted as defective unless it was intentionally (barring acts of malpractice).

2 Defective grantor trusts are viewed as being superior to Grantor Retained Annuity Trusts (GRATs) because there is no requirement that the grantor outlive the trust and because the GST exemption may be claimed up front.

3 One planning element commonly incorporated into a defective grantor trust is the ability to switch trustees, appointing an independent third party as the trustee. When that happens, the trust ceases being a grantor trust. Likewise, an independent third party trustee can be removed and the grantor appointed trustee, with the trust switching back to grantor mode.

the trust will be ignored for income tax purposes because the grantor trust is a disregarded entity.

Because the trust is irrevocable and is otherwise drafted to be outside of the grantor's estate, the property placed in the trust escapes estate taxation. To ensure this result and prevent the application of Code Section 2036, the grantor should set the trust up for someone else's benefit (e.g., the children). To avoid the application of the gift tax, the discounted value of property sold to the trust should equal the fair market value of the note.

Because the anti-freeze rules of Code Section 2702 may apply to a defective grantor trust, it may be advisable to prefund the trust with assets equal to 10 percent of the value of the property that will be sold to the trust. The property within the trust continues to appreciate in value while the value of the promissory note is fixed (the note earns a constant rate of return that is usually lower than the rate of appreciation of the assets within the trust). The value of the note will be included in the grantor's estate. Leveraging the lifetime estate and gift tax exclusion and discounting the value of partnership or LLC interests placed in the trust create significant estate tax savings. Additionally, because income taxes are paid by the grantor and do not constitute a gift to the trust,[4] additional wealth is shifted from the grantor's estate and into the trust.

A defective grantor trust would work particularly well for a start-up business or a new business opportunity. A start-up business, with low initial value but great upside potential, can be transferred to the trust at minimum value, with all the business growth occurring within the trust and outside the settlor's estate.

As a matter of fact, a business opportunity within a defective grantor trust calls for a slightly different structure to be optimally efficient. Where the trust requires little seed money to start the new business, it is advisable to have a client's parent, sibling, or other party seed the trust, with the client named as beneficiary. So long as the client is not treated as the grantor of the trust, Code Section 2036 issues do not arise. The client

---

4 A discharge of one's legal obligation is not a gift.

can then act as the trustee of the trust and will be the primary beneficiary.

As the trust makes interest payments on the note to the settlor, the settlor does not take the payments into income because the transaction is ignored for income tax purposes. However, it is unclear what happens on the death of the settlor when the trust loses its grantor status and the payments become taxable. Does the settlor's estate begin to recognize income? The answer is not entirely clear. It has been suggested that on the initial sale the settlor elect out of the installment method, thus accelerating all the gain realization on the sale. However, because at the time of the sale the trust has grantor status, the gain is not actually taxable to the grantor. At the time of death, the argument goes, there is no gain left to recognize. While there is no authority on this point, this strategy may work, and because there is no downside risk, the election out of the installment method should always be undertaken.

It is also possible to pay off the note prior to the settlor's death when the trust still has its grantor status. It is advisable in that case to pay off the note with highly appreciated assets that will get a step-up in basis on the death of the settlor. The assets within the trust will not get a step-up in basis on the grantor's death, which should be taken into account when evaluating the benefits of a defective grantor trust.

Although the grantor would be treated as owner of the trust for income tax purposes, he or she would clearly not have legal or equitable title to the trust's assets. Consequently, trust assets would not be available to the settlor's creditors, unless the trust was treated as a self-settled trust. Because grantors are usually not beneficiaries of defective grantor trusts to avoid inclusion of trust corpus under Code Section 2036, the trust should not be treated as a self-settled trust.

The trust can further be drafted as a spendthrift or a discretionary trust. Further, because the note received from the trust is an interest-only, balloon note, the payment to a creditor of the grantor cannot be accelerated.

Another alternative is to draft the note so that it is personal to the settlor and nonnegotiable. It is possible that making the note nonnegotiable will reduce its value. In that case, the face amount of the note should be increased to ensure that the fair market value of the note equals the value of the property transferred to the trust.

This advanced planning appendix was written by Jacob Stein, Esq., who is with the law firm of Boldra, Klueger & Stein, located in Woodland Hills, California. His asset protection Web site is www.maximumassetprotection.com.

Foreign LLC and Trust Combos

Generally, foreign trusts are most effective when they hold foreign assets. A judge can vest in the creditor any U.S. asset of the debtor, even if the asset is titled in a foreign trust. For cash and marketable securities, the trust can only hold the assets directly, because they can be moved offshore quickly. The same is not true for real estate or a business operated within the United States. In that case it is important to ensure that (a) the choice of law analysis points offshore, and (b) when the real estate is liquidated, the proceeds go offshore.

The best way to achieve both of those goals is by holding the real estate through a limited liability company organized offshore. This structure has the additional benefits of availing the client of the valuation discounts found in an LLC,[1] and obtaining the additional asset protection by way of the LLC charging order statute of the jurisdiction where the entity is organized.

FOREIGN LLCs

Many foreign jurisdictions have enacted LLC statutes. Many of these jurisdictions are so-called tax havens, which generally means that an entity organized in that jurisdiction will not be taxed by

---

1 Obtaining a valuations discount by using an LLC is a complex area of law, based primarily on the Code Section 2036 analysis, and is outside the scope of this outline.

that jurisdiction if the entity is not conducting any business in the jurisdiction. If a U.S. business or U.S. real estate is owned by an entity organized in a tax haven, the entity will not be doing any business in the tax haven and will not be taxed there.[2] It is important to remember that a foreign entity that does not want to be taxed as a corporation for U.S. tax purposes should make an affirmative election to be taxed as a partnership by filing Form 8832.

Pursuant to the traditional choice of law analysis, the law of the jurisdiction where an entity is organized will govern the entity, even if the business is transacted elsewhere. For example, California Corporations Code Section 17450(a) provides:

> The laws of the state or foreign country under which a foreign limited liability company is organized shall govern its organization and internal affairs and the liability and authority of its managers and members.

The only time when this choice of law will not be respected is when the application of the laws of the foreign jurisdiction will violate the public policy of the state where the LLC is conducting business. Because the LLC statutes of offshore jurisdictions are very similar to the U.S. LLC statutes, it is unlikely that the offshore statutes will be ignored for public policy reasons. Such is the case of a California resident who organized a Nevis LLC to hold Idaho real estate. The Nevis charging order statute limits the creditor to the charging order, with no right to foreclose.[3] Some U.S. jurisdictions (like Nevada) similarly restrict creditors to the charging order, with no right to foreclose. With all else being equal, the advantages of a foreign LLC to a domestic LLC are the extra costs and expenses incurred by a creditor in pursuing a debtor to a foreign jurisdiction and the favorable asset protection laws of the foreign jurisdiction.

THE COMBINED BENEFITS

Combining an LLC and a trust, both organized offshore, has advantages for both entities. In this structure, the foreign trust

---

2 Although the entity will not be "taxed" by the jurisdiction, it will still be subject to annual registration fees.

3 Nevis Limited Liability Company Ordinance Section 43.

owns the LLC as a sole member, or, at the very least, the trust holds a super-majority interest in the LLC. This provides further insulation to the assets within the LLC, because now a creditor has to first penetrate the foreign trust, then obtain a charging order against the LLC, and then collect on the charging order—technically possible, but not practical.

For a debtor to avail itself of the impossibility defense in a contempt situation, the debtor must not have any control over trust assets. However, if the trust owns the LLC, and the debtor is appointed as the LLC's manager, without an ownership interest, the debtor can control the assets without being in control of the trust.

In the event of threatened litigation, the debtor can be either removed as the manager of the LLC, or, preferably, the LLC agreement should give the trust veto power over certain distributions, actions, and decisions by the manager. For example, the trust should have veto power over liquidation of the LLC, a distribution exceeding a certain amount, or issuance of a membership interest to a new member.

Jacob Stein, Esq., of Boldra, Klueger & Stein, located in Woodland Hills, California, addresses this fully on his asset protection Web site: www.maximumassetprotection.com.

Countries of Interest

It is not my intent to recommend outrageous U.S. strategies; I have found that most don't work. But there are many legitimate structures and countries you may want to familiarize yourself with.

There are certain jurisdictions that stand out from the rest of the pack—the Cook Islands in the South Pacific, Nevis, and St. Vincent and the Grenadines in the West Indies. The reason these countries are so attractive to offshore investors is that they do not recognize foreign judgments and the settlor/beneficiary can retain some control.

Offshore trusts in general do not protect assets from creditors, but they do shield money from perfunctory investigations while providing jurisdictional immunity. It's not enough simply to put a veil over your assets to shelter them from prying eyes.

Note: Many of these countries rewrote their laws in an attempt to attract offshore investors, but be forewarned—it is not the same world that it was 10 years ago. Today, even the Cayman Islands demands references and letters of recommendation from your bank.

The following countries (jurisdictions) offer asset protection. Please check out further information on the page numbers provided.

ANTIGUA AND BARBUDA
Background

Antigua was "discovered" in 1493 by Columbus, who named it Santo Maria de la Antigua. Early settlements by the Spanish and French were succeeded by the English who formed a colony in 1667. Slavery, established to run the sugar plantations on Antigua, was abolished in 1834. The islands became an independent state within the British Commonwealth of Nations in 1981.

Location

The Caribbean islands of Antigua and Barbuda lie east-southeast of Puerto Rico. Antigua is the main island, covering about 108 square miles. Lying to the north of Antigua and covering 75 square miles is Barbuda.

Time Zone

UTC–4

Capital

Saint John's (Antigua)

Population

Antigua: 65,000; Barbuda: 1,500

Religion

The dominant religion is Christian (predominantly Anglican with other Protestant sects, and some Roman Catholic).

Languages

English is the official language, and a variety of local dialects are spoken.

Currency Risk and Strength

The national currency is the East Caribbean dollar (XCD), which has a moderate correlation to the U.S. dollar. US$1 currently equals XCD$2.6882. U.S. currency is also widely used and is accepted everywhere. Antigua and Barbuda is a member of the Eastern Caribbean Central Bank.

Government

The government of Antigua and Barbuda is a constitutional democracy with a U.K.-style parliament. There is a Governor General appointed by the Queen. The Prime Minister and Cabinet exercise executive power and there is both a Legislative Assembly with elected members and a Senate with appointed members. The current governing party has been in power since 1967, except for a five-year period following the 1971 general election. Democratic elections are held at least every five years. Antigua and Barbuda is a member of the British Commonwealth, the United Nations, and other international institutions.

Economy

Tourism is the driving force of the economy, accounting for more than half of the GDP. Weak tourist arrival numbers since early 2000 have slowed the economy, however, and pressed the government into a tight fiscal corner. Prospects for economic growth in the medium term will continue to depend on income growth in the industrialized world, especially in the United States, which accounts for slightly more than one-third of tourist arrivals.

Antigua has the highest per capita income of the Eastern Caribbean. The lack of a personal income tax results in higher levels of disposable income than in most Caribbean territories.

Attractive fiscal incentives are offered to investors in the manufacturing area. There is also a new Free Trade Zone. Government revenues are derived for the most part by various indirect taxes that include duties on imported goods, tourist-related taxes, and licensing fees.

Geopolitical Risk

Geopolitical risk is low. There are no serious issues of unrest in the Antigua and Barbuda. While it is considered a minor transshipment point for narcotics bound for the United States and Europe, Antigua and Barbuda has more significance as an offshore financial center. It is a politically stable, safe, and private jurisdiction for offshore companies and offshore bank accounts.

Infrastructure

Six major airlines serve the country with regularly scheduled flights to Europe, North America, and the Caribbean. Antigua is 3½ hours from New York, 2½ hours from Miami, 4½ hours from Toronto, and 8 hours from London.

Some of the world's largest cruise ships dock at the Deep Water Harbor or at the Heritage Quay Pier in the capital city of St. John's, allowing passengers to enjoy the attractions of Antigua at the duty-free shopping center and other tourist locations. Eleven shipping lines also provide shipping services to North America, Europe, the Caribbean, and Central America.

The telephone system is as good as any in North America, with undersea fiber-optic cable providing long-distance, Internet, and data transmission services. Express courier service by Federal Express, UPS, and other companies is readily available to and from Antigua.

Legal System

The legal system is based on and embodies the principles of English statutory and common law, making it particularly attractive for certain transactions not easily structured under civil law systems.

Because Antigua and Barbuda is an independent nation, it is not affected by the UK/EU regulations concerning the tax status of the British Dependent Territories.

Antigua and Barbuda are party to various conventions on drugs and money-laundering issues. The Proceeds of Crime Act, passed in 1993, established areas of cooperation with the United States and the United Kingdom. An extradition treaty with the United States was signed in 1995, providing for extradition in cases of dual criminality. A Money Laundering Act was also passed in 1996, establishing guidelines for offshore banking.

Offshore Investment Considerations

The nation of Antigua and Barbuda provides the traditional services of an Offshore Financial Center, including the formation of Antigua offshore companies, banks, and the provision of financial services.

Legislation governing offshore companies is contained in the International Business Corporations Act of 1982, with amendments. The Act (as amended) provides excellent confidentiality and privacy. The Act prohibits the disclosure of information imparted under conditions of business or professional confidence. The Act applies to banks and professionals (including attorneys, accountants, government officers, secretaries, etc.) and includes all commercial transactions arising in Antigua and Barbuda and continues to apply whether inside or outside of Antigua and Barbuda.

The advantages of incorporating an offshore company in Antigua are

- There is a 50-year tax exemption. This exemption applies to most forms of income, dividends, interest, and royalties paid by and to foreigners.
- There are no exchange controls, and the unrestricted operation of bank accounts is permitted.
- An International Business Company (IBC) benefits from the absence of capital gains and estate taxes in Antigua.
- An IBC is not subject to mandatory auditing.
- There is no minimum capital requirement, and shares may have a nominal or no par value.
- Bearer shares may be issued.
- An IBC may increase or reduce its authorized capital by way of an amendment to its Articles of Incorporation.
- An IBC may have a sole shareholder.
- An IBC may have a sole director, and directors need not be natural persons.
- There are no citizenship or residence requirements for directors, officers, or shareholders.
- Meetings of directors and shareholders may be held outside Antigua.
- Shareholders may vote by proxy.
- There are no requirements to file any audited statements or corporate reports with the government.
- The company's records and its operating office may be located anywhere.
- There are inward and outward domiciliary provisions.

BELIZE

Background

Territorial disputes between the United Kingdom and Guatemala delayed the independence of Belize (formerly British Honduras) until 1981. Guatemala refused to recognize the new nation until 1992.

Location

The Central American country of Belize, situated between Guatemala and Mexico and bordering the Caribbean Sea, is the only country in Central America without a coastline on the North Pacific Ocean.

Time Zone

UTC–6

Capital

Belmopan

Population

287,730 (July 2006 est.) Thirty-three percent of the population lives below the poverty level.

Religion

The Roman Catholic religion predominates with 49.6 percent of the population, followed by Protestant (27 percent). Other significant religions are Pentecostal (7.4 percent), Anglican (5.3 percent), Seventh-Day Adventist (5.2 percent), Mennonite (4.1 percent), Methodist (3.5 percent), and Jehovah's Witnesses (1.5 percent).

Languages

English is the official language but Spanish, Mayan, Garifuna (Carib), and Creole are also spoken.

Currency Risk and Strength

The national currency is the Belizean dollar (BZD), which currently has a 2 to 1 correlation to the U.S. dollar.

Government

The form of government is a parliamentary democracy.

Economy

In this small, essentially private enterprise economy, the tourism industry is the number one foreign exchange earner and the mainstay of the economy. The government's expansionary monetary and fiscal policies, initiated in September 1998, led to sturdy GDP growth averaging nearly 5 percent in 1999 to 2005. Major concerns continue to be the sizable trade deficit and foreign debt. A key short-term objective remains the reduction of poverty with the help of international donors.

Geopolitical Risk

There is moderate geopolitical risk in Belize. The country remains plagued by high unemployment, growing involvement in the South American drug trade, and increasing urban crime. Guatemalan squatters continue to settle in the largely uninhabited rain forests of Belize's border region. Belize is a major transshipment point for cocaine, a small-scale illicit producer of cannabis for the international drug trade, and money-laundering activity related to narcotics trafficking and the offshore sector is prevalent.

Infrastructure

Belize has 43 airports, but only 5 with paved runways. There is an above-average telephone system. Internet users are growing. Belize City is host to the largest port and terminal.

Legal System

The legal system operates under English law. The chief justice of the Supreme Court is appointed by the governor general on the advice of the prime minister.

Offshore Investment Considerations

Legislation has been created in Belize in the form of the International Business Company (IBC) Act to provide a vehicle to attract offshore investors. The uses of an IBC are practically unlimited. The government preserves investors' privacy and, at the same time, the integrity of its financial services industry. Directors of IBCs remain anonymous; names of shareholders are not recorded other than at the company's registered office and may not be divulged to any authority. Shares may be issued as Bearer Shares and the company may have "nominee" directors.

There are no restrictions on trade from Belize, enabling an IBC to trade globally in total privacy. Banking secrecy is rigidly enforced by law, and bank records cannot be made available to the authorities of any jurisdiction.

Belize has no tax treaties with any other nation and has no interest in the requests of other nations to enter into such treaties.

Banking secrecy in Belize is strictly enforced by law. Access to bank records is available only to signatories on an account and no one else. No details of the directors, shareholders, or beneficial owners can be obtained by any tax authorities, and the banks will not reveal even the existence of any account. A Belize IBC's assets cannot be touched by any authority.

There are no personal or corporate taxes in Belize so tax avoidance and even tax evasion are not considered criminal matters. In fact, as there are no taxes, there are no statutes relating to taxes.

Offshore banks are regulated far more strictly than banks in the United States and must, by law, hold much greater reserves. They are rigorously audited by the Central Banks, safeguarding the banking systems. Bank deposits are fully insured.

All normal banking services are available, such as current accounts, investment accounts, and portfolio funds, with Internet account access. Checking accounts and Gold debit and credit cards are also provided, with no credit checks. If a business has a merchant account, the card receipts can be credited to an IBC's offshore account.

An IBC can be incorporated in Belize and the bank account in another jurisdiction, if the investor so desires.

Precious metals, real estate, improved property, valuable collections, and shares of beneficial interest can be held by an offshore company.

In retirement planning and estate planning, assets and funds can be shifted into the IBC, where there is no tax payable, no death duties, and beneficiaries can gain access to the assets offshore, according to one's will.

In litigious countries such as the United States, it has become common practice for individuals and companies to seek offshore protection against lawsuits. Investors can trade through their offshore IBC's brokerage account and pay no tax on the profits.

The Belize Asset Protection Trust

The enactment of the Belize Trust Act of 1992 was a much-anticipated event. The Act itself was well received. For all its apparent success, however, the Act has remained largely misunderstood (particularly its asset protection provisions). It is not uncommon, for instance, for commentators, especially those doing fairly superficial reviews, to list Belize as a jurisdiction that has not repealed the so-called law of fraudulent conveyances as it relates to trusts created in Belize. In fact, the opposite is true; the Belize Trust Act expressly excludes the operation of this law.

BERMUDA

Background

Bermuda was first settled in 1609 by shipwrecked English colonists headed for Virginia. Tourism to the island to escape North American winters first developed in Victorian times. A referendum on independence was soundly defeated in 1995.

Location

Bermuda is a group of islands located in the western Atlantic Ocean approximately 800 miles from New York City and some 570 nautical miles due east of Cape Hatteras, North Carolina. The largest island in the group is Great Bermuda Island, which is 14 miles in length.

Time Zone

Atlantic UTC–4

Capital

Hamilton

Population

Bermuda's population is slightly greater than 60,000.

Religion

The major religions of Bermuda are Anglican (23 percent), Roman Catholic (15 percent), African Methodist Episcopal (11 percent), other Protestant sects (18 percent).

Languages

English is the official language; Portuguese is also spoken.

Currency Risk and Strength

The national currency is the Bermuda dollar (BMD). The Bermuda dollar has a fixed rate pegged to the U.S. dollar (1 to 1). Both the Bermuda dollar and the U.S. dollar, which are at par with each other, are regularly accepted as currency. Banks will set up accounts in either currency.

Government

As an overseas territory of the United Kingdom, Bermuda is a parliamentary British overseas territory with internal self-government.

Economy

Bermuda has developed into a highly successful offshore financial center. Tourism continues to be important to the island's economy, although international business has overtaken it in recent years.

Bermuda enjoys one of the highest per capita incomes in the world, nearly equal to that of the United States. Its economy is primarily based on providing financial services for international business and luxury facilities for tourists. The effects of September 11, 2001 have had both positive and negative ramifications for Bermuda. On the positive side, a number of new reinsurance companies have located on the island, contributing to the expansion of an already robust international business sector. On the negative side, Bermuda's tourism industry—which derives over 80 percent of its visitors from the United States—was severely hit as American tourists chose not to travel. Tourism rebounded in 2002 through 2005.

Geopolitical Risk

There is currently no significant unrest in Bermuda, and geopolitical risk is low.

Infrastructure

There is one main airport and one main seaport. Bermuda has a good digital telephone system with fiber-optic cables.

Legal System

Bermuda operates under the English Law system. The judicial system consists of a Supreme Court, Court of Appeal, and Magistrate Courts.

Offshore Investment Considerations

The Bermuda Stock Exchange (BSX) was established in 1971, and is owned by the three commercial banks in Bermuda: the Bank of Butterfield, Ltd.; the Bank of Bermuda, Ltd.; and Bermuda Commercial Bank, Ltd. There is a very sophisticated banking community on Bermuda, and Bermuda can rightfully claim to be one of the world's leading banking centers. Bermuda's banks are very conservative: loans typically constitute less than 15 percent of total deposits, creating a very low loan portfolio exposure. Following the downfall of Lloyd's of London, Bermuda probably has risen to be the world's insurance and reinsurance capital.

The country has no income tax or other form of taxation for profits or capital gains.

Bermuda has a well-developed modern trust law. Some professional advisors have complained that Bermuda trust companies are difficult to work with, but it is hard to say whether these are isolated incidents or whether it represents a pattern of conduct sufficient to cause one to avoid Bermuda for these purposes.

Bermuda offers a wealth of sophisticated corporate management services, local management consultants, and management services companies, as well as trust companies and brokerage firms. There are also a number of law firms in Bermuda that cater to the needs of international clients.

Bermuda is a good offshore location for U.S. clients located along the Atlantic coast, as there are daily flights from most major cities to Bermuda. Bermuda is probably the offshore location of choice for most eastern U.S. citizens. For the same reason, however, Bermuda is not as readily accessible to clients from the western United States as, say, the Cayman Islands or Belize. Also, Bermuda can be relatively cold (compared to the Caribbean) during the winter months. Moreover, because Bermuda sits alone in the Atlantic, there is no nearby location that can easily be visited from Bermuda, unlike the Caribbean.

THE CAYMAN ISLANDS

Background

The Cayman Islands was colonized from Jamaica by the British during the eighteenth and nineteenth centuries and administered by Jamaica after 1863. In 1959, the islands became a territory within the Federation of the West Indies, but when the Federation dissolved in 1962, the Cayman Islands chose to remain a British dependency.

Location

The Cayman Islands is located between Cuba and Central America in the Caribbean Sea. Three islands make up the country: Grand Cayman, Cayman Brac, and Little Cayman. The Cayman Islands is located 240 km south of Cuba and 268 km northwest of Jamaica.

Time Zone

The Cayman Islands is in the Eastern time zone, five hours behind Greenwich Mean Time.

Capital

George Town (Grand Cayman)

Population

45,436 (July 2006 est.). Most of the population lives on Grand Cayman.

Religion

United Church (Presbyterian and Congregational), Anglican, Baptist, Church of God, other Protestant sects, and Roman Catholic

Language

English

Currency and Banking

The Cayman Islands has its own currency. First issued in 1972, the basic unit is the dollar, issued in notes with denominations of CI $100, $50, $25, $10, $5, and $1 and coins valued at 25 cents, 10 cents, 5 cents, and 1 cent. The CI dollar has a fixed exchange rate with the US dollar of CI $1.00 equals US $1.25 OR US $1.00 equals CI $.80.

The CI $1 note bears a portrait of her Majesty Queen Elizabeth II and the Cayman Islands coat of arms. The reverse side of the CI $5 note features a schooner sailing off George Town harbor. The watermark on all notes (which may be seen by holding them up to the light) features a turtle printed into the design on the left-hand side. All the coins also bear the effigy of the Queen.

There is no need for visitors to exchange their US dollars into local currency. Many traders quote their prices in both CI dollars and US dollars and visitors can pay in either currency. Major credit cards (with the exception of the Discover Card) and traveler's checks are widely accepted. Canadian dollars and pounds sterling can be exchanged for CI dollars at local banks. The bank rate of exchange is more favorable for traveler's checks at a rate of CI $.82. If you change cash at a bank you will receive CI $.80 for US $1.00. Most banks will also honor cash advances on Visa and MasterCard at the rate of CI $.82 for each US $1.00. Pounds sterling are not readily accepted by local merchants or restaurants, but may be changed at one of the larger banks on the island at the current exchange rate, which may vary daily. Coins are not accepted.

There is no limit to the amount of non-Caymanian currency that may be brought into the island.

Type of Government

British Crown Colony

Economy

Tourism is a mainstay of the economy, accounting for about 70 percent of GDP and 75 percent of foreign currency earnings. The tourist industry is aimed at the luxury market and caters mainly to visitors from North America. Total tourist arrivals exceeded 1.2 million in 1997, with 600,000 from the United Staes. About 90 percent of the islands' food and consumer goods must be imported. The Caymanians enjoy one of the highest outputs per capita and one of the highest standards of living in the world.

Geopolitical Risk

Low. No international disputes. Defense is the responsibility of the United Kingdom. The location of the Cayman Islands makes the country vulnerable to drug transshipment to the United States and Europe.

Infrastructure

There are two airports with paved runways and two ports: Cayman Brac and George Town. There is a reasonably good telephone system and three cable TV stations. (The liberalization of the telecom market in 2003 is reflected in falling prices and improved services.)

Although Grand Cayman now has more than 692 licensed banks, only a handful are full-service "A-class" banks providing full customer banking services as visitors know them. These include Barclays Bank, Scotiabank, Bank of Butterfield, Royal Bank of Canada, Cayman National Bank, Canadian Imperial Bank of Commerce, and British American Bank.

Legal System

The legal system operates under British common law and local statutes. The judicial branch consists of a Summary Court, Grand Court, and Cayman Islands Court of Appeal.

Offshore Investment Considerations

With no direct taxation, the islands are a thriving offshore financial center. More than 40,000 companies were registered in the Cayman Islands as of 1998, including almost 600 banks and trust companies; banking assets exceed $500 billion. A stock exchange was opened in 1997.

THE COOK ISLANDS

Background

Named after British naval explorer, Captain Cook, who sighted them in 1770, the islands became a British protectorate in 1888. By 1900, administrative control was transferred to New Zealand; in 1965, residents chose self-government in free association with New Zealand.

Location

The Cook Islands are located in Oceania, a group of islands in the South Pacific Ocean about one-half of the way from Hawaii to New Zealand.

Time Zone

UTC–10

Capital

Avarua

Population

21,388 (July 2006 est.)

Religion

The Cook Islands Christian Church is predominant with 55.9 percent of the population belonging to that church. There are also a significant number of Roman Catholics (16.8 percent).

Languages

The official language is English; Maori is also spoken.

Currency Risk and Strength

The New Zealand dollar (NZD) has a high correlation to the U.S. dollar (1.53 to 1 in 2005).

Government

The Cook Islands are a self-governing parliamentary democracy.

Economy

Agriculture provides the economic base. Trade deficits are offset by remittances from emigrants and by foreign aid, overwhelmingly from New Zealand. In the 1980s and 1990s, the country lived beyond its means, maintaining a bloated public service and accumulating a large foreign debt. Subsequent reforms, including the sale of state assets, the strengthening of economic management, the encouragement of tourism, and a debt restructuring agreement, have rekindled investment and growth.

Like many other South Pacific island nations, the Cook Islands' economic development is hindered by the isolation of the country from foreign markets, the limited size of domestic markets, lack of natural resources, periodic devastation from natural disasters, and inadequate infrastructure. The emigration of skilled workers to New Zealand and government deficits are continuing problems.

Geopolitical Risk

There are no significant transnational issues to consider, and geopolitical risk is low.

Offshore Investment Considerations

If you have a legitimate reason, it's perfectly legitimate to set up an offshore trust in the Cook Islands. For most people, it's not appropriate and not cost effective.

The Cook Islands permit the incorporation of companies under the International Companies Act of 1981 with a minimum capital of $1,000,000 without fees based on the capital. There is a one-time fee of $1,000 and annual $500 fees are payable to the government.

CYPRUS

Background

A former British colony, Cyprus became independent in 1960 following years of resistance to British rule. Tensions between the Greek Cypriot majority and Turkish Cypriot minority came to a head in December 1963, when violence broke out in the capital of Nicosia. Despite the deployment of UN peacekeepers in 1964, sporadic intercommunal violence continued, forcing most Turkish Cypriots into enclaves throughout the island. In 1974, a Greek government-sponsored attempt to seize control of Cyprus was met by military intervention from Turkey, which soon controlled more than a third of the island. In 1983, the Turkish-held area declared itself the "Turkish Republic of Northern Cyprus," but it is recognized only by Turkey. The latest two-year round of UN-brokered talks—between the leaders of the Greek Cypriot and Turkish Cypriot communities to reach an agreement to reunite the divided island—ended when the Greek Cypriots rejected the UN settlement plan in an April 2004 referendum. The entire island entered the EU on May 1, 2004, although the EU *acquis*—the body of common rights and obligations—applies only to the areas under direct Republic of Cyprus control, and is suspended in the areas administered by Turkish Cypriots. At present, every Cypriot carrying a CyprusUS passport has the status of a European citizen; however, EU laws do not apply to north Cyprus. Nicosia continues to oppose EU efforts to establish direct trade and economic links to north Cyprus as a way of encouraging the Turkish Cypriot community to continue to support reunification.

Location

Middle East, island in the Mediterranean Sea, south of Turkey

Time Zone

Eastern European Time (EET) (UTC+2); Summer: EEST (UTC+3)

Capital

Nicosia

Population

784,301 (July 2006 est.)

Religions

Greek Orthodox (78 percent), Muslim (18 percent), Maronite, Armenian Apostolic, and other sects (4 percent)

Languages

Greek, Turkish, English

Currency Risk and Strength

Republic of Cyprus: Cypriot pound (CYP); Turkish Cypriot area: Turkish New lira (YTL). Exchange rates: Cypriot pounds per U.S. dollar—0.45. Turkish lira per U.S. dollar—1.552 million

Government

Republic

Economy

The Republic of Cyprus has a market economy dominated by the service sector, which accounts for 76 percent of GDP. Tourism and financial services are the most important sectors. Erratic growth rates over the past decade reflect the economy's reliance on tourism, which often fluctuates with political instability in the region and economic conditions in Western Europe. Nevertheless, the economy grew a healthy 3.7 percent per year in 2004 and 2005, well above the EU average. Cyprus joined the European Exchange Rate Mechanism (ERM2) in May 2005. The government has initiated an aggressive austerity program, which has cut the budget deficit to below 3 percent, but continued fiscal discipline is necessary if Cyprus is to meet its goal of adopting the euro on January 1, 2008. As in the area administered by Turkish Cypriots, water shortages are a perennial problem; a few desalination plants are now on line. After 10 years of drought, the country received substantial rainfall from 2001 to 2003, alleviating immediate concerns. The Turkish Cypriot economy has roughly one-third of the per capita GDP of the south, and economic growth tends to be volatile, given north Cyprus's relative isolation, bloated public sector, reliance on the Turkish lira, and small market size. The Turkish Cypriot economy grew 15.4 percent in 2004, fueled by growth in the construction and education sectors, as well as increased employment of Turkish Cypriots in the Republic of Cyprus. The Turkish Cypriots are heavily dependent on transfers from the Turkish Government. Under the 2003 to 2006 economic protocol, Ankara plans to provide around $550 million to the "TRNC." Agriculture and services, together, employ more than half of the work force.

Geopolitical Risk

Moderate. Hostilities in 1974 divided the island into two de facto autonomous entities, the internationally recognized Cypriot government and a Turkish-Cypriot community (north Cyprus). The

1,000-strong UN Peacekeeping Force in Cyprus (UNFICYP) has served in Cyprus since 1964 and maintains the buffer zone between north and south. March 2003 reunification talks failed, but Turkish-Cypriots later opened their borders to temporary visits by Greek Cypriots. In 2004, the Greek Cypriot and Turkish Cypriot communities voted in simultaneous and parallel referenda on whether to approve the UN-brokered Annan Plan that would have ended the 30-year division of the island by establishing a new "United Cyprus Republic." A majority of Greek Cypriots voted "no." In May 2004, Cyprus entered the European Union still divided, with the EU's body of legislation and standards (*acquis communitaire*) suspended in the north.

Cyprus is a minor transit point for heroin and hashish via air routes and container traffic to Europe, especially from Lebanon and Turkey. There are some cocaine transits as well. Despite a strengthening of anti-money-laundering legislation, Cyprus remains vulnerable to money laundering. Reporting of suspicious transactions in the offshore sector remains weak.

Infrastructure

There are 16 airports, 13 with paved runways. Cyprus has 8 broadcast stations, plus two in North Cyprus. The telephone system is excellent in both Republic of Cyprus and north Cyprus areas. Technology includes open-wire, fiber-optic cable, microwave radio relay, three coaxial and five fiber-optic submarine cables.

Legal System

The legal system is based on common law, with civil law modifications. Cyprus accepts compulsory ICJ jurisdiction, with reservations. The highest court is the Supreme Court (judges are appointed jointly by the president and vice president). *Note:* There is also a Supreme Court in north Cyprus.

Offshore Investment Considerations

The offshore regime in Cyprus has changed as a result of agreements with the Organization for Economic Cooperation and

Development (OECD) and due to the island's inclusion in the EU. Cyprus was omitted from the OECD's tax haven blacklist in response to a commitment to amend its tax practices.

Cyprus's 10 percent corporate tax is one of the lowest rates in the EU.

GIBRALTAR

Background

Strategically important, Gibraltar was reluctantly ceded to Great Britain by Spain in the 1713 Treaty of Utrecht; the British garrison was formally declared a colony in 1830. In a referendum held in 1967, Gibraltarians voted overwhelmingly to remain a British dependency. Although the current 1969 Constitution for Gibraltar states that the British government will never allow the people of Gibraltar to pass under the sovereignty of another state against their freely and democratically expressed wishes, a series of talks were held by the United Kingdom and Spain between 1997 and 2002 on establishing temporary joint sovereignty over Gibraltar. In response to these talks, the Gibraltarian government set up a referendum in late 2002 in which a majority of the citizens voted overwhelmingly against any sharing of sovereignty with Spain. Since the referendum, tripartite talks have been held with Spain, the United Kingdom, and Gibraltar.

Location

Southwestern Europe, bordering the Strait of Gibraltar, which links the Mediterranean Sea and the North Atlantic Ocean, on the southern coast of Spain

Time Zone

Central European Time (CET) (UTC+1); Summer CEST (UTC+2)

Capital

Gibraltar

Population

27,928 (July 2006 est.)

Religions

Roman Catholic (78.1 percent), Church of England (7 percent), other Christian (3.2 percent), Muslim (4 percent), Jewish (2.1 percent), Hindu (1.8 percent), other or unspecified (0.9 percent), none (2.9 percent) (2001 census)

Languages

English (used in schools and for official purposes), Spanish, Italian, Portuguese

Currency

Gibraltar pounds per U.S. dollar—0.57.
Note: The Gibraltar pound is at par with the British pound.

Government

Overseas territory of the United Kingdom

Economy

Self-sufficient Gibraltar benefits from an extensive shipping trade, offshore banking, and its position as an international conference center. The British military presence has been sharply reduced and now contributes about 7 percent to the local economy, compared with 60 percent in 1984. The financial sector, tourism (almost 5 million visitors in 1998), shipping services fees, and duties on consumer goods also generate revenue. The financial sector, the shipping sector, and tourism each contribute 25 to 30 percent of GDP. Telecommunications accounts for another 10 percent. In recent years, Gibraltar has seen major structural change from a public to a private sector economy, but changes in government spending still have a major impact on the level of employment.

Geopolitical Risk

Low. Defense is the responsibility of the United Kingdom. The last British regular infantry forces left Gibraltar in 1992, replaced by the Royal Gibraltar Regiment.

Infrastructure

Gibraltar has one airport, an adequate telephone system, and adequate international facilities. Within Gibraltar, the main form of transport is the car. Motorbikes are popular and there is a good modern bus service. Unlike other British territories, traffic drives on the right, as it shares a land border with Spain.

There is a cable car that runs from ground level to the top of the rock, with an intermediate station at the apes' den.

The only transport link with Spain is by land, as the government of Spain currently prohibits all air and ferry links with Gibraltar. Despite this, Gibraltar Airport maintains regular flight connections to London and Manchester. Flights to Morocco were canceled after insufficient demand to sustain the service.

Motorists, and on occasion pedestrians, crossing the border with Spain are randomly subjected to long delays and searches by the Spanish authorities. Spain has closed the border during disputes with Gibraltar authorities, including when the *Aurora* cruise ship called at Gibraltar and during a dispute after a Spanish fishing vessel was impounded.

Gibraltar has a digital telephone exchange supported by a fiber-optic and copper infrastructure. The telephone operator also operates a GSM network. International subscriber dialing is provided, and Gibraltar has been allocated the access code 350 by the International Telecommunication Union. Dial-up, ADSL, and high-speed Internet are also available. The Gibraltar Broadcasting Corporation operates a television and radio station on UHF, VHF, Medium Wave, and with Internet streaming of the radio service.

Legal System

The legal system is English law. The judicial branch consists of the Supreme Court and Court of Appeal.

Offshore Investment Considerations

Although residents of Gibraltar pay reasonably high income taxes, and there is estate duty, there are several tax-efficient mechanisms for making investments through Gibraltar.

Nonresidents are taxable on their income received in Gibraltar, but not if it is channeled through a trust or an exempt company. Bank interest is exempt from tax, although the EU's Savings Tax Directive, which came into effect in July 2005, means that payments of interest and other savings returns made to EU citizens are reported to their home tax authorities.

Residents can make use of High Net-Worth Individual (HNWI) status, and some expatriate executives are given tax-privileged regimes; in both cases the total tax bill is capped, so that additional income over the cap is free of tax.

High Net-Worth Individuals are permitted to hold shares in an exempt company, and to hold deposits in Gibraltar banks; income from these sources is only taxable (for the company) if paid to the HNWI for his or her own use in Gibraltar.

The main types of investment available through Gibraltar are investment funds, real estate, pension investments, and bank deposits.

HONG KONG

Background

Occupied by the United Kingdom in 1841, Hong Kong was formally ceded by China the following year. Various adjacent lands were added later in the nineteenth century. Pursuant to an agreement signed by China and the United Kingdom on December 19, 1984, Hong Kong became the Hong Kong Special Administrative Region (SAR) of China on July 1, 1997. In this agreement, China has promised that, under its "one country, two systems" formula, China's socialist economic system will not be imposed on Hong Kong and that Hong Kong will enjoy a high degree of autonomy in all matters except foreign and defense affairs for the next 50 years.

Location

Hong Kong is in Eastern Asia, bordering the South China Sea and China.

Time Zone

HKT UTC+8

Capital

None

Population

6,940,432 (July 2006 est.)

Religion

Hong Kong has an eclectic mixture of local religions (90 percent) and Christian sects (10 percent).

Language

There are two official languages: Chinese (Cantonese) and English.

Currency Risk and Strength

The national currency is the Hong Kong dollar (HKD). Currently, the correlation to one U.S. dollar is 7.76 HKD.

Government

The government of Hong Kong is a limited democracy. Hong Kong is a special administrative region of China.

Economy

Hong Kong has a free market, entrepot economy, highly dependent on international trade. Even before Hong Kong reverted to Chinese administration on July 1, 1997, it had extensive trade and investment ties with China. Hong Kong has been further integrating its economy with China because China's growing openness to the world economy has made manufacturing in China much more cost effective. Hong Kong's re-export business to and from China is a major driver of growth. Per capita GDP is comparable to that of the four big economies of Western Europe. GDP growth averaged a strong 5 percent from 1989 to 2005, but Hong Kong suffered two recessions in the past eight years because of the Asian financial crisis in 1997 through 1998 and the global downturn in 2001 through 2002. Although the Severe Acute Respiratory Syndrome (SARS) outbreak also battered Hong Kong's economy, a solid rise in exports, a boom in tourism from the mainland because of China's easing of travel restrictions, and a return of consumer confidence resulted in the resumption of strong growth from late 2003 through 2005.

Hong Kong has become the world's eighth largest trading economy calculated in terms of total value of trade undertaken. Hong Kong is the seventh biggest importer of goods and the ninth biggest exporter. This is an astonishing achievement for a territory with a population of only 6 million. After the Second World War, many of the Shanghai traders set up shop in Hong Kong. The British administration, consistent with British imperial tradition, allowed their businesspeople maximum freedom. This combination has resulted in a standard of living for Hong Kong residents that is now higher than Germany or France. Clearly, freedom pays extraordinary benefits when combined with hard-working and smart businesspeople.

The takeover of Hong Kong by mainland China has generated much speculation about Communist intentions. The Chinese are businesspeople first, and socialism has been redefined to mean whatever works. The reality of what has in fact happened on the ground supports the view that Hong Kong is taking over China.

Geopolitical Risk

Historically, Hong Kong has been somewhat politically unstable. There are no international disputes with Hong Kong, and geopolitical risk is low. Hong Kong makes strenuous law enforcement efforts, but faces difficult challenges in controlling transit of heroin and methamphetamine to regional and world markets. The modern banking system provides a conduit for money laundering. There is rising indigenous use of synthetic drugs, especially among young people.

Infrastructure

Hong Kong has a highly developed and sophisticated transport network, encompassing both public and private transport. The Octopus card stored-value smart card payment system can be used to pay for fares on almost all railways, buses, and ferries in Hong Kong. The Octopus card uses RFID (Radio Frequency Identification) to allow users to scan their cards without taking them out of their wallets or bags. All parking meters in Hong Kong accept payment by Octopus card only, and Octopus card payment can be made at various car parks.

Hong Kong Island is dominated by steep, hilly terrain, which required the development of unusual methods of transport up and down the slopes. In Central and Western districts there is an extensive system of escalators and moving sidewalks, including the longest outdoor covered elevator system in the world, the Mid-levels Escalator.

Hong Kong has several different modes of public rail transport. The two metro systems for the city are the MTR and KCR (KCR also operates a light rail system in northwest New Territories), which are operated by the MTR Corporation Limited and the Kowloon-Canton Railway Corporation, respectively. The tramway system covers the northern parts of Hong Kong Island and is the only tram system in the world run exclusively by double-deckers.

Five separate companies operate franchised public bus services in Hong Kong. Double-decker buses were introduced to Hong Kong in 1949. They are now used almost exclusively in Hong Kong, just as in Dublin and London. However, single-decker buses remain in use for routes with lower demand or roads with lower carrying capacity and are used exclusively in South Lantau. Most normal franchised bus routes in Hong

Kong operate until 1 a.m. Public light buses run the length and breadth of Hong Kong, through areas that standard bus lines cannot reach or do not reach as frequently, quickly, or directly. Taxis are also widely used throughout Hong Kong. Ninety-nine percent of taxis in Hong Kong run on liquefied petroleum gas; the rest are still diesel operated.

Most ferry services are provided by licensed ferry operators, which serve outlying islands, new towns, and inner-Victoria Harbor. The two routes operated by the Star Ferry, operating for over 100 years, are franchised. Additionally, 78 "kai-to" ferries are licensed to serve remote coastal settlements.

Hong Kong has one active international airport known as Hong Kong International Airport located at Chek Lap Kok. This replaced the famous airport of Kai Tak International Airport located in Kai Tak, Kowloon, in 1998. After dreadful delays in the cargo systems in the first few months, the airport now serves as a transport hub for Southeast Asia, and as the hub for Cathay Pacific Airways, Dragonair, Air Hong Kong, and Hong Kong Express. Additionally, both Hong Kong International Airport and Cathay Pacific Airways have been voted best in the world, in the airport and airline criteria, respectively, by Skytrax from 2001 to 2005. Hong Kong International Airport served more than 36 million passengers in the year 2004, and increased to over 40 million passengers in 2005.

Access to the airport includes "Airport Express," "CityFlyers," and "Airbuses." These services connect the airport to the rest of Hong Kong. The Airport Express zooms passengers to Central on Hong Kong Island in just 23 minutes. The recent opening of Sunny Bay Station of the MTR allows easy access to the Disneyland Resort.

While the traffic in mainland China drives on the right, Hong Kong still maintains its own road rules, with traffic continuing to drive on the left. There are about 517,000 registered vehicles in Hong Kong, 64 percent of which are privately owned passenger cars. As a metropolis for luxury in Asia, Hong Kong is world famous for having the most Rolls-Royce cars per capita in the world.

Legal System

Hong Kong's legal system is based on English Common Law.

Offshore Investment Considerations

What this former British colony lacks in political stability, it makes up for in sheer financial sophistication. As well as being a major trading center, Hong Kong is also one of the world's major financial centers and the expertise of the banks reflects this. The Hong Kong banking system is one of the most efficient in the world, and Hong Kong banks are particularly well prepared to process letters of credit and import/export documentation and also to open accounts through which stocks and shares can be traded on the world's major stock exchanges.

The concept of residence has no applicability to Hong Kong tax law. Only Hong Kong source income is subject to Hong Kong tax. For this reason, Hong Kong is a suitable base from which to administer an offshore company without tax consequence, provided that company does not do business with other Hong Kong residents. This is one of the reasons why the use of offshore companies by Hong Kong residents has proliferated to such a great extent. Offshore companies can conveniently have Hong Kong–based directors, a Hong Kong bank account, and a Hong Kong office address without being brought into the Hong Kong tax net.

Most other countries of the world operate a residency-based tax system and care, therefore, needs to be taken to ensure that the offshore company doesn't establish a permanent place of business within those countries or is managed and controlled from those countries. For example, an offshore company that had U.K.–based directors or established a place of business within the United Kingdom may become liable to U.K. tax on its worldwide income.

A Hong Kong company does not have to state its registered office address or place of incorporation on its letterhead. This would give the non–Hong Kong offshore company the added respectability of a Hong Kong persona combined with the added flexibility and ease of administration of an offshore company.

There is a capital duty of 0.6 percent and an annual fee of HK$75. There are no double tax treaties and no restrictions on dealings in currencies. Bearer shares are not permitted; registration takes three weeks; but shelf corporations are readily available.

LABUAN

Background

Well known among the business community as an International Offshore Financial Centre, Labuan is also fast becoming popular as an island resort. Once a part of the Sultanate of Brunei, Labuan was ceded to the British in 1846. It remained under British rule for 115 years except for three years when it was under Japanese occupation. With the increasing change in colonization, Labuan was ceded to the state of Sabah in 1963. Subsequently, its administration was handed to the Federal Government of Malaysia in 1984. Recognizing Labuan's strategic location and proximity to major shipping routes and offshore oil and gas fields, the Federal Government launched a long-term development program to jump-start Labuan's stagnating economy and to encourage the influx of both domestic and foreign investments. As Malaysia's only deepwater anchorage, Labuan is a free port, a Federal Territory, and an International Offshore Financial Centre (IOFC).

Location

Labuan is an island off the coast of the state of Sabah at the mouth of the Brunei Bay. It comprises one main island and six smaller ones. It is also centrally located in the middle of the Asia-Pacific region.

Time Zone

MST (UTC+8)

Capital

Bandar Labuan/Victoria

Population

More than 53 percent of the island's 80,000 population claim Brunei-Malay descendants. Numbering slightly less are the Kedayan, who claim Java origins. There are also Chinese as well as immigrant Fillipinos and Indonesians. Labuan's inhabitants are very cosmopolitan. They come from all walks of life and from various regions around the world, thus creating a diverse and stimulating society.

Religion

Islam is the official religion of Malaysia but the constitution guarantees the right of people to practice other religions.

Language

The Malay language (Bahasa Melayu) is the national language of the country. English is the second language, but other languages can be freely used and practiced. Similarly the Malay culture is dominant in the country because the Malays are the dominant race in Malaysia and in the region. But there is a free intermingling of different cultures.

Currency

Malaysian Ringgit (MYR). Exchange rate 3.64 MYR per U.S. dollar.

Government

Under Malaysian Federal Government. The island has a progressive local government that is one of the most efficient in Malaysia. This is attributable to its status as a federal territory of Malaysia. This is the result of a 1984 political delineation that conceded the island a high degree of administrative autonomy at par with any of the 13 states in Malaysia.

Economy

The Malaysian government's attempts to turn Labuan into an international banking center have had only limited success, but the government still offers incentives to try to lure in new investors. With land utilization geared more toward property and industrial use, there is little agricultural activity. Most of the island's prime land, waterfront, and suburbs are utilized for residential and tourism development. A sizeable area on the southwestern side of the island is occupied by shipbuilding, manufacturing, and oil and gas industries. Within recent decades Labuan has undergone significant improvements in infrastructure and services.

Geopolitical Risk

Low. Malaysia is one of the most politically stable countries in the world. The rule of law is one of the fundamentals in Malaysia's constitution. Everyone is subject to the law and also equal before the law. Malaysia is one of the safest countries in the world. Its crime rate is relatively low.

Infrastructure

Labuan is one of the most accessible islands in the world today. It is well connected by air, sea, land, and via the information highway. Labuan boasts a modern satellite telecommunication system and well-developed infrastructure. There is a full range of telecommunication facilities such as telephones, cellular mobile service, intelsat business satellite services, cable, telex, telefax, data and integrated services digital network (ISDN) which allows video conferencing, high-speed fax, and multimedia applications. Other services include Centrex, Digitaline, high-speed international private leased circuits, and VSATs.

Malaysian Airlines and Air Asia offer daily flights from Kuala Lumpur, Kota Kinabalu, and Kuching. Kota Kinabalu in the Borneo state of Sabah also offers regular flights every day. There are also high-speed air-conditioned ferries daily to Labuan from Kota Kinabalu, Sarawak, and Brunei. Another alternative is the vehicle ferry from Menumbok to Labuan.

Legal System

Labuan's legal system is based on Malaysian Common Law. Malaysia practices the British system of justice with an independent and dependable judiciary.

Offshore Investment Considerations

In 1990, Labuan was declared as an International Offshore Financial Centre. The 65 foreign banks operating on the island offer sophisticated offshore banking services and numbered accounts facilities to the world's rich and famous. Compared to International Offshore Financial Centers in Europe and the Caribbean, Labuan offers many advantages. First, it is in a low-operating-cost environment in terms of physical facilities and professional fees.

Second, apart from easy accessibility, Labuan shares a similar time zone with major cities in Asia; this means phone calls can be made during the same office hours. Third, the corporate tax rate imposed on offshore companies is among the lowest in the world: 3 percent of net profit or merely MYR 20,000, whichever is chosen by the company.

Fourth, dealing with the government is easy, as there is a one-stop regulatory agency, the Labuan Offshore Financial Services Authority. Offshore businesses are regulated by a separate set of offshore regulations. Numerous double tax agreements and Investment Guarantee Agreements have been signed with many countries. The latter provide foreign investors with, among other things, protection against nationalization and expropriation. Only "fit and proper" persons are allowed to operate in Labuan. Finally, the operations of offshore institutions are completely free from exchange control regulations when dealing with nonresidents.

Labuan's GDP was estimated at RM145 million in 1991 and RM196 million in 1995, giving a per capita GDP of RM2,650 and RM3,010 respectively. In 2000, GDP per head was estimated to be RM3,579. The mining sector, largely represented by oil and gas production and its related industries, is the biggest contributor to Labuan's economy, followed by the manufacturing, wholesale, retail, hotel, and restaurant sectors.

Although still not a major economic contributor, the finance sector is gaining significantly with its GDP contribution increasing from 5.7 percent in 1991 to nearly 10 percent in 2000. In the future, the manufacturing and mining sectors are expected to play a less significant role.

The government expects Labuan to register an average GDP growth of 10.1 percent per annum during the planning period 1995 through 2015. By the year 2015, Labuan's total GDP is projected to be RM1.335 million with a per capita GDP of RM9,315.

Malaysia's ambitions for Labuan to become a financial center to challenge Singapore and Hong Kong remain unfulfilled, but the island has become a major conduit for FDI into the surrounding economies, especially Korea. It is thought that somewhere between one-third and one-half of the 2,500 companies registered on the island are somehow linked to Korea. Many Korean companies themselves have invested back into Korea through Labuan.

MARSHALL ISLANDS

Background

After almost four decades under U.S. administration as the easternmost part of the UN Trust Territory of the Pacific Islands, the Marshall Islands attained independence in 1986 under a Compact of Free Association. Compensation claims continue as a result of U.S. nuclear testing on some of the atolls between 1947 and 1962. The Marshall Islands hosts the U.S. Army Kwajalein Atoll (USAKA) Reagan Missile Test Site, a key installation in the U.S. missile defense network.

Location

The Marshall Islands is an independent sovereign country located in the North Pacific Ocean, about halfway between Hawaii and Australia. The country includes the atolls of Bikini, Enewetak, Kwajalein, Majuro, Rongelap, and Utirik.

Time Zone

UTC+12

Capital

Majuro

Population

60,422 (July 2006 est.)

Religion

The majority of the population is Protestant (54.8 percent), followed by Assembly of God (25.8 percent), Roman Catholic (8.4 percent), Bukot nan Jesus (2.8 percent), Mormon (2.1 percent), other Christian sects (3.6 percent), other (1 percent), none (1.5 percent).

Languages

Marshallese is the principal language, spoken by 98.2 percent of the population. English is widely spoken as a second language, and both Marshallese and English are official languages.

Currency Strength and Risk

The U.S. dollar is the legal tender of the Marshall Islands.

Government

The government is a constitutional one in free association with the United States; the Compact of Free Association was entered into force October 21, 1986, and the Amended Compact entered into force in May 2004.

Economy

U.S. government assistance is the mainstay of this tiny island economy. Agricultural production, primarily subsistence, is concentrated on small farms; the most important commercial crops are coconuts and breadfruit. Small-scale industry is limited to handicrafts, tuna processing, and copra. The tourist industry, now a small source of foreign exchange employing less than 10 percent of the labor force, remains the best hope for future added income. The islands have few natural resources, and imports far exceed exports.

Geopolitical Risk

Geopolitical risk is low. There are no international disputes. The Marshall Islands has no military force, and defense of the country is the responsibility of the U.S. government.

Infrastructure

There are 15 airports, four with paved runways, two television broadcast stations (both U.S. military). There are at least six Internet hosts and over 2,000 users. Modern telephone services include telex, cellular, Internet, international calling, caller ID, and leased data circuits digital switching equipment. Majuro Atoll and Ebeye and Kwajalein islands have regular, seven-digit, direct-dial telephones; other islands are interconnected by high-frequency radiotelephone (used mostly for government purposes) and mini-satellite telephones. The U.S. government has a satellite communications system on Kwajalein.

Legal System

The Marshall Islands legal system is based on adapted Trust Territory laws, acts of the legislature, municipal, common, and customary laws.

Offshore Investment Considerations

The Marshall Islands has few restrictions on the business that a company can engage in. This is one of the few jurisdictions where the offshore company can be taken public; can raise capital from the public; carry out third-party trading of securities; act as an investment advisor; invest funds for other people; and so on. It can carry out virtually any legal business activity, except banking, insurance, trust, and online gaming.

Unlike other jurisdictions, "true" bearer shares are allowed. The only other jurisdictions providing "true" bearer shares are

Antigua, Panama, Samoa, and the Seychelles. "True" bearer shares are those that can be held in one's possession and do *not* have to be held at the Registered Office and the owner declared.

The Marshall Islands has no tax information exchange treaties and refuses to cooperate with the OECD on information exchange.

Directors and owners are confidential and information does not have to be provided to either the government or the public. No audited accounts or annual returns are required to be provided to the government.

The names of the directors and shareholders are not required to be filed with the government or registered agent, and are not held in the public record. Names are required to be filed with the registered agent if the company is engaged in soliciting funds from the public and/or engaged in other similar investment activities on behalf of other persons or companies.

Any name that is identical or similar to an existing Marshall Islands company cannot be used.

MAURITIUS (GATEWAY TO INDIA)
Background

Mauritius, an independent member of the British Commonwealth, is a mountainous island in the Indian Ocean east of Madagascar. Discovered by the Portuguese in 1505, Mauritius was subsequently held by the Dutch, French, and British before independence was attained in 1968. A stable democracy with regular free elections and a positive human rights record, the country has attracted considerable foreign investment and has earned one of Africa's highest per capita incomes. Recent poor weather and declining sugar prices have slowed economic growth, leading to some protests over standards of living in the Creole community.

Mauritius is a minor consumer and transshipment point for heroin from South Asia; small amounts of cannabis produced and consumed locally; significant offshore financial industry creates potential for money laundering, but corruption levels are relatively low and the government appears generally to be committed to regulating its banking industry.

Location

Southern Africa, island in the Indian Ocean, east of Madagascar

Time Zone

UTC+4

Capital

Port Louis

Population

1,240,827 (July 2006 est.) Mauritian society is highly multicultural. Island residents are the descendants of people from the Indian subcontinent, Africa, Madagascar, France, England, China, plus a few other places.

Religion

The major religion is Hindu (48 percent) followed by Roman Catholic (23.6 percent). Muslims make up 16.6 percent of the population and other Christian sects account for 8.6 percent.

Languages

The official language of Mauritius is English. French is still widely spoken despite France having lost its colonial dominion over the island nearly 200 years ago. The French-derived Mauritian Creole, with major influences from the other dialects, is widely spoken (80 percent) on the island and is considered the lingua franca of the country. Several other languages, including Arabic; Indian languages such as Urdu, Hindi, Punjabi, Tamil, Telugu, Marathi, Bhojpuri, Gujarati; or dialects of Chinese like Cantonese, Hakka, and Mandarin are also spoken.

The latter South Asian languages are spoken by descendants of the laborers brought from British India during the British rule.

Currency Risk and Strength

The Mauritian rupee (MUR) is the national currency. It has a very low correlation to the U.S. dollar: 29.14 Mauritian rupees to the U.S. dollar as of 2005.

Government

The government of Mauritius is a parliamentary democracy.

Economy

Since independence in 1968, Mauritius has developed from a low-income agriculturally based economy to a middle-income diversified economy with growing industrial, financial, and tourist sectors. For most of the period, annual growth has been in the order of 5 to 6 percent. This remarkable achievement has been reflected in more equitable income distribution, increased life expectancy, lowered infant mortality, and a much improved infrastructure. Sugarcane is grown on about 90 percent of the cultivated land area and accounts for 25 percent of export earnings. The government's development strategy centers on expanding local financial institutions and building a domestic information telecommunications industry. Mauritius has attracted more than 9,000 offshore entities, many aimed at commerce in India and South Africa, and investment in the banking sector alone has reached over $1 billion.

Geopolitical Risk

There is little geopolitical risk. There are two international disputes: Mauritius claims the Chagos Archipelago (U.K.-administered British Indian Ocean Territory) and its former inhabitants, who reside chiefly in Mauritius, were granted U.K. citizenship,but no right to patriation in the United Kingdom; it also claims French-administered Tromelin Island.

Infrastructure

Five airports, one international, two with paved runways. Port Louis is the main seaport. There are no railways or waterways. The telephone system is small with good service; there are HF radio-telephone links to several countries; fiber-optic submarine cable (SAT-3/WASC/SAFE) provides connectivity to Europe and Asia.

Legal System

The legal system is based on French civil law system with elements of English Common Law in certain areas. Mauritius accepts compulsory ICJ jurisdiction, with reservations.

Offshore Investment Considerations

At present, there are two main fiscally advantageous companies in Mauritius: "Ordinary Offshore Companies" (governed by the General Companies Act, 1984, as amended by the Mauritius Offshore Business Activities Act, 1992) and "International Companies" (governed by the International Companies Act, 1994). The former can avail of the Mauritian double taxation treaty network while the latter are directly analogous to West Indian "Tax Free" IBC Companies and do not enjoy tax treaty benefits. To enjoy the substantial benefits afforded by the Mauritian/Indian Double Taxation Treaty, which interestingly was signed in 1983 and hence before much of the Mauritian tax-planning legislation, it is necessary to prove that the recipient is resident.

Mauritius has a significant number of local lawyers and accountants who can provide resident directors, maintain local bank accounts, record official minutes, hold board meetings, and submit the annual audited accounts.

According to the Income Tax Act the proscribed rate of tax for an Ordinary Offshore Company is 0 percent, unless otherwise elected, up to a maximum rate of 35 percent. This provision exists for tax-planning and anti-avoidance reasons. In other words, it is quite possible for a Mauritian Ordinary Offshore Company to have no indigenous tax consequences. The question then becomes at what level will India impose withholding taxes on investments? Under the Treaty, once a Mauritian company holds an investment stake of 10 percent or more in an Indian company (known as a participation exemption) India will only impose a withholding tax rate of 5 percent on dividend distributions. In addition, tax on realized capital gains from the disposition of shares is fully exempted from Indian taxes.

The withholding tax on interest payments is merely 10 percent compared to the 20 percent rate levied in the case of Mauritius.

Mauritius permits the incorporation of companies under the International Companies Act of 1994 and exempts them from all taxes and fees except for a $100 annual fee. Bearer and no par value shares are permitted. No information need be given to the authorities prior to incorporation or prior to exempt tax status being granted. There is no information open to the public about exempt companies and there is no restriction on where meetings may be held. A registered office and a representative are required, and certain documents must be kept at the agent's office. Exempt companies cannot, however, take advantage of double taxation treaties, the most important of which is with India.

Mauritius offers substantial advantages for investors who are active in India. In addition, exempt companies, which may not avail themselves of the double tax treaty, are nevertheless private and inexpensive and may be appropriate in many other situations.

NAURU

Background

Nauru's phosphate deposits began to be mined early in the twentieth century by a German-British consortium; the island was occupied by Australian forces in World War I. Nauru achieved independence in 1968 and joined the UN in 1999.

Location

An island in the South Pacific Ocean, Nauru lies south of the Marshall Islands. Nauru is one of the three great phosphate rock islands in the Pacific Ocean; the others are Banaba (Ocean Island) in Kiribati and Makatea in French Polynesia.

Time Zone

UTC+12

Capital

Yaren

Population

13,287 (July 2006 est.) Of the island's residents, 58 percent are Nauruan, 26 percent other Pacific Islanders, 8 percent Chinese, and 8 percent Europeans.

Religion

The main religion practiced on the island is Christianity (two-thirds Protestant, one-third Roman Catholic). The Constitution provides for freedom of religion; however, the government restricts this right in some circumstances, and has restricted the practice of religion by the Church of Jesus Christ of Latter-day Saints and members of Jehovah's Witnesses, most of whom are foreign workers employed by the Nauru Phosphate Corporation.

Language

Nauruan (a distinct Pacific Island language) is the official language, but English is widely understood, spoken, and used for most government and commercial purposes.

Currency Risk and Strength

The national currency is the Australian dollar (AUD), which has a high correlation to the U.S. dollar. As of 2005, the exchange rate was 1.31 Australian dollars per U.S. dollar.

Government

Nauru is the world's smallest independent republic.

Economy

Revenues of this tiny island have traditionally come from exports of phosphates, but reserves are now depleted. Few other resources exist, with most necessities being imported, mainly from Australia, its former occupier and later major source of support. The rehabilitation of mined land and the replacement of income from phosphates are serious U.S. long-term problems.

In anticipation of the exhaustion of Nauru's phosphate deposits, substantial amounts of phosphate income have been invested in trust funds to help cushion the transition and provide for Nauru's economic future. As a result of heavy spending from the trust funds, the government faces virtual bankruptcy. To cut costs the government has called for a freeze on wages, a reduction of overstaffed public service departments, privatization of numerous U.S. government agencies, and closure of some overseas consulates. In 2005, the deterioration in housing, hospitals, and other capital plants continued, and the cost to Australia of keeping the government and economy afloat has substantially mounted. Few comprehensive statistics on the Nauru economy exist, with estimates of Nauru's GDP varying widely.

Geopolitical Risk

There is low geopolitical risk in Nauru. There are currently no international disputes. Nauru remains on the Financial Action Task Force Non-Cooperative Countries and Territories List for its continued failure to address deficiencies in money-laundering control regime.

Infrastructure

Nauru has one paved road that circles the island. There is one artificial harbor at Anibare Bay. The island's airport consists of a stretch of road that serves as a runway and an airline terminal. Air service was provided by Air Nauru. However, the national carrier Air Nauru had been teetering on the edge of bankruptcy for years and had its last remaining plane impounded in December 2005, leaving the future of flights to Nauru unclear. There is one harbor: Nauru.

Nauru has one government-owned radio station and two television stations. One TV station is government-owned and mainly rebroadcasts CNN and the other is a private sports network. The island's Internet service is provided by CenPacNet.

The telephone system is adequate. Local and international radiotelephone communications are provided via Australian facilities. There is one AM radio station, no FM.

Legal System

Acts of the Nauru Parliament and British Common Law; accepts compulsory ICJ jurisdiction, with reservations.

Offshore Investment Considerations

Nauru offers the possibility of setting up a bank with no requirement for local directors or any local presence apart from a registered office and company secretary in Nauru. These services would normally be provided by a management organization.

Nauru will accept applications for unrestricted licenses or for in-house-type banks but, in practice, the authorities are unwilling to grant unrestricted licenses to anybody other than an existing bank and would also impose a requirement that the applicant set up an office and associated infrastructure in Nauru. The capital requirements for an in-house bank are low (U.S. $100,000), and the time scale is in the order of one to three months.

A Nauru in-house bank is prohibited from dealing with anybody other than associated companies and individuals, but it would be possible for investors to set up a finance company that conducted a broader range of activities. For example, the finance company could take deposits from third parties and would then deposit the money with the bank. Any literature that was drafted could make clear reference to the fact that the finance company was a wholly owned subsidiary of XYZ Bank LTD and contain further details about the bank. The costs for obtaining this type of license would be in the order of U.S. $20,000 and the timescale would be one to two months.

NEVIS

Background

The island was named *Oualie* ("Land of Beautiful Waters") by the Caribs and *Dulcina* ("Sweet Island") by the early British settlers. The name *Nevis* is derived from Spanish, *Nuestra Señora de las Nieves* ("Our Lady of the Snows"), a name given the island in 1493 by Christopher Columbus who thought the clouds over Nevis Peak made the island resemble a snow-capped mountain. Nevis was united with Saint Kitts and Anguilla in 1882, and they became an associated state with full internal autonomy in 1967, though Anguilla seceded in 1971. Together, Saint Kitts and Nevis became independent on September 19, 1983. On August 10, 1998, a referendum on Nevis to separate from Saint Kitts had 2,427 votes in favor and 1,498 against, falling short of the two-thirds majority needed. Since independence from the United Kingdom in 1983, the Nevis Island Administration and the Federal Government have been involved in several conflicts over the interpretation of the new constitution that came into effect at independence.

Location

Together with Saint Kitts, Nevis constitutes the Federation of Saint Kitts and Nevis. The two islands are separated by a 2-mile-wide channel. Nevis lies in the Caribbean near the top of the Lesser Antilles archipelago, about 220 miles (350 km) southeast of Puerto Rico and 50 miles (80 km) west of Antigua. The 36-square-mile (93 km²) island is part of the Leeward Islands and is located at latitude 17.15°N and longitude 62.58°W. Nevis is conical in shape, with a volcanic peak at the center. It is fringed by long strands of golden sand beaches and has a coastline intermittently protected by coral reefs. The pale yellow to black sand is a result of the mixture of coral, foraminifera, and volcanic sand. The most famous beach is the 4-mile-long Pinneys Beach on the west coast. The islands have a pleasant, healthy climate, warm with cool breezes throughout the year, low humidity, and no real demarcated rainy season. Average annual rainfall is about 55 inches, most of it in the fall, which is also the hurricane season. The official tourist season is from December 15 to April 14, only because that's when weather is nastiest in the northern hemisphere and the Caribbean islands are most fashionable. Temperatures year-round average 78 to 85 degrees Fahrenheit, and from November through January the islands experience increased "Christmas winds," as they are called locally.

Time Zone

GMT–4

Capital

Charlestown. About 1,200 of the island's 9,300 inhabitants live in the town, founded in 1660, a place full of ancient buildings with fanciful galleries, elaborate gingerbread woodwork, shutters, color-ful hanging plants—and a small but effective cadre of international corporate and asset protection experts, both lawyers and bankers.

Population

39,129 (July 2006 est.) The majority of the population is of African descent. Most St. Kitts–Nevis islanders are descendants of African slaves imported by the British and French, the original American West Indian natives being long since extinct. The population is 94 percent black, 40 percent urban. English is the official and spoken language, but with a lilting West Indian accent, "mon."

Religion

Anglican, other Protestant sects, Roman Catholic

Language

English is the official language and the literacy rate, 98 percent, is one of the highest in the Western Hemisphere.

Currency

Although it was formerly a member of the British sterling bloc, the country's official currency is now the Eastern Caribbean

Dollar (XCD) used by several CARICOM nations. The XCD is pegged to the U.S. dollar at a rate hovering around XCD2.60 to 2.70 to the U.S. dollar. U.S. currency is freely accepted, but change will be given in EC dollars.

Type of Government

The political structure for the Federation of Saint Kitts and Nevis is based on the Westminster Parliamentary system, but it is a unique structure in that Nevis has its own unicameral legislature, consisting of Her Majesty's representative (the Deputy Governor General) and members of the Nevis Island Assembly. Nevis has considerable autonomy in its legislative branch. The constitution actually empowers the Nevis Island Legislature to make laws that cannot be abrogated by the National Assembly. In addition, Nevis has a constitutionally protected right to secede from the federation, should a two-thirds majority of the island's population vote for independence in a local referendum. The current Premier of Nevis, Vance Amory, leader of the Concerned Citizens Movement (CCM), has made an initiative of sovereign independence for Nevis from the Federation of Saint Kitts and Nevis part of his party's agenda.

Nevis has its own premier, its own government, the Nevis Island Administration, and the island collects its own taxes and has a separate budget. The Administration has managed to produce a balanced budget and a current account surplus, even with an ambitious infrastructure development program in progress, including a transformation of the Charlestown port, construction of a new deepwater harbor, resurfacing and widening the Island Main Road, a new airport terminal and control tower, and a major airport expansion, which required the relocation of an entire village in order to make room for the runway extension. Nevis has also managed to produce one of the highest growth rates in gross national product and per capita income in the Caribbean.

Economy

The major source of revenue for Nevis is tourism. The island focuses on an upscale market in order to keep the island uncrowded. The introduction of new legislation has made offshore financial ser-vices a rapidly growing economic sector in Nevis. Incorporation of companies—international insurance and reinsurance—as well as several international banks, trust companies, and asset man-agement firms have created a boost in the economy. The growing employment and economic activity on Nevis are reflected in the latest numbers presented by the minister of finance. During 2005, the Nevis Island Treasury collected $94.6 million in annual rev-enue, compared to $59.8 million during 2001.

Geopolitical Risk

Low. Transshipment point for South American drugs destined for the United States and Europe; some money-laundering activity.

Infrastructure

Nevis has good interisland and international connections; inter-island links via fiber optic-cable; construction of enhanced wire-less infrastructure launched in November 2004. International calls are carried by submarine cable or Intelsat. Nevis has the only five-star hotel in the Caribbean. Three exclusive restored plantation inns and a couple of smaller hotels are currently in operation, but larger developments have recently been approved and are in the process of being developed. There is one televi-sion broadcast station, three FM, and three AM radio stations. There is an international airport.

Offshore Investing

This tiny West Indies island nation has become very big in cer-tain exclusive international financial circles because Nevis has no taxes, extremely user-friendly incorporation and trust laws, and an official attitude of hearty welcome to foreign offshore corporations and asset protection trusts.

A low-key economic promotional program authorized by the 1984 "Citizenship Act" offers nationality and a passport in return for a $200,000 investment, usually the purchase price of a seaside condominium and certain "fees." Citizenship for the investor and spouse are included in the deal. (A less expensive route to citizenship is marriage, since St. Kitts and Nevis is one of the few countries that gives instant citizenship upon marriage to a spouse of either sex.)

Based on the Island Assembly's adoption of the "Business Corporation of 1984," Nevis has an established, decade-long record of catering to foreign offshore corporations, with the welcome mat always out. Patterned after the extremely liberal (toward business) corporation laws of the American State of Delaware, English commercial law is also blended into the statute, so U.K. solicitors should have little fear about navigating its provisions. The corporation statute allows complete confidentiality for company officials and shareholders, and there is no requirement for public disclosure of ownership, management, or financial status of a business.

Although they must pay an annual fee of U.S.$450, "international business corporations," or "IBCs" as the law calls them, are otherwise exempt from taxes—no withholding, stamps, fees, or taxes on income or foreign assets. Individually negotiated government-guaranteed tax holidays are available in writing for IBCs, provided they carry on no business locally. Official corporate start-up costs can be under U.S.$1,000, including a minimum capitalization tax of U.S.$200 and company formation fees of U.S.$600. These low government levies compare very favorably with those imposed by other corporate-friendly havens, like the high-profile, high-cost Cayman Islands.

On Nevis there are no exchange controls, no tax treaties with other nations (including the United States), and the government will not exchange tax or other information with any other foreign revenue service or government. Principal corporate offices and records may be maintained by Nevis companies anywhere in the world the owners wish.

The Nevis corporation law is almost unique in that it contains a very modern legal provision allowing the international portability or transfer of an existing foreign company from its country of origin to the island. Known as the "redomiciling provision," this allows the smooth and instantaneous transfer of an existing American, British, Panamanian, or any other nation's corporation and retention of its original name and date of incorporation—all without interruption of business activity or corporate existence. The only requirement is the amendment of existing articles of incorporation to conform with local laws.

New company creation and registration is fast in Nevis— accomplished by the simple payment of the capitalization tax and fees mentioned earlier to the Register of Corporations. Within 10 days thereafter, formal incorporation documents must be filed, but there are corporate service firms waiting to assist the foreign incorporator with ready-made paperwork. Small wonder that in the 10 years since the law's original adoption, thousands of foreign corporate owners have established their companies in Charlestown, Nevis.

In 1995 Nevis enacted the Limited Liability Company Ordinance, which provides for the existence of what is some-times known as a Limited Duration Company, or LLC, with the added benefit that the company may be structured in such a way as to be treated as a partnership under U.S. tax laws.

Asset Protection Trusts—A New Offshore Service. Building on their record for statutory corporate cordiality, on April 28, 1994, the Island Assembly adopted the "Nevis International Trust Ordinance," a comprehensive, clear, and flexible asset protection trust (APT) law comparable to, and in many ways better, than that of the Cook Islands in the South Pacific, already well-known as an APT world center.

The new Nevis law incorporates the best features of the Cook Islands law, but in many ways is more flexible. The basic aim of the law is to permit foreign citizens to obtain protection against threats to their property and assets by transferring title to an APT established in Charlestown, Nevis.

Nevis simply is taking advantage of the fact that in many parts of the world, especially the United States, medical, legal, and professional malpractice lawsuits, as well as legislative and judicial imposition of no-fault personal liability on corporate officers and directors, have become a nasty fact of business life. A Nevis trust places personal assets beyond the reach of potential foreign governments, litigious plaintiffs, creditors, and contingent-fee lawyers.

Under the new law, the Nevis judiciary will not recognize any nondomestic court orders regarding its domestic APTs. This forces a foreign judgment creditor to start all over again, retrying in Nevisian courts, with Nevisian lawyers, the original claim that gave rise to the foreign judgment. A plaintiff who sues an APT must first post a U.S.$25,000 bond with the government to cover court and other costs before a suit will be accepted for filing. And the statute of limitations for filing legal challenges to a Nevisian APT runs out one year from the date of the trust creation. In cases where fraudulent intent on the part of the trust or its officers or beneficiaries is alleged, the law places the burden of proof on the foreign claimant.

Nevis has an established international bar and local trust experts who understand and can assist in furthering APT objectives. The APT act has proven very popular, and a considerable number of trusts have been registered in Nevis.

Under the statute, basic trust documents are not required to be filed with the Nevis government and are not a matter of public record. The only public information needed to establish an APT is a standard form or letter naming the trustee, the date of trust creation, the date of the filing, and the name of the local trust company representing the APT. The only governmental fee charged is U.S.$200 upon filing, and an equal annual fee to maintain the filing.

Once established, the Nevis asset protection trust can consist of as little as a trust account in a local bank offering international services. These established banks have full international departments. Most international banks offer U.S. dollar–denominated accounts that often pay better interest rates than U.S. institutions. With modern fax machines, telex, telephones, instant communications, and international banking facilities, it is just as convenient to hold assets and accounts in Nevis as it is in any major financial center—and a lot safer in many personal and financial respects.

Under the provisions of the Nevis International Trust Ordinance, the same person can serve in the triple role of creator (settlor), beneficiary, and protector of the APT, allowing far greater control over assets and income than U.S. domestic law permits. Generally, Anglo-American common law forbids a settlor to create a trust for his or her own benefit.

The basic structure of a foreign asset protection trust differs little from an Anglo-American trust.

The settlor creates the trust by executing a formal declaration describing the purposes to which he transfers assets to be administered according to the declaration by the named trustees. Usually there are three trustees named, two in the settlor's country and one in Nevis, the latter known as a "protector." Named trust beneficiaries can vary according to the settlor's estate-planning objectives, and under Nevis law the settlor may be the primary beneficiary.

Nevis requires the appointment of a trust "protector" who, as the title indicates, oversees its operation to ensure trust objectives are met and the law is followed. A protector does not manage the trust, but possibly can veto some actions—and Nevis allows a beneficiary to serve in the dual role as protector.

Tax and Legal Advantages for Americans: Under U.S. tax law, foreign asset protection trusts are "tax-neutral." They are considered as domestic trusts, meaning income from the trust is treated by the Internal Revenue Service as the settlor's personal income and taxed accordingly. Because the settlor retains some control over the transfer of his or her assets to any foreign trust, including those established in Nevis, U.S. gift taxes can usually be avoided. Although Nevis has no estate taxes, U.S. estate taxes are imposed on the value of trust assets for the settlor's estate, but all existing exemptions for combined marital assets can be used. Foreign asset protection trusts are not subject to the 35 percent U.S. excise tax otherwise imposed on transfers of property to a "foreign person."

One device a settlor may employ to retain optimal control of assets is to form a limited partnership, making the Nevisian trust a limited partner. This allows a general managing partner/settlor to retain active control over all assets he or she transfers to the Nevis trust/limited partner, while trust assets are protected from creditors or other legal assaults.

NEW ZEALAND

Background

New Zealand is well known to most readers and requires little introduction. The Polynesian Maori reached New Zealand in about A.D. 800. In 1840, their chieftains entered into a compact with Britain, the Treaty of Waitangi, in which they ceded sovereignty to Queen Victoria while retaining territorial rights. In that same year, the British began the first organized colonial settlement. A series of land wars between 1843 and 1872 ended with the defeat of the native peoples. The British colony of New Zealand became an independent dominion in 1907 and supported the U.K. militarily in both World Wars. New Zealand's full participation in a number of defense alliances lapsed by the 1980s. In recent years, the government has sought to address long-standing Maori grievances.

Location

Approximately the size of Colorado, New Zealand is located in the South Pacific Ocean southeast of Australia.

Time Zone

NZST UTC+12; in summer (Oct.–Mar.) NZDT UTC+13

Capital

Wellington

Population

4,134,200

Religions

Not including the indigenous religions, the main religions are Anglican (14.9 percent), Roman Catholic (12.4 percent), Presbyterian (10.9 percent), Methodist (2.9 percent), Pentecostal (1.7 percent), Baptist (1.3 percent), and other Christian sects (9.4 percent).

Language

There are two official languages: English and Maori.

Currency Risk and Strength

The national currency is the New Zealand dollar (NZD). It has a high correlation to the U.S. dollar—currently, 1.64 NZD to the U.S. dollar.

Government

The government of New Zealand is a parliamentary democracy.

Economy

Over the past 20 years the government has transformed New Zealand from an agrarian economy dependent on concessionary British market access to a more industrialized, free market economy that can compete globally. This dynamic growth has boosted real incomes (but left behind many at the bottom of the ladder), broadened and deepened the technological capabilities of the industrial sector, and contained inflationary pressures. Per capita income has risen for six consecutive years and is now more than $24,000 in purchasing power parity terms. New Zealand is heavily dependent on trade—particularly in agricultural products—to drive growth. Exports are equal to about 20 percent of GDP. Thus far the economy has been resilient, and the Labor Government promises that expenditures on health, education, and pensions will increase proportionately to output.

Geopolitical Risk

Geopolitical risk is low. It is a safe, stable, and secure country that offers considerable benefits to those involved in international tax planning.

Offshore Investment Considerations

If properly structured, a New Zealand resident company can operate as a tax-free offshore company.

New Zealand resident companies are usually taxable. A New Zealand Special Purpose Company, however, which is structured as the trustee of a nonresident New Zealand trust is not taxable. The trust and its beneficiaries are also nontaxable, except on income with a New Zealand source.

If the New Zealand company and trust have no connection to New Zealand, the complete structure is nontaxable in New Zealand. The company owner and trust beneficiary may be the same person.

Once incorporated, the company is generally free to do business, open bank accounts, or invest anywhere in the world. In effect, it can operate as a tax-free offshore company but without the "tax haven" implications of the traditional offshore centers. In addition, it benefits from the asset protection features of the trust, as funds may be moved into and out of the trust as required. The complete structure costs a little more than the traditional offshore company.

The structure is quick and simple to establish. The only connection with New Zealand is that it will be a New Zealand resident company with a New Zealand registered office.

PANAMA

Overview

The Republic of Panama is considered one of the oldest and safest tax havens in the world. Since its independence from Colombia in 1903, Panama has had convenient and attractive legislation for offshore operations, based exclusively on the territorial principle of not taxing foreign source income. With U.S. backing, Panama seceded from Colombia in 1903 and promptly signed a treaty with the United States allowing for the construction of a canal and U.S. sovereignty over a strip of land on either side of the structure (the Panama Canal Zone). The Panama Canal was built by the U.S. Army Corps of Engineers between 1904 and 1914. On September 7, 1977, an agreement was signed for the complete transfer of the Canal from the United States to Panama by the end of 1999. Certain portions of the Zone and increasing responsibility over the Canal were turned over in the intervening years. With U.S. help, dictator Manuel Noriega was deposed in 1989. The entire Panama Canal, the area supporting the Canal, and remaining U.S. military bases were turned over to Panama by or on December 31, 1999.

Location

Panama is located in Central America between Colombia and Costa Rica and borders both the Caribbean Sea and the North Pacific Ocean.

Time Zone

UTC–5

Capital

Panama City

Population

3,191,319 (July 2006 est.)

Religion

The predominant religion is Roman Catholic (85 percent), followed by Protestant (15 percent).

Language

Spanish is the official language; however, English is also spoken and many Panamanians are bilingual.

Currency Risk and Strength

There are two currencies used in Panama: the balboa (PAB) and the U.S. dollar. The PAB is equal to the U.S. dollar.

Government

The government is a constitutional democracy.

Economy

Panama's dollarized economy rests primarily on a well-developed services sector that accounts for four-fifths of GDP. Services include operating the Panama Canal, banking, the Colon Free Zone, insurance, container ports, flagship registry, and tourism. A slump in Colon Free Zone and agricultural exports, the global slowdown, and the withdrawal of U.S. military forces held back economic growth in 2000 through 2003; growth picked up in 2004 and 2005 led by export-oriented services and a construction boom stimulated by tax incentives. The government has been backing tax reforms, reform of the social security program, new regional trade agreements, and development of tourism. Unemployment remains high.

Geopolitical Risk

However, geopolitical risk is currently low while Panama is politically stable. Central America is known for a great deal of unrest. Organized illegal narcotics operations in Colombia operate within the border region of Panama. It is a major cocaine transshipment point and primary money-laundering center for narcotics revenue. Money-laundering activity is especially heavy in the Colon Free Zone. Although monitoring of financial transactions is improving, official corruption remains a major problem.

Infrastructure

Panama has excellent international transportation and communication systems. There are 109 airports, 47 with paved runways. Telephone system: domestic and international facilities are well developed. As of 2005, there were 7,013 Internet hosts and 300,000 Internet users.

Legal system

Panama's legal system is based on a civil law system with judicial review of legislative acts in the Supreme Court of Justice. Panama accepts compulsory ICJ jurisdiction, with reservations.

Offshore Investment Considerations

Due to its structure, geographical position, political stability, and characteristics of its economy, Panama has become one of the most important tax havens of the Western Hemisphere. The U.S. dollar has been a currency of legal tender for more than 90 years in Panama; there are no exchange controls or government regulations and there is a complete freedom in the movement of funds. Also, confidentiality and banking secrecy are recognized by law.

Panama's success as a tax haven is primarily based on its tax structure. According to article 694 of the Fiscal Code, the income earned by any person, either an individual or a corporation, from sources outside of Panama is exempt from taxes. Legislation expressly provides that the following transactions are not subject to income tax in Panama:

- Invoicing to a company abroad from an office located in Panama the sale of goods for an amount greater than that at which said goods were invoiced to the office located in Panama, provided those goods are handled exclusively abroad.
- Directing or managing, from an office located in Panama, operations and transactions that are executed, completed, or take effect abroad.
- Distributing dividends from income earned by a company when that income is produced or earned abroad.

Also, the Fiscal Code exempts from income tax:

- The interest paid by banks located in Panama to their customers for savings accounts and time deposits kept in Panama
- The salary or fees earned by Directors, Officers, and Executives of Panamanian corporations located abroad

Panamanian Foundations—Panama has copied much of Liechtenstein's *Stiftung* legislation (see Liechtenstein), giving investors the option of the Panamanian Foundation.

The Panamanian Foundation is modeled after the *Stiftung*, with some important differences. The Foundation is formed by the filing of a Charter, and is treated as a separate legal entity. As an entity, it can hold title to assets in its own name like a corporation. However, it can also make discretionary payments to the Founder or beneficiaries, like a trust. When used for this latter function, the entity is sometimes referred to as a "Family Foundation."

Panamanian law permits the appointment of one or more protectors to oversee the three or more members of the Foundation Council. The members of the Council are required to apply the Foundation's assets for the benefit of its beneficiaries or some beneficial purpose as set out in the Charter. As with the *Stiftung*, the Foundation is mostly controlled by its Regulations (bylaws) that are not required to be registered or publicly disclosed.

Panama has a three-year statute of limitation for fraudulent transfer challenges to contributions to the Foundation. If gifting is utilized to fund the Foundation, there will be a three-year window available for creditors to attempt to void the gifts. For this reason, the Foundation should be initially funded with a small gift, but if it is desired that the Foundation hold significant assets, then the Foundation should be funded by some alternative for-value transfer method, such as an installment note sale or private annuity.

Once past the three-year limitation, however, the assets are probably safe from creditors. Panamanian law specifically provides that the Foundation assets may not be applied toward the debts of either the Founder or any beneficiary. But perhaps the greatest advantage of the Panamanian Foundation over the *Stiftung* is that the Panamanian version is relatively inexpensive to form and maintain. Another advantage is that Panama is in the same time zone, making administration of the Foundation from the United States easier.

As with the *Stiftung*, probably the best use of the Panamanian Foundation is not to hold assets but rather to own an entity that is used as a management company. From a creditor's viewpoint, the management company will be owned by a Panamanian charity with three Panamanian residents as members of the Foundation's Council. The creditor will likely not see that the U.S. settlor has appointed one or more protectors to make sure that the Council members carry out the purposes of the Foundation as set forth in the charter. It will thus be very difficult for a creditor to claim that the U.S. owner of the asset being managed has any ties to or control over the Foundation. However, in 1984 new provisions on trusts were enacted by means of Law No. 1 of January 5th, to complement other legal instruments and benefits provided by Panama as a tax haven to the international financial community. This legislation introduced new and modern concepts to update the former law on trusts in order to make them more flexible and convenient to foreigners who were searching for a place to execute a trust overseas.

The most important features of the Panamanian trust are

- *Liberty of bargaining:* The trust can contain any lawful clause as the needs of the settlor may require. According to articles 5 and 9 of Law No. 1, the trust may be created for any purpose provided it is not contrary to the law or public policy.

- *Simplicity in its execution:* The trust shall be created in a private document, with the only formality that the signature of settlor and trustee must be authenticated by a Panamanian Notary, so confidentiality is guaranteed. It is not necessary that the trust be executed in a public deed or be registered in any public register unless real property located in Panama is given in trust.

- *Duration:* The trust is not perpetual unless so stated by the settlor in the trust. The trust should have its duration expressly stated. Also, it may be revocable or terminated before its expiration if it is so provided by the settlor in the trust agreement.

- *Confidentiality:* Article 37 of Law No. 1 expressly guarantees the confidentiality for the execution of the trust. It provides that the trustee and his representative or employees or any other person involved in the execution of the trust must uphold the secrecy of the operation. The violation of this provision is penalized with imprisonment of up to six (6) months and a fine of up to US$50,000.

- *Corporations may be used:* Both the settlor and the trustee and/or beneficiary may be a corporation. They do not need to be individuals.
- *Special tax benefits:* To be consistent with the tax principles already mentioned, Law No. 1 expressly states that the acts of executing, modifying, and terminating a trust as well as the transfer, conveyance, or encumbrance of trust funds and the income or interest produced by the assets and properties given in trust are exempt from all taxes, contributions, assessments, or encumbrances, provided the trust involves the following assets:
  - Properties or assets located abroad;
  - Funds that are not from a Panamanian source or subject to taxes in Panama;
  - Shares of stocks or securities of any kind, issued by corporations whose income is not produced in Panama, even though those shares or securities may be deposited in Panama;
  - Time deposits or savings accounts kept in banks located in Panama. The previous tax limitation will not be applicable when the trust funds are invested in housing projects or the development of industrial parks in Panama, in which cases the income earned in those commercial operations will be tax free.
- *Separate estate:* The assets of the trust shall constitute an estate separate from the assets of the trustee. Therefore, they cannot be attached, seized, or subject to any lien as a result of obligations of the trustee. The assets of the trust only answer for liabilities of the trust itself.
- *Assets subject to trust:* The trust fund may consist of properties or assets of any kind, present or future. The settlor may increase or add other assets to the trust fund after the execution of the trust.
- *Applicability of foreign law and jurisdiction:* Although the trust shall be regulated by Panamanian law, the settlor and the trustee may agree that foreign law will be applicable. Also, the trust and the trust fund may be transferred to another jurisdiction or country.

- *Trust of other jurisdictions:* Trusts created pursuant to foreign law may be governed by Panamanian law provided they are subject to the formalities of the law on trusts.
- *Trustee:* The trustee can be any person, either an individual or a corporation, duly authorized by law. Also, the settlor may replace the trustee if so provided in the trust agreement.

The problem really is the judges that enforce such statutes, and the fact that it is an entity only found in Common Law nations (such as the Bahamas, Canada, and the United States). Because many judges have gone the route of "re-interpreting" the law in such a way that the Trust structure is not as secure as one would be led to believe, our advice is to take a look at the Panamanian Foundation instead. Why? For one thing it does have some attributes that actually make it superior to a trust in many ways, and, perhaps more importantly, it is a vehicle backed by a civil law country.

The Panamanian Foundation structure was codified into law in 1995. While this structure is a fairly new entity for Panama, the Foundation structure itself has existed in Liechtenstein for quite some time and the Panamanian structure was in fact modeled after the Liechtenstein legislation. Some advantages a Panamanian foundation has over a Liechtenstein foundation include the following:

It is far less expensive to create. (A Panamanian Foundation costs less than $3,000 while some firms have charged as much as $10,000 to create a Liechtenstein foundation.)

It is far less expensive to maintain.

It offers more flexibility.

To understand the idea and benefits of the foundation structure, you should first understand the difference between a trust and a corporation. It is also important to note the difference between English-speaking countries that use Common Law and many non-English speaking countries that use Civil Law.

I think most people understand the idea behind a corporation and how it works. The corporation structure is used worldwide basically to carry out a business enterprise and keep the owners' business assets (and liabilities) separate from his or her own personal assets. As a separate entity, the corporation usually has its own tax identification number and is what can be termed a *juridical person*. Certainly it is not a human being, but it has all of the rights and responsibilities of a natural person under the law. The key point is that the assets and liabilities of the corporation are separate and distinct from those of the shareholders.

The trust structure, however, is a vehicle usually only found in Common Law countries and is most commonly used as an estate-planning mechanism.

How to create a Panamanian Foundation: The Panamanian Foundation can be created by one or more natural persons or by a juridical entity, such as a corporation. A foundation charter is created, which, in essence, is similar to the incorporation documents created for a Panamanian company. Like the incorporation documents, the foundation charter document is public record. The foundation structure is directed by a council of three or more members. This is similar to a corporation, which is directed by three directors or board members. These directors of the foundation are called Council Members. In addition, like a trust, a private protector may be named to have special oversight authority.

The position of a protector is not required, but it is advisable. While the position of protector can be a private agreement between the foundation and the person acting as protector, extra protection is given to the client when this position is spelled out in the foundation charter.

The Foundation Charter must contain:

- *Name of the Foundation*—The name of the foundation can be expressed in any language, but must contain the term *foundation* as part of the title to indicate that the entity is in fact a foundation structure.
- *The Initial Patrimony*—The initial patrimony is the amount used to fund the foundation. The foundation can be funded in any currency, but the initial patrimony cannot be less than the equivalent of U.S.$10,000. An important point to note is that this initial funding or contribution does not have to be done at the time the foundation is created. Rather it can be done after the fact. In reality, there is no public record of the foundation assets other than the fact it was originally funded with U.S.$10,000.

- *Council Members*—The foundation structure must have a minimum of three council members who are natural persons or a juridical person, such as a corporation that has three natural persons as directors. The names and addresses of the council members are public record.
- *The Purpose of the Foundation*—The foundation may be created for any lawful purpose. Examples of such purposes could include: the maintenance and welfare of minor children, a college scholarship fund for any person, the maintenance and welfare of the founder upon his or her retirement, the maintenance of a building or property, the benefit of any charitable foundation or organization, or any other purpose that the founder can think of that is within the confines of the law.
- *Beneficiaries*—The foundation structure, like a trust document, must name beneficiaries and also what percentage each beneficiary is entitled to. The foundation charter must also indicate how assets are to be distributed upon its dissolution. The founder of the foundation, or the client, can be named as a beneficiary.
- *Domicile*—The domicile of the foundation can be located or indicated as any desired jurisdiction, but it is suggested that Panama or another civil law jurisdiction be used.
- *Resident Agent*—The foundation must have a local resident agent which is a duly authorized lawyer or law firm, with a physical presence in Panama.
- *Duration of the Foundation*—The foundation can have a limited life span if the client wishes to indicate it as such.

Advantages of the Panamanian Foundation: The assets placed inside a Panamanian Foundation are sole and separate property and cannot be seized to satisfy any personal judgments or obligations of the founder or the foundation's beneficiaries. Assets inside a Panamanian Foundation cannot be attached in order to satisfy any claims against the founder, including judgments for divorce, lawsuit, and other liabilities.

The Panamanian Foundation offers the best of a trust and the best of an offshore corporation. While the foundation cannot technically engage in business activities, it can own the shares of a company engaged in business activities. It is also permissible for the foundation to engage in any activity that will increase the value of assets. This means that a foundation can be the owner of bank accounts, securities brokerage accounts, and real estate holdings.

Since there are no shares of ownership in a Panamanian Foundation, the founder does not own the foundation and, as such, gains important tax-reporting and protection benefits with this.

ST. VINCENT AND THE GRENADINES
Background

Disputed between France and the United Kingdom in the eighteenth century, Saint Vincent was ceded to the latter in 1783. Autonomy was granted in 1969 and independence in 1979.

Location

The Grenadines are a chain of islands stretching from St. Vincent in the north to Grenada in the south. St. Vincent, the largest island, is a densely green and mountainous island. St. Vincent and the Grenadines are among the most beautiful islands in the Eastern Caribbean.

Time Zone

UTC–4

Capital

Kingstown

Population

117,848 (July 2006 est.)

Religion

Anglican (47 percent), Methodist (28 percent), Roman Catholic (13 percent); and the rest are Hindu, Seventh-Day Adventist, and other Protestant sects

Language

English, French patois

Currency

St. Vincent and the Grenadines is a member of the Eastern Caribbean Central Bank. The local currency is the Eastern Caribbean dollar, which is pegged to the U.S. dollar (U.S. $1 equals EC $2.6882). U.S. currency is also widely used and is acceptable everywhere.

Government

St. Vincent and the Grenadines is a parliamentary democracy, an independent sovereign state within the Commonwealth. St. Vincent and the Grenadines is a member of the British Commonwealth with a Governor General appointed by Queen Elizabeth II of the United Kingdom. There is universal suffrage for all persons 18 years of age and over. The Prime Minister is the leader of the governing party and, together with his or her cabinet, forms the executive branch of the government.

Economy

Economic growth in this lower-middle-income country hinges upon seasonal variations in the agricultural and tourism sectors. Tropical storms wiped out substantial portions of crops in 1994, 1995, and 2002, and tourism in the Eastern Caribbean has suffered low arrivals following September 11, 2001. Saint Vincent is also a producer of marijuana and is being used as a transshipment point for illegal narcotics from South America.

Geopolitical Risk

There is some instability as St. Vincent and the Grenadines is a transshipment point for South American drugs destined for the United States and Europe. There is also small-scale cannabis cultivation.

Infrastructure

St. Vincent does not have an international jet airport. There are turboprop aircraft serving the island, with international connections through Grenada, Barbados, Antigua and San Juan, Puerto Rico. St. Vincent has an excellent communications system with an undersea fiber-optic cable linking it to the world. Direct dial, facsimile, Internet, and computer modem facilities are available. There are also excellent postal and courier services.

Legal System

The legal system is based on English Common Law. Legislation governing offshore companies is contained in the International Business Companies Act, 1996.

Offshore Investment Considerations

In 1996 there were comprehensive legislative changes to its IBC Act, bringing St. Vincent to the forefront of the world's offshore financial centers as one of the safest and most private jurisdictions. These legislative changes concentrated on two specific policies in St. Vincent's approach to offshore financial law: ultimate privacy and maximum asset protection. These policies are also reinforced in the new offshore finance laws proclaimed in 1997 and 1998.

IBCs incorporated in St. Vincent are completely free of all taxes for a period of 25 years. There is no requirement to disclose the beneficial owner of the IBC, and bearer shares are allowed. There are no exchange controls. There are no tax information exchange treaties with any country. There is no requirement for books or audited reports to be presented to any authority.

St. Vincent is an independent sovereign nation and will therefore not be affected by the impending U.K./EU legislation impacting the British Dependent Territories, the Isle of Man, and the Channel Islands.

The Confidential Relationships Preservation (International Finance) Act, 1996, is a further expression of the privacy theme of the new legislative policy. This law elevates the protection of professional confidential relationships and information to a matter of state "public policy." To make this perfectly clear the "Confidential Relationships Preservation (International Finance) Act, 1996 specifically says, "The Court hearing an application for directions under this section shall not allow the giving in evidence of confidential information in connection with the enforcement or prosecution of the civil or criminal revenue or tax laws of another state, territory or other political jurisdiction."

The Government has reaffirmed that the right to privacy in financial affairs is a basic right of offshore companies and financial institutions in St. Vincent and that it will not help other governments collect their taxes, directly or under the guise of investigations or prosecutions of other purported offenses.

The International Business Companies Act, 1996, contains provisions assuring that the privacy of persons will be protected. These provisions reduce the amount of information to be contained in government registers and curtails the right of the public to inspect the registers.

The original bearer shares are required by law to be kept at the Registered Office.

The offshore IBC must have at least one Director. If there is more than one shareholder, it must have at least two Directors. Directors may be individuals or may be Corporations. Directors may be of any nationality and may reside anywhere. Nominee Directors may be used and are provided by Maritime International Ltd. at no extra cost.

An annual meeting of the Board of Directors is required. This meeting, however, may be held anywhere and may be by telephone, if desired.

There is no requirement for an annual meeting of shareholders. Shareholders' meetings may be conducted by telephone.

St. Vincent and the Grenadines is a member of the British Commonwealth, the United Nations, CARICOM, and other international organizations.

There are no exchange controls on the monetary transactions of St. Vincent offshore companies. Funds can be freely moved on and off the island.

SEYCHELLES

Background

A lengthy struggle between France and Great Britain for the islands ended in 1814, when they were ceded to the latter. Independence came in 1976. Socialist rule was brought to a close with a new constitution and free elections in 1993. The most recent presidential elections were held in 2001; President Rene, who had served since 1977, was re-elected. In April 2004, Rene stepped down and Vice President James Michel was sworn in as president.

Location

The Seychelles is an archipelago in the Indian Ocean, northeast of Madagascar. The Seychelles comprises a group of approximately 115 islands in the Indian Ocean some 5 degrees NE of Madagascar, most of which are situated between 4 and 5 degrees south of the equator.

Time Zone

GMT+4 (same working day as Europe, Asia, and Africa)

Capital

Victoria

Population

81,541 (July 2006 est.)

Religion

Roman Catholic (82.3 percent), Anglican (6.4 percent), Seventh Day Adventist (1.1 percent), other Christian sects (3.4 percent), Hindu (2.1 percent), Muslim (1.1 percent), other non-Christian sects (1.5 percent), unspecified (1.5 percent), none (0.6 percent) (2002 census).

Language

Creole (91.8 percent), English (4.9 percent), (official), other 3.1 percent, unspecified (0.2 percent) (2002 census).

Currency

Seychelles rupee (SCR). Seychelles rupees per U.S. dollar— 5.46

Government

An Independent Republic within the British Commonwealth, Seychelles has a democratically elected Government.

Economy

The economy was primarily based on tourism and commercial fishing, but now has a rapidly expanding offshore financial services industry. Encouraged by favorable tax policies, incentives, and Free Trade Zone, inward investment is also on the increase, especially in hotels.

Since independence in 1976, per capita output has expanded to roughly seven times the old near-subsistence level. Growth has been led by the tourist sector, which employs about 30 percent of the labor force and provides more than 70 percent of hard currency earnings, and by tuna fishing. In recent years the government has encouraged foreign investment in order to upgrade hotels and other services. At the same time, the government has moved to reduce the dependence on tourism by promoting the development of farming, fishing, and small-scale manufacturing. Sharp drops illustrated the vulnerability of the tourist sector in 1991 through 1992 due largely to the Gulf War, and once again following the September 11, 2001, terrorist attacks on the United States. Growth slowed in 1998 through 2002, and fell in 2003, due to sluggish tourist and tuna sectors, but resumed in 2004, erasing a persistent budget deficit. Growth turned negative again in 2005. Tight controls on exchange rates and the scarcity of foreign exchange have impaired short-term economic prospects. The black-market value of the Seychelles rupee is half the official exchange rate; without a devaluation of the currency, the tourist sector may remain sluggish as vacationers seek cheaper destinations such as Comoros, Mauritius, and Madagascar.

Geopolitical Risk

Low. Seychelles has good political stability, no international disputes.

Infrastructure

There are 15 airports, 7 with paved runways. Victoria is the main seaport. The Seychelles has an effective telephone system and radiotelephone communications between islands in the archipelago and direct radiotelephone communications with adjacent island countries and African coastal countries.

Legal System

The Seychelles legal system is based on English Common Law, French civil law, and customary law.

Offshore Investing Considerations

In contrast to the "worldwide" income tax regimes in place in most OECD and EU states, Seychelles has in place a "territorial" tax system whereby residents' income is only taxed on Seychelles sourced income. Seychelles residents enjoy no tax on foreign-derived earnings.

Seychelles entered the offshore financial services industry in December 1994, following the enactment of the International Business Companies Act 1994 and other legislation regulating offshore trusts, offshore banking, offshore insurance, and international shipping and aircraft registration. In 1997, legislation was enacted to provide for Seychelles-based mutual funds. Free trade zone laws are also in effect, aimed at encouraging inward investment.

Seychelles IBCs: Seychelles IBCs have proved to be highly popular in the global marketplace. Major factors in this are

Attractive corporate features

Rapid processing

Time zone

The competitive pricing

A Seychelles IBC offers clients all the features and benefits of offshore companies in better-known Caribbean jurisdictions, but a greater availability of company names and competitive pricing. Some of the attractive features of Seychelles IBCs are

- They may be incorporated by just one person who may be the sole director and sole shareholder of an offshore company [IBC].
- They have zero taxation—in Seychelles, nil taxation is levied on income and profits made by an offshore company [IBC].
- There is no stamp duty on transferring shares in an IBC.
- Privacy—no public register of shareholders or directors is maintained. In addition, the name of the beneficial owner (the client) is not required to be filed with the Seychelles offshore company registry. Nominee Corporate Shareholders and Directors are permitted—use of nominee shareholders and directors gives added protection for clients seeking to maximize privacy.
- Minimal paperwork is required. This means less cost, less inconvenience, and very limited publicly available

information on the IBC, which in turn gives clients a high degree of protection against third-party claimants.

- Asset protection—in view of an IBC's privacy features, any third-party claimant pursuing an IBC owner personally will face difficulties both in finding assets held offshore by an IBC and proving that an owner beneficially owns the IBC.

Offshore bank accounts maintained by IBCs allow the client to hold assets offshore in a private banking environment that affords the client a high degree of asset protection. Seychelles IBCs may be used and/or owned by Seychelles residents or nonresidents, though they are both subject to a statutory prohibition against using an IBC to carry on business in Seychelles (i.e., there is no advantage to nonresidents over residents).

Seychelles entered the offshore financial services industry in December 1994, following the enactment of the International Business Companies Act 1994 and other legislation regulating offshore trusts, offshore banking, offshore insurance, and international shipping and aircraft registration. In 1997 legislation was enacted to provide for Seychelles-based mutual funds. Free trade zone laws are also in effect, aimed at encouraging inward investment.

Seychelles is in the process of taking further offshore industry development steps, with the imminent enactment of new laws providing for low tax holding companies (3 percent tax rate and will have access to double taxation avoidance agreements), nil tax limited liability partnerships, interactive gambling, and protected cell companies.

TURKS & CAICOS ISLANDS
Background

The islands were part of the United Kingdoms's Jamaican colony until 1962, when they assumed the status of a separate crown colony upon Jamaica's independence. The governor of The Bahamas oversaw affairs from 1965 to 1973. With Bahamian independence, the islands received a separate governor in 1973. Although independence was agreed upon for 1982, the policy was reversed and the islands remain a British overseas territory.

Location

Caribbean, two island groups in the North Atlantic Ocean, southeast of The Bahamas, north of Haiti.

Time Zone

UTC–5

Capital

Grand Turk

Population

21,152 (July 2006 est.)

Religion

Baptist (40 percent), Anglican (18 percent), Methodist (16 percent), Church of God (12 percent), other (14 percent) (1990)

Language

English (official)

Currency

U.S. dollar (USD)

Government

N/A. Overseas territory of the United Kingdom.

Economy

The Turks and Caicos economy is based on tourism, fishing, and offshore financial services. Most capital goods and food for domestic consumption are imported. The United States is the leading source of tourists, accounting for more than half of the annual 93,000 visitors in the late 1990s. Major sources of government revenue also include fees from offshore financial activities and customs receipts.

Geopolitical Risk

Low. Defense is the responsibility of the United Kingdom. The country has received Haitians fleeing economic and civil disorder. It is a transshipment point for South American narcotics destined for the United States and Europe.

Infrastructure

The islands have no significant railways and 121 kilometers of highway, 24 kilometers paved and 97 kilometers unpaved. The territory's ports and harbors are on Grand Turk and Providenciales. The islands have seven airports. Four have paved runways, three of which are around 2,000 meters long and one around 1,000 meters long. Three have unpaved runways, two of which are around 1,000 meters long and one significantly shorter. The telephone system is connected to the mainland by two submarine cables and an Intelsat earth station. There is one television broadcast station, namely WIV TV; broadcasts from the Bahamas can also be received and cable television is available. The territory has two Internet service providers.

Legal System

The legal system is based on laws of England and Wales, with a few adopted from Jamaica and The Bahamas.

Offshore Investment Considerations

The Turks & Caicos Islands Government has constructed a regulatory regime that is highly favorable to offshore operations, especially since there is no taxation other than stamp duty and import duties. There are more than 15,000 companies registered in the Islands, including 13,000 International Business Companies.

The EU Council Directive on taxation of savings income in the form of interest payments came into effect in 2005, but the

TCI says it anticipates very little reduction in business in the islands since the Directive is applicable to individuals and not to corporate entities. Investments can be moved into corporate entities and investors have been advised to structure their operations to form corporate entities in the medium to long term.

In 1994 the government set up the Turks and Caicos Investment Agency ("TCInvest") to encourage sustainable economic growth by attracting new offshore investment and by encouraging entrepreneurial spirit among the local population.

In 1972, the islands enacted the Encouragement of Development Ordinance whereby approved development projects are granted relief from import duties and possible future taxes for a period of up to 35 years. The benefits under this Ordinance may apply to expansion as well as to the original establishment of development enterprises. Similar incentives apply to developments carried out by locals or foreigners on Crown land, provided the developments are not for private residences. In such cases, Crown lands can be acquired on long-term concessionaire leases or in special circumstances on a conditional purchase lease provided the developer completes the agreed improvements and meets other conditions within the option period.

Banking confidentiality and secrecy are governed by the Confidential Relationships Ordinance 1979, which provides for penalties and terms of imprisonment for professionals, including government officials, who make unauthorized disclosure of confidential information. The Companies Ordinance 1981 contains similar provisions in relation to exempted companies. Additionally the Common Law also imposes civil liability for breaches of professional privilege.

The duty to maintain confidentiality does not apply where it conflicts with the provisions of the Mutual Legal Assistance (USA) Ordinance 1991, which was passed to give effect to the treaty made between the United States and the United Kingdom to give assistance in criminal matters. However, this treaty does not extend to fiscal crime; the Islands have not entered into any double taxation treaties and there is therefore no scope for the local authorities to cooperate with requests by foreign investigators for assistance in investigating tax evasion.

Helpful Resources and Additional Information

GLOBAL SECURITIES AND FUTURES EXCHANGES

The following is a list of the names and addresses of major securities and futures exchanges around the world. Telephone numbers are provided, and the list is arranged alphabetically by country.

Argentina

Bolsa de Comercio de Buenos Aires
Sanniento 299, 2nd Floor
1353 Buenos Aires
(54) 1 313 7218

Australia

Adelaide
55 Exchange Place
Adelaide, S.A. 5000
(61) 8261 5000

Australian Stock Exchange Ltd.
20 Bond Street
Sydney NSW 2000
(61) 2227 0400

Brisbane
Riverside Centre
123 Eagle Street
Brisbane, QLD 4000
(61) 7 3 835 4000

Hobart
86 Collins Street
Hobart, Tasmania 7000
(61) 02347333

Melbourne
530 Collins Street
Melbourne, Vie 3000
(61) 396178611

Perth
2, the Esplanade
Perth, WA 6000

Sydney Futures Exchange
Grouner Street
Sydney, NSW 2000
(61) 2 256 0555

Sydney
Exchange Centre
20 Bond Street
Sydney, NSW 2000
(61) 2227 0000

Austria

Wiener Borse
Wipplingerstrasse 34
A-1013 Vienna
(43) 1 534990

Bahrain

Bahrain Stock Exchange
P.O. Box 3203
Manama
(973) 261260

Bangladesh

Dhaka Stock Exchange Ltd.
Stock Exchange Building
9F Motijheel Commercial Area
Dhaka 1000
(880) 2231 935

Chittagong Stock Exchange
Kashfia Plaza (First Floor), 923/A
Sk. Mujib Road
Chittagong

Belgium

Korte Klarenstraat 1
2600 Antwerp
(32) 3 233 8016

Van Antwerpen
Bourse de Bruxelles, Beurs Van
  Bnissel
Palais de la Bourse
1000 Brussels
(32) 2 509 1211

Bermuda

Bermuda Stock Exchange
3rd Floor Washington Mall
Church Street
Hamilton
(1-441) 292 7212

Botswana

Botswana Stock Exchange
5th Floor, Barclays House
Khama Crescent
P.O. Box 51015
Gabarone
(267) 357900

Brazil

Bolsa Brasileira de Futuros
Praca XV de novembro 20
6th Floor
Rio de Janeiro 20010-010
(55) 21 271 1086

Bolsa de Mercadorias & Futuros
Praca Antonio Prado, 48
Sao Paulo SP, 01010-901
(55 11) 232 5454

Bolsa de Valores do Rio de Janeiro
Praca XV Novembro 20
20010010 Rio de Janeiro/RJ
Bolsa de Valores de Sao Paulo
Rue XV de Novembro 275
01013 011 Sao Paulo SP
(55) 21 5324616

Bolsa Mercantil and de Futuros
Praca Antonio Prado, 48
Sao Paulo SP 01010
(5511) 239-5511

Bulgaria

Bulgarian Stock Exchange
1 Macedonia Square
1040 Sofia
(359) 2815 711

Canada

Alberta Stock Exchange
300 5th Avenue, S.W, 21st Floor
Calgary, Alberta T2P 3C4
(403) 262-7791

Montreal Exchange
Tour de la Bourse, P.O. Box 61
800 Victoria Square
Montreal, Quebec H4Z 1A9
(514) 871-3585

Toronto Futures Exchange
Toronto Stock Exchange
The Exchange Tower
2 First Canadian Place
Toronto, Ontario M5X 1J2
(416) 947-4325 (416) 947-4700

Vancouver Stock Exchange
609 Granville Street
Vancouver, British Columbia V7Y
  1H1
(604) 689-3334

**Winnipeg Commodity
  Exchange**
500 Commodity Exchange Tower
360 Main Street
Winnipeg, Manitoba R3C 3Z4
(204) 925-5000

Winnipeg Stock Exchange
2901-One Lombard Place
Winnipeg, Manitoba R3B 0Y2
(204) 942-8431

Chile

Bolsa de Comercio de Santiago
Casilla 123-D
Santiago
(56) 2 698 2001

Bolsa Electromca
Huerfanos 770, piso 14
Santiago
(56) 2 639 4699

Bolsa de Valparaiso
PRAT 798
Valparaiso
(56) 3 225 6955

China

Shanghai Metal Exchange
No. 430, Caoyang Road
Putuo District
Shanghai 200063
(86) 021 6 2445566

Shanghai Securities Exchange
15 Huang Pu Road
Shanghai
(86) 21 306 3291

Shenzhen Metal Exchange
1-3f, Block B
Zhongjian Overseas Decoration
  Building
Hua Fu Road
518031 Shenzhen Special Economic
  Zone
(86) 755 3343473 (information)

Shenzhen Stock Exchange
203 Honglixi Road
Shenzhen 518028
(86) 755 320 3431

Colombia

Bolsa de Bogota
Canera 8, #13-82, 7th Floor
Apdo. Aereo 3584
Santafe de Bogota, D.C.
(57) 1 243 6501

Bolsa de Medellin
Carrera 50, #50-48, 2nd Floor
Apdo. Aereo 3535
Medellin
(57) 4 260 3000

Bolsa de Occidente
Calle 8, #3-14, 17th Floor
Cali
(57) 4 260 3000

Congo

Congo Stock Exchange
5th Floor, Southhampton House
P.O. Box UA234
Union Avenue/1st Street
Harare
(263) 4736 861

Costa Rica

Bolsa Nacional de Valores
P.O. Box 1736-1000
San Jose
(506) 256 1180

Croatia

Zagrebacka Burza
Ksaver 208
Zagreb 10000
(385) 1 42 8455

Czech Republic

Prague Stock Exchange
Rybna 14
110 00 Prague 1
(420) 22183 2126

Denmark

Kobenhavns Fondsbors
2 Nikolaj Plads 2
1067 Copenhagen K
(45) 33 93 33 66

Ecuador

**Bolsa de Valores de Guayaquil
(BVG)**
Baquerizo Moreno 1112
Guayaquil
(593) 4 307 710

Boisa de Valores de Quito (BVQ)
Av. Rio Amazonas 540 y Jerommo
  Carrion
Quito
  (593) 2 526 805

**Bolsa de Valores de Cuenca
(SATI)**
Presidente Cordova 785 y Luis
  Cordero
Cuenca
(593) 7 841 600

Egypt

Cairo Stock Exchange
4a Shenfen Street
Cairo
(20) 2 392 1447/8968

Alexandria Stock Exchange
1 iTalat Harb Street
Menshia
Alexandria
(20) 3 483 5432

Finland

Helsingin Arvopapereriporssi Oy
Fabianinkatu 14
001310 Helsinki
(358) 9 1733 0399

France

MATIF SA
115 Rue Reaumur
75083 Paris CEDEX 02
(33) 1 40 28 82 82

**MONEP (Marche des Options
  Negociables de Paris)**
Societe de Compensation des
  Marches Conditionnels—SCMC
39 Rue Cambon
75001 Paris
(33) 1 4927 1800

SBF-Paris Bourse
39 Rue Cambon
75001 Paris
(33) 149271000

Germany

Baden-Wurttembergische Wertpapierborse zu Stuttgart
Konigstrasse 28
Postfach 100441
D-70003 Stuttgart
(49) 711290183

Bayerische Borse
Lenbachplatz 2 a
D-80333 Munich
(49) 89 5990-0

Berliner Borse
Fasanenstrasse 3
D-10623 Berlin
(49) 30 31 1091-0

Bremen Wertpapierborse
Oberstrasse 2-12
Postfach 1007 26
D-28007 Bremen
(49) 421 32 1282

Deutsche Borse AG
Borsenplatz 7-11
D-60313 Frankfurt/Main 1
(49) 69 2101 5371

Deutsche Temunborse (DTB)
60284 Frankfurt
(49) 69 2101-0

Frankfurter Wertpapierborse
Borsenplatz 7-11
D-60284 Frankfurt 4
(49) 69 2101-0

Hanseatische Wertpapierborse Hamburg
Schauenburgerstrasse 47
20415 Hamburg
(49) 44 36 1302-0

Niedersachsische Borse zu Hannover
Rathenstrasse 2
Postfach 4427
D-30044 Hanover
(49) 511 327661

Rheinisch-Westfalische Borse zu Dusseldorf
Emst-Schneider-Platz 1, Postfach 104262
D-40033 Dusseldorf 1
(49) 211 13890

Greece

Athens Stock Exchange
10 Sophocleous Street
Athens 10559
(30) 1 321 1301

Hong Kong

Stock Exchange of Hong Kong Ltd.
Hong Kong
(852) 522 11 22

The Stock Exchange of Hong Kong Ltd.
First Floor, 1&2 Exchange Square
P.O. Box 8888
Hong Kong
(852) 2522 1122

Hungary

Budapest Commodity Exchange
H-1373 P.O. Box
H-i 134 Budapest
(36) 1 269 8571

Budapest Stock Exchange
Deak Ferenc u.5
H-1364Bp.,Pf24
H-1052 Budapest
(36) 1117 5226

India

The Stock Exchange, Mumbai
25th Floor, Phiroze Jeejeebhoy Towers
Dalal Street
Mumbai 400 001
(91) 22 265 5581

Calcutta Stock Exchange
7 Lyons Range
Calcutta 700
(91) 33 2293 66

Delhi Stock Exchange
3 & 4/4B Asaf Mi Road
New Delhi 110002
(91) 11 27 1302

National Stock Exchange
Mahindra Towers, 1st Floor
Mumbai 400 018
A-Wing, RBC, Worli
(91) 22496 1525

**Over-the-Counter Exchange
  of India**
Sir Vithaldas Thackersey Marg.
New Marine Lines
Mumbai 400 020
(91) 22 204 3389

Indonesia

Jakarta Stock Exchange
Jln Jendral Sudinnan Kay. 52-53
Jakarta 12190
(62)21 515 0515

Surabaya Stock Exchange
Gedung Medan Pemuda
Jalan Permuda 2731
(62) 31 510 646

Ireland

Irish Stock Exchange
28 Anglesea Street
Dublin 2
(353) 1 677 8808

Israel

Tel Aviv Stock Exchange
54 Ahad Haam Street
Tel-Aviv 65202
(972) 3567 7411

Italy

Italian Stock Exchange
Piazza Degli Affari 6
20123 Milan
(39) 2 853 44636

Jamaica

Jamaica Stock Exchange
40 Harbour Street
P.O. Box 1084
Kingston
(1 809) 922 0806

Japan

Chubu Commodity Exchange
3-2-15
Nisiki Naka-ku
Nagoya 460
(81) 52 951 2170

Fukuoka Stock Exchange
14-2, Tenjin 2-chome
Chuo-ku
Fukuoka 810
(81) 92741 8231

Hiroshima Stock Exchange
14-18, Kanayama-cho
Naka-ku
Hiroshima 730
(81) 82 541 1121

Kanmon Commodity Exchange
1-5 Nabe-cho, Shimonoseki
Yamaguchi Pref 20750
(81) 832 31 1313

**Kansai Agricultural Commodities
  Exchange**
1-10-14 Awaza
Osaka 550
(81) 6531 7931

Kobe Raw Silk Exchange
126 Higashimachi
Chuo-ku

Kobe 650
(81) 78 331 7141

Kyoto Stock Exchange
66- Tachiurinishi-machi
  Higashinotoin-higashiiru
Shijo-dori Simogyo-ku
Kyoto 600
(81) 75 221 1171

**Maebashi Dried Cocoon
  Exchange**
1-49-1 Furuichi-machi
Maebashi 371
(81) 272 521401

Nagoya Stock Exchange
3-17, Sakae 3-chome
Naka-ku
Nagoya 460
(81) 522623171

Niigata Stock Exchange
1245, Hachiban-cho
Kamiohkawamae-dori
Niigata 951
(81) 252224181

Osaka Mercantile Exchange
2-5-28 Kyutaro-machi
Chuo-ku
Osaka 541
(81) 6 244 2191

Osaka Securities Exchange
8-16 Kitahama 1-Chome
Chuo-ku
Osaka 541
(81) 6229 8607

Sapporo Stock Exchange
14-1, Nishi 5-chome
Minami 1-jo
Chuo-ku
Sapporo 060
(81) 11 241 6171

Tokyo Commodity Exchange
36-2 Nihonbashi-Hakozakicho
Chuo-ku

Tokyo 103
(81) 3 3661 9191

Tokyo Grain Exchange
1-12-5 Nihonbashi kakigara-cho
Chuo-ku
Tokyo 103
(81) 33668 9321

**Tokyo International Financial
  Futures Exchange**
1-3-1 Marunouchi
Chiyoda ku
Tokyo 100
(81) 3 5223 2400

Tokyo Stock Exchange
2-1, Nihombashi-Kabuto
Chuo-ku
Tokyo 103
(81) 3 3666 0141

Yokohama Raw Silk Exchange
Silk Center
1 Yamashita-cho
Naka-ku
Yokohama 231
(81) 45 641 1341

Jordan

Amman Financial Market
Housing Bank Centre, 6th Floor
Anan
(962) 6607 171

Kenya

Nairobi Stock Exchange Ltd.
Nation Centre
P.O. Box 43633
Nairobi
(254) 2230 2692

Korea

Korea Stock Exchange
33 Yoido-dong
Youngdungpo-ku
Seoul 150-010
(82) 27802271

Lebanon

Bourse de Beyrouth
Sadat Tower, 2nd Floor
Sadat Street
Beirut
(961) 1 807 552

Luxembourg

**Societe de la Bourse de
  Luxembourg SA**
Avenue de la Porte-Neuve, BP 165
L-2011 Luxembourg
(352) 47 79 36-1

Malaysia

**Kuala Lumpur Commodity
  Exchange**
(KLCE)
4th Floor, Dayabumi Complex
Jalan Sultan Hishamuddin
P.O. Box 11260
50750 Kuala Lumpur
60 (3) 293-6822

Kuala Lumpur Stock Exchange
3rd, 4th, & 5th Floors, Exchange
  Square
Damansara Heights
Kuala Lumpur 50490
(60) 3 2546433/6662

Mexico

Bolsa Mexicana de Valores
Paseo de la Reforma 255
Col. Cuauhtemoc
06500, Mexico D.F.
(52) 5 726 6735

Morocco

Casablanca Stock Exchange
Avenue de L'Armeé Royale
Casablanca
(212) 245 2626

Netherlands

**Agricultural Futures Market
  Amsterdam**
Postbus 529
1000 AM Amsterdam
(31) 206382258

Amsterdam Exchanges
Beursplein 5
1012 JW Amsterdam
(31) 20550 4444

New Zealand

New Zealand Stock Exchange
8th Floor, Caltex Tower
282 Lambton Quay
Wellington
(64) 4 472 7599

**New Zealand Futures & Options
  Exchange (NZFE)**
P.O. Box 6734, Wellesley Street
Auckland
64 (9) 309 8308

Nigeria

Nigerian Stock Exchange
24 Customs Street
P.O. Box 2457
Lagos
(234) 1 266 0287

Norway

Bergen Branch
Olav Kyrresgt 11
5000 Bergen
(47) 55 32 3050

Oslo Bors
P.O. Box 460 Sentnim
0105 Oslo 1
(47) 234 1700

Trondheim Branch
Dronningens gt 12
7011, Trondheim
(47) 73 883115

Oman

Muscat Securities Market
P.O. Box 3265
Ruwi, Postal Code 112
(968) 702 665

Pakistan

Karachi Stock Exchange
Stock Exchange Building
Stock Exchange Road
Karachi
(92) 21 242 5502/3/4/8

Lahore Stock Exchange
19 Khayaban-e-Iqbal
Egerton Road
Lahore
(92) 426368111/8555

Islamabad Stock Exchange
Anees Plaza
Fazal-ul-Haq Road
Islamabad
(92) 51 216 040/41

Panama

Bolsa de Valores de Panama SA
Calle Elvira Mendez y Calle 52
Edif. Vallanno
Planta Baja
Panama City
(507) 0 269 1966

Peru

Bolsa de Valores de Lima
Pasaje Acuna 191
Lima
(51) 1 426 7939

Philippines

**Manila International Futures
Exchange (MIFE)**
PDCP Bank Centre, 7th Floor
Paseo de Roxas
Makati, Metro Manila
(63) 2 8185496

PSE (Malcati trading floor)
Ayala Tower
Ayala Avenue and Paseo de Roxas
Makati, Metro Manila
(63) 2 891 9001

Poland

Warsaw Stock Exchange
6/12 Nowy Swiat
00-400 Warsaw
(48) 22 628 3232

Portugal

Bolsa de Derivados do Oporto
Av da Boavista 3,433
4100 Oporto
(351) 2 618 5858

Bolsa de Valores de Lisboa
Edificio de Bolsa
Rua Soeiro Pereira Gomes
1600 Lisboa
(351) 1 790 9904

Russia

**Moscow Interbank Currency
Exchange**
119021 Moscow
4 Zubovsky Boulevard
(7) 095 201 2817

**Moscow International Stock
Exchange**
103084 Moscow
4, bld.2, Slavyanska pl.
(7) 095 924 8259

Russian Exchange
101000 Moscow
26 Myasnitskaya Street
(7) 095 262 2352

St. Petersburg Stock Exchange
St. Petersburg
274 Ligovsky pr.
(7) 812 296 0523

Yekaterinburg Stock Exchange
620 Yekaterinburg
109 Furmanova Street
(7) 3432 221 225

Vladivostok Stock Exchange
Vladivostok
62A Partizansky Prospect
(7) 4232 228 009

Sibirskaya Stock Exchange
630194 Novosibirsk
5 Frounze Street
(7) 3832 216 951

Scotland

The Stock Exchange
Stock Exchange House
P.O. Box 141
7 Nelson Mandela Place
Glasgow G2 1BU
(44) 141 221 7060

Singapore

Singapore Commodity Exchange
111 North Bridge Road #23-04/05
Peninsula Plaza
Singapore 179098
(65) 338 5600

Stock Exchange of Singapore Ltd.
20 Cecil Street #26-01/08
The Exchange
Singapore 049705
(65) 535-3788

**Singapore International
  Monetary Exchange (SIMEX)**
1 Raffles Place
07-00 OUB Centre
Singapore 048616
(65) 535 7382

Slovakia

Bratislava Stock Exchange
Vyosoka 17
P.O. Box 151
SK 814 99 Bratislava
(421) 7 5036 103

Slovenia

Ljubljana Stock Exchange
Slovenska 56
61000 Ljubljana
(386) 6117102 11

South Africa

Johannesburg Stock Exchange
17 Diagonal Street
P.O. Box 1174
Johannesburg 2000
(27) 11 377 2200

South African Futures Exchange
105 Central Street
Houghton Estate, 2198
P.O. Box 4406
Johannesburg 2000
(27) 11 7285960

South Korea

Korea Stock Exchange
33, Yoido-Dong
Youngdeungpo-Ku
Seoul 150-010

Spain

Bolsa de Barcelona
Paseo Isabel II, 1
08003 Barcelona
(34) 3 401 3555

Bolsa de Bilbao
Olavarri 1
48001 Bilbao (Vizcaya)
(34) 4423 6818

Bolsa de Madrid
Plaza de la Lealtad 1
Madrid 28014
(34) 1 589 2600

Bolsa de Valencia
San Vincente 23
46002 Valencia
(34) 6387 0100

MEFF Renta Fija
Via Layetana 58
08003 Barcelona
(34) 3412 1128

MEFF Renta Variable
Torre Picasso pl 26
28020 Madrid
(34) 1 585 0800

Sri Lanka

Colombo Stock Exchange
4104-01 West Block
World Trade Centre
Echelon Square
Colombo 1

Sweden

OM Stockholm AB
Box 16305
S-103 26, Stockholm
46 (8)7000600

Switzerland

Swiss Exchange and SOFFEX
Selnaustrasse 32
CH-802l Zurich
(41) 12292111

Swiss Exchange Geneva
8 Rue de la Confederation
CH-1204 Geneva 11
(41) 22 818 5830

Taiwan

**Taiwan Stock Exchange
 Corporation**
7–10th Floors, City Building
85 Yen-Ping Road
Taipei
(886) 2 311 4020

ROC (OTC) Exchange
3F, No. 51 Sec 2 Chung Ching
South Road
Taipei
(886) 2 322 5555

Thailand

Stock Exchange of Thailand
132 Sintorn Building, 2nd Floor
Wireless Road
Bangkok, 10330
(66) 2254 0960

Trinidad and Tobago

**Trinidad and Tobago Stock
 Exchange**
65 Independence Square
Port of Spain
Trinidad
(1 809) 6255107

Turkey

Istanbul Stock Exchange
Istinye 80860
Istanbul
(90) 212 298 2100

United Kingdom

International Petroleum Exchange
1 St. Katharine's Way
London El 9UN
(44) 171 481 0643

London International Financial Futures
Exchange (LIFFE)
Cannon Bridge
London EC4R 3XX
(44) 171 623 0444

London Metal Exchange (LME)
56 Leadenhall Street
London EC3A 2BJ
(44) 171 2645555

London Securities and Derivatives Exchange—OMLX
Milestone House, 6th Floor
107 Cannon Street
London EC4N 5AD
(44) 171 283 0678

London Stock Exchange
Old Broad Street
London EC2N 1HP
(44) 171 797 1000

Regional Offices/London Stock Exchange
MIDLANDS & WEST
The Stock Exchange
Margaret Street
Birmingham B3 3JL
(44) 1212369181

NORTH WEST
The Stock Exchange
76 King Street
Manchester M2 4NH
(44) 161 833 0931

NORTH EAST
The Stock Exchange
Enterprise House
12 St. Paul's Street
Leeds LS 1 2LQ
(44) 113 243 0738

Northern Ireland

The Stock Exchange
Northern Bank House
10 High Street
Belfast BT1 2BP
(44) 1232321 094

United States

American Stock Exchange (AMEX)
86 Trinity Place
New York, New York 10006-1881
(212) 306-1841

Boston Stock Exchange (BSE)
One Boston Place
Boston, Massachusetts 02108
(617) 723-9500

Chicago Board of Trade (CBO)
141 West Jackson Boulevard
Chicago, Illinois 60604-2994
(312) 435-3500

Chicago Board Options Exchange (CBOE)
400 South LaSalle Street
Chicago, Illinois 60605
(312) 786-5600

Chicago Mercantile Exchange (CME)
30 South Wacker Drive
Chicago, Illinois 60606
(312) 930-1000

Chicago Stock Exchange (CHX)
440 South LaSalle Street
Chicago, Illinois 60605
(312) 663-2222

Cincinnati Stock Exchange (CSE)
400 South LaSalle Street
Chicago, Illinois 60605
(312) 786-8803

Kansas City Board of Trade (KCBT)
4800 Main Street, Suite 303
Kansas City, Missouri 64112
(816) 753-7500

MidAmerica Commodity Exchange (MIDAM)
141 West Jackson Boulevard
Chicago, Illinois 60604
(312) 341-3000

Midwest Stock Exchange (MSE)
440 South LaSalle Street
Chicago, Illinois 60605
(312) 663-2222

Minneapolis Grain Exchange (MGE)
130 Grain Exchange Building
400 South Fourth Street
Minneapolis, Minnesota 55415
(612) 321-7101

New York Futures Exchange (NYFE)
20 Broad Street
New York, New York 10005
(212) 748-1248

New York Mercantile Exchange (NYMEX)
One North End Avenue
New York, New York 10282
(212) 292-2000

New York Stock Exchange (NYSE)
11 Wall Street
New York, New York 10005
(212) 656-2065

Pacific Exchange (PCX)
301 Pine Street
San Francisco, California 94104
(415) 393-4000

Philadelphia Stock Exchange (PHLX)
Philadelphia Board of Trade (PBOT)
1900 Market Street
Philadelphia, Pennsylvania 19103
(215) 496-5000, 496-5165

Uruguay

Bolsa de Valores de Montevideo
Misiones 1400
Montevideo
(598) 2 965 051

Venezuela

Bolsa de Valores de Caracas
Apartado Postal 62724-A
Chacao
(58) 29055511

Bolsa de Valores de Maracaibo
Edif. Banco Central de Venezuela
Ave 5 de Julio y Las Delicias
Piso 9
Maracaibo, Edo. Zulia
(58) 61 226 833

Bolsa Electronica de Valores de Venezuela
Ave. Bolivar
Camara de Comercio de Valencia
Valencia, Edo. Carabobo
(58) 41 575 109/115

Zambia

Lusaka Stock Exchange
1st Floor, Stock Exchange Building
Cairo Road
Lusaka
(260) 1 228391

ABBREVIATIONS AND ACRONYMS

A

A	Includes extra (or extras) (in stock listings of newspapers)
AAII	American Association of Individual Investors
AB	Aktiebolag (Swedish stock company)
ABA	American Bankers Association
ABA	American Bar Association
ABLA	American Business Law Association
ABS	Automated Bond System
ABWA	American Business Women's Association
ACRS	Accelerated Cost Recovery System
A-D	Advance-Decline Line
ADB	Adjusted Debit Balance
ADR	American Depositary Receipt
ADR	Automatic Dividend Reinvestment
ADRS	Asset Depreciation Range System
ADS	American Depositary Shares
AE	Account Executive
AFL-CIO	American Federation of Labor-Congress of Industrial Organizations
AICPA	American Institute of Certified Public Accountants
AID	Agency for International Development
AIM	American Institute for Management
AG	Aktiengesellschaft (German stock company)
AGI	Adjusted Gross Income
AIP	Automatic Investment Plan
AMA	American Management Association
AMA	Asset Management Account
AMBAC	American Municipal Bond Assurance Corporation
AMEX	American Stock Exchange
AMPS	Auction Market Preferred Stock
AMT	Alternative Minimum Tax
AON	All or None
APB	Accounting Principles Board
APR	Annual Percentage Rate
APS	Auction Preferred Stock
ARB	Airport Revenue Bond
Arb	Arbitrageur

ARF	American Retail Federation
ARM	Adjustable Rate Mortgage
ARPS	Adjustable Rate Preferred Stock
ART	Annual Renewable Term (insurance)
ASAP	As Soon As Possible
ASE	American Stock Exchange
ASE	Amsterdam Stock Exchange
ASPIRIN	Australian Stock Price Riskless Indexed Notes
ASX	Australia Stock Exchange
ATM	Automatic Teller Machine
ATP	Arbitrage Trading Program

B

B	Annual rate plus stock dividend (in stock listings of newspapers)
BAC	Business Advisory Council
BAN	Bond Anticipation Note
BBB	Better Business Bureau
BD	Bank Draft
BD	Bills Discontinued
B/D	Broker-Dealer
BE	Bill of Exchange
BEACON	Boston Exchange Automated Communication Order-routing Network
BEARS	Bond Enabling Annual Retirement Savings
BF	Brought Forward
BFP	Basic Formula Price (milk)
BIC	Bank Investment Contract
BIF	Bank Insurance Fund
BL	Bill of Lading
BLS	Bureau of Labor Statistics
BMA	Bond Market Association
BO	Branch Office
BO	Buyer's Option
BOM	Beginning of the Month
BOP	Balance of Payments
BOT	Balance of Trade
BOT	Bought
BOT	Board of Trustees

BOVESPA	Bolsa de Valores de Sao Paulo
BPW	Business and Professional Women's Foundation
BR	Bills Receivable
BS	Balance Sheet
BS	Bill of Sale
BS	Bureau of Standards
BSE	Boston Stock Exchange
BSE	Brussels Stock Exchange
BTCI	Bankers Trust Commodity Index
BVRJ	Bolsa de Valores de Rio de Janiero
BW	Bid Wanted

C

C	Liquidating dividend (in stock listings of newspapers)
CA	Capital Account
CA	Chartered Accountant
CA	Commercial Agent
CA	Credit Account
CA	Current Account
CACM	Central American Common Market
CAD	Cash against Documents
CAF	Cost Assurance and Freight
CAMPS	Cumulative Auction Market Preferred Stocks
C&F	Cost and Freight
CAPM	Capital Asset Pricing Model
CAPS	Convertible Adjustable Preferred Stock
CARDS	Certificates for Amortizing Revolving Debts
CARS	Certificate for Automobile Receivables
CATS	Certificate of Accrual on Treasury Securities
CATV	Community Antenna Television
CBA	Capital Builder Account
CBA	Cost Benefit Analysis
CBD	Cash before Delivery
CBO	Collateralized Bond Obligation
CBOE	Chicago Board Options Exchange
CBT	Chicago Board of Trade
CC	Chamber of Commerce
CCH	Commerce Clearing House

CD	Certificate of Deposit
CD	Commercial Dock
CDN	Canadian Dealing Network
CEA	Council of Economic Advisors
CEO	Chief Executive Officer
CF	Certificates (in bond listings of newspapers)
CF	Carried Forward
CFA	Chartered Financial Analyst
CFC	Chartered Financial Counselor
CFC	Consolidated Freight Classification
CFI	Cost, Freight, and Insurance
CFO	Chief Financial Officer
CFP	Certified Financial Planner
CFTC	Commodities Futures Trading Commission
CH	Clearing House
CH	Custom House
ChFC	Chartered Financial Consultant
CHX	Chicago Stock Exchange
CIa	Compañilla (Spanish company)
Cie	Compagnie (French company)
CIF	Corporate Income Fund
CIF	Cost, Insurance, and Freight
CIPs	Cash Index Participations
CLD	Called (in stock listings of newspapers)
CLN	Construction Loan Note
CLU	Chartered Life Underwriter
CME	Chicago Mercantile Exchange
CMO	Collateralized Mortgage Obligation
CMV	Current Market Value
CN	Consignment Note
CN	Credit Note
CNS	Continuous Net Settlement
CO	Cash Order
CO	Certificate of Origin
Co.	Company
COB	Close of Business (with date)
COBRA	Consolidated Omnibus Budget Reconciliation Act
COD	Cash on Delivery

COD	Collect on Delivery
CODA	Cash or Deferred Arrangement
COFI	Cost of Funds Index
COLA	Cost-of-Living Adjustment
COLTS	Continuously Offered Longer-Term Securities
COMEX	Commodity Exchange (New York)
COMSAT	Communications Satellite Corporation
CONNIE LEE	College Construction Loan Insurance Association
COO	Chief Operating Officer
CPA	Certified Public Accountant
CPCI	Chase Physical Commodity Index
CPD	Commissioner of Public Debt
CPFF	Cost Plus Fixed Fee
CPI	Consumer Price Index
CPM	Cost per Thousand
CPPC	Cost Plus a Percentage of Cost
CR	Carrier's Risk
CR	Class Rate
CR	Company's Risk
CR	Current Rate
CRB	Commodity Research Bureau
CRT	Charitable Remainder Trust
CSCE	Coffee, Sugar and Cocoa Exchange
CSE	Cincinnati Stock Exchange
CSE	Copenhagen Stock Exchange
CSVLI	Cash Surrender Value of Life Insurance
CUBS	Calls Underwritten by Swanbrook
CUNA	Credit Union National Association
CUSIP	Committee on Uniform Securities Identification Procedures
CV	Convertible Security (in bond and stock listings of newspapers)
CWO	Cash with Order
D	
DA	Deposit Account
DA	Documents against Acceptance
DAC	Delivery Against Cost
DAF	Defined Asset Fund

D&B	Dun and Bradstreet
DAPS	Dutch Auction Preferred Stock
DBA	Doing Business As
DC	Deep discount issue (in bond listings of newspapers)
DCFM	Discounted Cash Flow Method
DDB	Double-Declining-Balance depreciation method
DENKS	Dual-Employed, No Kids
DEWKS	Dual Employed, With Kids
DF	Damage Free
DIDC	Depository Institutions Deregulatory Committee
DINKS	Dual-Income, No Kids
DISC	Domestic International Sales Corporation
DJIA	Dow Jones Industrial Average
DJTA	Dow Jones Transportation Average
DJUA	Dow Jones Utility Average
DK	Don't Know
DN	Debit Note
DNI	Do Not Increase
DNR	Do Not Reduce
D/O	Delivery Order
DOT	Designated Order Turnaround
DP	Documents against Payment
DPI	Disposable Personal Income
DS	Days after Sight
DTB	Deutsche Terminbourse
DTC	Depository Trust Company
DUNS	Data Universal Numbering System (Dun's Number)
DVP	Delivery Versus Payment

E

E	Declared or paid in the preceding 12 months (in stock listings of newspapers)
EAFE	Europe and Australasia, Far East Equity Index
E&OE	Errors and Omissions Excepted
EBIT	Earnings before Interest and Taxes
EBITA	Earnings before Interest, Taxes, Depreciation, and Amortization
EBS	Swiss Electronic Bourse
EC	European Community

ECB	European Central Bank
ECM	Emerging Company Marketplace
ECM	European Common Market
ECOA	Equal Credit Opportunity Act
ECT	Estimated Completion Time
ECU	European Currency Unit
EDD	Estimated Delivery Date
EEC	European Economic Community
EEOC	Equal Employment Opportunity Commission
EMF INDEX	Emerging Market Free Index
EMP	End-of-Month Payment
EMS	European Monetary System
ENMET	Energy and Metals Index
EOA	Effective On or About
EOD	Every Other Day (advertising)
EOE	European Options Exchange
EOM	End of Month
EPR	Earnings Price Ratio
EPS	Earnings per Share
ERISA	Employee Retirement Income Security Act of 1974
ERM	Exchange Rate Mechanism
ERTA	Economic Recovery Tax Act of 1981
ESOP	Employee Stock Ownership Plan
ESP	Exchange Stock Portfolio
ETA	Estimated Time of Arrival
ETD	Estimated Time of Departure
ETLT	Equal To or Less Than
ETM	Escrowed to Maturity
ETS	Energy Trading System (on the International Petroleum Exchange)
EU	European Union
EXIMBANK	Export-Import Bank

F

F	Dealt in flat (in bond listings in newspapers)
FA	Free Alongside
FACT	Factor Analysis Chart Technique
F&F	Furniture and Fixtures

FAS	Free Alongside
FASB	Financial Accounting Standards Board
FAT	Fixed Asset Transfer
FAX	Facsimile
FB	Freight Bill
FCA	Fellow of the Institute of Chartered Accountants
FCBA	Fair Credit Billing Act
FCC	Federal Communications Commission
FCFAC	Federal Credit Financial Assistance Corporation
FCRA	Fair Credit Reporting Act
FCUA	Federal Credit Union Administration
FDIC	Federal Deposit Insurance Corporation
Fed	Federal Reserve System
FET	Federal Excise Tax
FFB	Federal Financing Bank
FFCS	Federal Farm Credit System
FGIC	Financial Guaranty Insurance Corporation
FHA	Farmers Home Administration
FHA	Federal Housing Administration
FHFB	Federal Housing Finance Board
FHLBB	Federal Home Loan Bank Board
FHLMC	Federal Home Loan Mortgage Corporation (Freddie Mac)
FIBOR	Frankfurt Interbank Offered Rate
FICA	Federal Insurance Contributions Act
FICB	Federal Intermediate Credit Bank
FICO	Financing Corporation
FIFO	First In, First Out
FINEX	Financial Derivatives Division of New York Cotton Exchange
FIRREA	Financial Institutions Reform and Recovery Act
FIT	Federal Income Tax
FITW	Federal Income Tax Withholding
FLB	Federal Land Bank
FLEX	Flexible Exchange Options
FMAN	February, May, August, November cycle
FMC	Federal Maritime Commission
FNMA	Federal National Mortgage Association (Fannie Mae)
FOB	Free on Board

FOC	Free of Charge
FOCUS	Financial and Operations Combined Uniform Single Report
FOI	Freedom of Information Act
FOK	Fill or Kill
FOMC	Federal Open Market Committee
FOOTSIE	*Financial Times*—SE 100 Index of U.K. Stocks
FOR	Free on Rail (or Road)
FOT	Free on Truck
FOX	Finnish Options Index
FP	Floating Policy
FP	Fully Paid
FPM	Fixed-Payment Mortgage
FRA	Federal Reserve Act
FRB	Federal Reserve Bank
FRB	Federal Reserve Board
FRD	Federal Reserve District
FREDDIE MAC	Federal Home Loan Mortgage Corporation
FREIT	Finite Life Real Estate Investment Trust
FRS	Federal Reserve System
FS	Final Settlement
FSC	Foreign Sales Corporation
FSLIC	Federal Savings and Loan Insurance Corporation
FTC	Federal Trade Commission
FTI	Federal Tax Included
FUTA	Federal Unemployment Tax Act
FVO	For Valuation Only
FX	Foreign Exchange
FY	Fiscal Year
FYA	For Your Attention
FYI	For Your Information

G

G	Dividends and earnings in Canadian dollars (in stock listings of newspapers)
GAAP	Generally Accepted Accounting Principles
GAAS	Generally Accepted Auditing Standards
GAl	Guaranteed Annual Income
GAO	General Accounting Office

GATT	General Agreement on Tariffs and Trade
GDP	Gross Domestic Product
GDR	Global Depositary Receipt
G-8	Group of Eight Finance Ministers
GEM	Growing Equity Mortgage
GIC	Guaranteed Investment Contract
GINNIE MAE	Government National Mortgage Association
GIT	Guaranteed Income (or Investment) Contract
GM	General Manager
GmbH	Gesellschaft mit beschrankter Haftung (German limited liability company)
GNMA	Government National Mortgage Association
GNP	Gross National Product
GO	General Obligation Bond
GPM	Graduated Payment Mortgage
GRIT	Grantor Retained Income Trust
GSA	General Services Administration
GSCI	Goldman Sachs Commodity Index
GSE	Government Sponsored Entity
GTC	Good Till Canceled
GTM	Good This Month
GTW	Good This Week
GULP	Group Universal Life Policy

H

H	Declared or paid after stock dividend or split-up (in stock listings of newspapers)
HEL	Home Equity Loan
HEX	Helsinki Stock and Derivatives Exchange
H/F	Held For
HFR	Hold for Release
HIBOR	Hong Kong Interbank Offered Rate
HLT	Highly Leveraged Transaction
HO	Home Owner's Insurance Policy
HQ	Headquarters
HR	U.S. House of Representatives
HR	U.S. House of Representatives Bill (with number)
HUD	Department of Housing and Urban Development

I

I	Paid this year, dividend omitted, deferred, or no action taken at last dividend meeting (in stock listings of newspapers)
IAFP	International Association for Financial Planning
I/B/E/S	Institutional Broker's Estimate System
I-Bonds	Inflation-indexed Savings Bonds
IBRD	International Bank for Reconstruction and Development (World Bank)
ICC	Interstate Commerce Commission
ICEP	Institute of Certified Financial Planners
ICFTU	International Confederation of Free Trade Unions
ICI	Investable Commodity Index
ICI	Investment Company Institute
ICMA	Institute of Cost and Management Accountants
IDB	Industrial Development Bond
IDEM	Italian Derivatives Market
IET	Interest Equalization Tax
IFC	International Finance Corporation
ILA	International Longshoremen's Association
ILGWU	International Ladies' Garment Workers' Union
ILO	International Labour Organization (UN)
IMF	International Monetary Fund
IMM	International Monetary Market of the Chicago Mercantile Exchange
Inc.	Incorporated
INSTINET	Institutional Networks Corporation
IO	Interest Only
IOC	Immediate-or-Cancel Order
IOU	I Owe You
IPE	International Petroleum Exchange
IPO	Initial Public Offering
IR	Investor Relations
IRA	Individual Retirement Account
IRB	Industrial Revenue Bond
IRC	Internal Revenue Code
IRR	Internal Rate of Return
IRS	Internal Revenue Service
ISBN	International Standard Book Number

ISE	International Stock Exchange of the U.K. and the Republic of Ireland
ISE	Italian Stock Exchange
ISIS	Intermarket Surveillance Information System
ISO	Incentive Stock Option
ISRO	International Securities Regulatory Organization
ISSN	International Standard Serial Number
ITC	Investment Tax Credit
ITS	Intermarket Trading System

J

JA	Joint Account
JAJO	January, April, July, October cycle
JPMCI	J.P. Morgan Commodity Index
JSE	Johannesburg Stock Exchange
JTWROS	Joint Tenancy with Right of Survivorship

K

K	Declared or paid this year on a cumulative issue with dividends in arrears (in stock listings of newspapers)
K	Kilo- (prefix meaning multiplied by 1,000)
KCBT	Kansas City Board of Trade
KD	Knocked Down (disassembled)
KIBOR	Kuala Lumpur Interbank Offered Rate
KK	Kabushiki-Kaisha (Japanese stock company)
KEOFFE	Kuala Lumpur Options & Financial Futures Exchange (Barhad)
KESE	Kuala Lumpur Stock Exchange
KW	Kilowatt
KWH	Kilowatt-hour
KYC	Know Your Customer rule

L

L	Listed (securities)
LBO	Leveraged Buyout
L/C	Letter of Credit
LCL	Less-Than-Carload Lot
LCM	Least Common Multiple (mathematics)
LDC	Less Developed Country

LEAPS	Long-Term Equity Anticipation Securities
LEl	Leading Economic Indicators
LESOP	Leveraged Employee Stock Ownership Plan
LI	Letter of Intent
LIBOR	London Interbank Offered Rate
LIFFE	London International Financial Futures and Options Exchange
LIFO	Last In, First Out
LISBOR	Lisbon Interbank Offered Rate
LME	London Metal Exchange
LMRA	Labor-Management Relations Act
LP	Limited Partnership
LSE	Lisbon Stock Exchange
LSE	London Stock Exchange
Ltd	Limited (British corporation)
LTV	Loan to Value

M

M	Matured bonds (in bond listings in newspapers)
M	Milli- (prefix meaning divided by 1,000)
M	Mega- (prefix meaning multiplied by 1,000,000)
M	One thousand (Roman numeral)
MACD	Moving Average Convergence/Divergence
MACRS	Modified Accelerated Cost Recovery System
M&L	Matched and Lost
MATH	Marche a Terme International de France
MAX	Maximum
MBA	Master of Business Administration
MBIA	Municipal Bond Insurance Association
MBO	Management by Objective
MRS	Mortgage-Backed Security
MC	Marginal Credit
M-CATS	Municipal Certificates of Accrual on Tax-exempt Securities
MCE	Malaysia Commodity Exchange
MD	Months after Date
ME	Montreal Exchange (Bourse de Montreal)
MFN	Most Favored Nation (tariff regulations)
MGE	Minneapolis Grain Exchange
MG	Milligram

MHR	Member of the U.S. House of Representatives
MIBOR	Madrid Interbank Offered Rate
MICEX	Moscow Interbank Currency
MIG-1	Moody's Investment Grade
MIMC	Member of the Institute of Management Consultants
Mm	Minimum
MIS	Management Information System
Misc	Miscellaneous
MIT	Market If Touched
MIT	Municipal Investment Trust
MJSD	March, June, September, December cycle
MLP	Master Limited Partnership
MLR	Minimum Lending Rate
MM	Millimeter (metric unit)
MMDA	Money Market Deposit Account
MO	Money Order
MOB	Municipals over Bonds
MOC	Market-on-Close Order
MONEP	Marche des Options Negociables de Paris
MPC	Market Performance Committee
MSA	Medical Savings Account
MSB	Mutual Savings Bank
MSCI	Morgan Stanley Capital International
MSE	Madrid Stock Exchange (Bolsa de Madrid)
MSE	Mexican Stock Exchange
MSRB	Municipal Securities Rulemaking Board
MTN	Medium-Term Note
MTU	Metric Units
MUD	Municipal Utility District
MW	Mercato Italiano Futures Exchange

N

N	New issue (in stock listings of newspapers)
NA	National Association (National Bank)
NAFTA	North American Free Trade Agreement
NAIC	National Association of Investors Corporation
NAM	National Association of Manufacturers
NAPA	National Association of Purchasing Agents
NAPFA	National Association of Personal Financial Advisors

NAPM	National Association of Purchasing Management
NAR	National Association of Realtors
NASA	National Aeronautics and Space Administration
NASD	National Association of Securities Dealers
NASDAQ	National Association of Securities Dealers Automated Quotation
NATO	North Atlantic Treaty Organization
NAV	Net Asset Value
NBS	National Bureau of Standards
NC	No Charge
NCUA	National Credit Union Administration
NCV	No Commercial Value
ND	Next Day Delivery (in stock listings of newspapers)
NEMS	National Exchange Market System
NEO	Nonequity Options
NFCC	National Foundation for Consumer Credit
NH	Not Held
NIC	Net Interest Cost
NICS	Newly Industrialized Countries
NIP	Normal Investment Practice
NIT	Negative Income Tax
NL	No Load
NLRA	National Labor Relations Act
NLRB	National Labor Relations Board
NMAB	National Market Advisory Board
NMB	National Mediation Board
NMS	National Market System
NMS	Normal Market Size
NNP	Net National Product
NOB	Notes over Bonds
NOL	Net Operating Loss
NOW	National Organization for Women
NOW	Negotiable Order of Withdrawal
NP	No Protest (banking)
NP	Notary Public
NP	Notes Payable
NPV	Net Present Value

NPV	No Par Value
NQB	National Quotation Bureau
NQB	No Qualified Bidders
NR	Not Rated
NSBA	National Small Business Association
NSCC	National Securities Clearing Corporation
NSE	National Stock Exchange (India)
NSF	Not Sufficient Funds (banking)
NSTS	National Securities Trading System
NTU	Normal Trading Unit
NV	Naamloze Vennootschap (Dutch corporation)
NYCE	New York Cotton Exchange
NYCSCE	New York Coffee, Sugar and Cocoa Exchange
NYFE	New York Futures Exchange
NYMEX	New York Mercantile Exchange
NYSE	New York Stock Exchange
NYZE	New Zealand Stock Exchange
NZFOE	New Zealand Futures and Options Exchange

O

O	Old (in options listing of newspapers)
O	APEC Organization of Arab Petroleum Exporting Countries
OB	Or Better
OBV	On-Balance Volume
OCC	Option Clearing Corporation
OD	Overdraft, overdrawn
ODE	Oporto Derivatives Exchange (Bolsa de Derivados de Oporto) in Portugal
OECD	Organization for Economic Cooperation and Development
OEX	Standard & Poor's 100 Stock Index
OID	Original Issue Discount
OMB	Office of Management and Budget
OMLX	London Securities and Derivatives Exchange
OPD	Delayed Opening
OPEC	Organization of Petroleum Exporting Countries
OPM	Options Pricing Model
OPM	Other People's Money

OSE	Oslo Stock Exchange
O/T	Overtime
OTC	Over the Counter
OTS	Office of Thrift Supervision
OW	Offer Wanted

P

P	Paid this year (in stock listings of newspapers)
P	Put (in options listings of newspapers)
PA	Power of Attorney
PA	Public Accountant
PA	Purchasing Agent
PAC	Planned Amortization Class
PAC	Put and Call (options market)
PACE	Philadelphia Automated Communication and Execution System
PAL	Passive Activity Loss
P&I	Principal and Interest
P&L	Profit and Loss statement
PAYE	Pay As You Earn
PBGC	Pension Benefit Guaranty Corporation
PBOT	Philadelphia Board of Trade
PBR	Price-to-Book Value Ratio
PC	Participation Certificates
PCX	Pacific Exchange
PE	Price to Earnings ratio (in stock listings of newspapers)
PEFC	Private Export Funding Corporation
PER	Price Earnings Ratio
PERCS	Preferred Equity Redemption Cumulative Stock
PERLS	Principal Exchange-Rate-Linked Securities
PFD	Preferred Stock
PHLX	Philadelphia Stock Exchange
PIG	Passive Income Generator
PIK	Payment-in-Kind Securities
PIN	Personal Identification Number
PITI	Principal, Interest, Taxes, and Insurance
PL	Price List
PLC	Public Liability Company

PLC	(British) Public Limited Company
PMI	Private Mortgage Insurance
PMV	Private Market Value
PN	Project Note
PN	Promissory Note
PO	Principal Only
POA	Power of Attorney
POD	Pay on Delivery
POE	Port of Embarkation
POE	Port of Entry
POR	Pay on Return
PPI	Producer Price Index
PPP	Penultimate Profit Prospect
PPS	Prior Preferred Stock
PR	Public Relations
PRE-RE	Pre-refunded Municipal Note
PRIME	Prescribed Right to Income and Maximum Equity
Prop	Proprietor
PSE	Philippine Stock Exchange
PSR	Price/Sales Ratio
PUC	Public Utilities Commission
PUHCA	Public Utility Holding Company Act of 1935
PVR	Profit/Volume Ratio

Q

QB	Qualified Buyers
QC	Quality Control
QI	Quarterly Index
QT	Questioned Trade
QTIP	Qualified Terminable Interest Property Trust

R

R	Declared or paid in the preceding 12 months plus stock dividend (in stock listings of newspapers)
R	Option not traded (in option listings in newspapers)
RAM	Reverse Annuity Mortgage
RAN	Revenue Anticipation Note
R&D	Research and Development

RCIA	Retail Credit Institute of America
RCMM	Registered Competitive Market Maker
REA	Rural Electrification Administration
REDs	Refunding Escrow Deposits
REFCORP	Resolution Funding Corporation
REIT	Real Estate Investment Trust
RELP	Real Estate Limited Partnership
REMIC	Real Estate Mortgage Investment Conduit
Repo	Repurchase Agreement
RIA	Registered Investment Adviser
RICO	Racketeer Influenced and Corrupt Organization Act
ROC	Return on Capital
ROE	Return on Equity
ROI	Return on Investment (Return on Invested Capital)
ROL	Reduction-Option Loan
ROP	Registered Options Principal
ROS	Return on Sales
RP	Repurchase Agreement
RPA	Retirement Protection Act of 1994
RRP	Reverse Repurchase Agreement
RRSP	Registered Retirement Savings Plan
RT	Royalty Trust
RTC	Resolution Trust Corporation
RTS	Russian Trading System
RTW	Right to Work

S

S	No option offered (in option listings of newspapers)
S	Signed (before signature on typed copy of a document, original of which was signed)
S	Split or stock dividend (in stock listings of newspapers)
SA	Sociedad Anónima (Spanish corporation)
SA	Société Anonyme (French corporation)
SAA	Special Arbitrage Account
SAB	Special Assessment Bond
SAFEX	South African Futures Exchange
SAW	Savings Association Insurance Fund
SALLIE MAE	Student Loan Marketing Association

SAM	Shared Appreciation Mortgage
S&L	Savings and Loan
S&L	Sale and Leaseback
S&P	Standard & Poor's
SAX	Stockholm Automatic Exchange
SB	Savings Bond
SB	U.S. Senate Bill (with number)
SB	Short Bill
SBA	Small Business Administration
SBIC	Small Business Investment Corporation
SBLI	Savings Bank Life Insurance
SBWEI	Salomon Brothers World Equity Index
SCORE	Special Claim on Residual Equity
SD	Standard Deduction
SDB	Special District Bond
SDBL	Sight Draft, Bill of Lading Attached
SDRs	Special Drawing Rights
SE	Shareholders' Equity
SEAQ	Stock Exchange Automated Quotations
SEC	Securities and Exchange Commission
Sen	Senator
SEP	Simplified Employee Pension Plan
SES	Stock Exchange of Singapore
SET	Securities Exchange of Thailand
SET	Stock Exchange of Thailand
SF	Sinking Fund
SFE	Sydney Futures Exchange
SG&A	Selling, General and Administrative Expenses
SHSE	Shanghai Securities Exchange
SIA	Securities Industry Association
SIAC	Securities Industry Automation Corporation
SIDE	Spanish Stock Market Interconnection System
SIC	Standard Industrial Classification
SICA	Securities Industry Committee on Arbitration
SIMPLE IRA	Savings Incentive Match Plan for Employees Individual Retirement Account
SIPC	Securities Investor Protection Corporation
SL	Sold

SLMA	Student Loan Marketing Association (Sallie Mae)
SLO	Stop-Limit Order; Stop-Loss Order
SMA	Society of Management Accountants
SMA	Special Miscellaneous Account
SN	Stock Number
SOES	Small Order Entry (or Execution) System
SOFFEX	Swiss Options and Financial Futures Exchange
SOP	Standard Operating Procedure
SOYD	Sum of the Years' Digits Method
SpA	Società per Aziom (Italian corporation)
SPDA	Single Premium Deferred Annuity
SPDR	Standard & Poor's Depository Receipt
SPLI	Single Premium Life Insurance
SPQR	Small Profits, Quick Returns
SPRI	Société de Personnes a Responsabilité Limitée (Belgian corporation)
SPX	Standard & Poor's 500 Stock Index
Sr	Senior
SRO	Self-Regulatory Organization
SRP	Salary Reduction Plan
SRT	Spousal Remainder Trust
SS	Social Security
SSA	Social Security Administration
SSE	Stockholm Stock Exchange
STAGS	Sterling Transferable Accruing Government Securities
STh	Special Tax Bond
STRIPS	Separate Trading of Registered Interest and Principal of Securities
SU	Set Up (freight)
SZSE	Shenzhen Stock Exchange

T

T-	Treasury (as in T-bill, T-bond, T-note)
TA	Trade Acceptance
TA	Transfer Agent
TAB	Tax Anticipation Bill
TAC	Targeted Amortization Class
TAN	Tax Anticipation Note

T&E	Travel and Entertainment Expenses
TASE	Tel Aviv Stock Exchange
TBA	To Be Announced
TBE	Tenancy by the Entirety
TC	Tax Court of the United States
TD	Time Deposit
TED	Spread Treasury Bills versus Eurodollar Futures
TEFRA	Tax Equity and Fiscal Responsibility Act of 1982
TFE	Toronto Futures Exchange
TIC	Tenancy in Common
TWFE	Tokyo International Financial Futures Exchange
TIGER	Treasury Investors Growth Receipt
TIP	To Insure Promptness
TE	Trade-Last
TM	Trademark
TOCOM	Tokyo Commodity Exchange
TOPIX	Tokyo Stock Price Index
TRA	Taxpayer Relief Act of 1997
TSE	Taiwan Stock Exchange
TSE	Toronto Stock Exchange
TT	Testamentary Trust
TVA	Tennessee Valley Authority

U	
UAW	United Automobile Workers
UCC	Uniform Commercial Code
UCOM	United Currency Options Market
UGMA	Uniform Gifts to Minors Act
	Unit Investment Trust
UL	Underwriters' Laboratories
ULC	Underwriter's Laboratories of Canada
ULI	Underwriter's Laboratories, Inc.
UMW	United Mine Workers
UN	United Nations
UPC	Uniform Practice Code
US	United States (of America)
USA	United States of America

USBS	United States Bureau of Standards
USC	United States Code
USCC	United States Chamber of Commerce
USIT	Unit Share Investment Trust
USJCC	United States Junior Chamber of Commerce (JAYCEES)
USS	United States Senate
USS	United States Ship
UTMA	Uniform Transfer to Minors Act
UW	Underwriter

V

VA	Veterans Administration
VAT	Value Added Tax
VD	Volume Deleted
Veep	Vice President
VELDA SUE	Venture Enhancement & Loan Development Administration for Smaller Undercapitalized Enterprises
VI	In bankruptcy or receivership; being reorganized under the Bankruptcy Act; securities assumed by such companies (in bond and stock listings of newspapers)
VIP	Very Important Person
VE	Value Line Investment Survey
VOL	Volume
VP	Vice President
VRM	Variable Rate Mortgage
VSE	Vancouver Stock Exchange
VSE	Vienna Stock Exchange
VTC	Voting Trust Certificate

W

WAM	Weighted Average Maturity
WB	Waybill
WCA	Workmen's Compensation Act
WCE	Winnipeg Commodity Exchange
WD	When Distributed (in stock listings of newspapers)
WEBS	World Equity Benchmark Shares
WHOOPS	Washington Public Power Supply System
WI	When Issued (in stock listings of newspapers)

WR	Warehouse Receipt
WSJ	*Wall Street Journal*
WT	Warrant (in stock listings of newspapers)
W/Tax	Withholding Tax
WTO	World Trade Organization
WW	With Warrants (in bond and stock listings of newspapers)

X

X	Ex-interest (in bond listings of newspapers)
XAM	AMEX Market Value Index
XD	Ex-Dividend (in stock listings of newspapers)
X-Dis	Ex-Distribution (in stock listings of newspapers)
XMI	AMEX Major Market Index
XR	Ex-Rights (in stock listings of newspapers)
XW	Ex-Warrants (in bond and stock listings of newspapers)

Y

Y	Ex-dividend and sales in full (in stock listings of newspapers)
YLD	Yield (in stock listings of newspapers)
YTB	Yield to Broker
YTC	Yield to Call
YTD	Year to Date
YTM	Yield to Maturity

Z

Z	Zero
ZBA	Zero Bracket Amount
ZBB	Zero-Based Budgeting
ZR	Zero Coupon Issue (Security) (in bond listings of newspapers)

CURRENCIES

This is a list of the currencies of most of the countries on earth. The countries are listed alphabetically, with the name of the currency, the symbol used to look up the currency on computerized foreign exchange systems, and the denomination that currency is broken down into. For example, one dollar is made up of 100 cents. This listing should be useful to anyone traveling or doing business in any of these countries.

Afghanistan 1 afghani (At) = 100 puls

Albania 1 lek (L) = 100 qintars

Algeria 1 Algerian dinar (DA) = 100 centimes

American Samoa 1 U.S. dollar (US$) = 100 cents

Andorra 1 Andorran franc (F) = 100 centimes; (1/1 to French franc); 1 Andorran peseta (pta) = 100 centimos (1/1 to Spanish peseta); Euro

Angola 1 new kwanza (Kz) = 100 lwei

Anguilla 1 EC dollar (EC$) = 100 cents

Antarctica Each Antarctic base uses the currency of its home country

Antigua and Barbuda 1 EC dollar (EC$) = 100 cents

Argentina 1 austral (AA) = 100 centavos

Armenia 1 dram (Ar) = 100 luma

Aruba 1 Aruban guilder (also known as form or gulden) (Af) = 100 cents

Australia 1 Australian dollar (A$) = 100 cents

Austria 1 Austrian schilling (5) = 100 groschen; euro

Azerbaijan 1 manat = 100 gopik

Bahamas 1 Bahamian dollar (B$) = 100 cents

Bahrain 1 Bahraini dinar (BD) = 1,000 fils

Bangladesh 1 taka (Tk) = 100 paisa (poisha)

Barbados 1 Barbadian dollar (Bds$) = 100 cents

Belarus Balarusian rubel (BR)

Belgium 1 Belgian franc (BF) = 100 centimes; euro

Belize 1 Belizean dollar (BZ$) = 100 cents

Benin 1 CFA franc (CFAF) = 100 centimes; euro

Bermuda 1 Bermudian dollar (Bd$) = 100 cents

Bhutan 1 ngultrum (Nu) = 100 chetrum; Indian currency also legal tender

Bolivia 1 boliviano (Bs) = 100 centavos

Bosnia 1 B.H. dinar = 100 para

Botswana 1 pula (P) = 100 thebe

Brazil 1 real (R$) = 100 centavos

British Virgin Islands 1 U.S. dollar (US$) = 100 cents

Brunei 1 ringgit, also known as Bruneian dollar (B$) = 100 sen or cents

Bulgaria 1 leva (Lv) = 100 stotinki

Burkina Faso 1 CFA franc (CFAF) = 100 centimes; euro

Burma (see Myanmar)

Burundi 1 Burundi franc (FBu) = 100 centimes

Cambodia 1 new riel (CR) = 100 sen

Cameroon 1 CFA franc (CFAF) = 100 centimes; euro

Canada 1 Canadian dollar (Can$) = 100 cents

Cape Verde Islands 1 Cape Verdean escudo (CVEsc) = 100 centavos

Cayman Islands 1 Caymanian dollar (CI$) = 100 cents

Central African Republic 1 CFA franc (CFAF) = 100 centimes; euro

Chad 1 CFA franc (CFAF) = 100 centimes; euro

Chile 1 Chilean peso (Ch$) = 100 centavos

China 1 yuan renminbi (Y) = 10 jiao = 100 fen

Christmas Island 1 Australian dollar (A$) = 100 cents

Cocos (Keeling) Islands 1 Australian dollar (A$) = 100 cents

Colombia 1 Colombian peso (Col$) = 100 centavos

Comoros 1 Comoran franc (CF) = 100 centimes; euro

Congo, Democratic Republic of 1 CFA franc (CFAF) = 100 centimes; euro

Cook Islands 1 New Zealand dollar (NZ$) = 100 cents

Costa Rica 1 Costa Rican colon (C) = 100 centimos

Côte d'Ivoire 1 CFA franc (CFAF) = 100 centimes; euro

Croatia 1 Croatian kuna (HRK) = 100 lipas

Cuba 1 Cuban peso (Cu$) = 100 centavos

Cyprus 1 Cypriot pound (SC) = 100 cents; Northern Cyprus = 1
  Turkish lira (TL) = 100 kurus

Czech Republic 1 koruna (Kc) = 100 haleru

Denmark 1 Danish krone (DKr) = 100 øre

Djibouti 1 Djibouti franc (DF) = 100 centimes

Dominica 1 EC dollar (EC$) = 100 cents

Dominican Republic 1 Dominican peso (RD$) = 100 centavos

Ecuador 1 sucre (SI) = 100 centavos

Egypt 1 Egyptian pound (CE) = 100 piasters or 1,000 milliemes

El Salvador 1 Salvadoran colon (c) = 100 centavos

Equatorial Guinea 1 CFA franc (CFAF) = 100 centimes; euro

Eritrea 1 birr (Br) = 100 cents

Estonia 1 Estonian kroon (KR) = 100 senti

Ethiopia 1 birr (Br) = 100 cents

European Union 1 Euro = 100 cents

Faeroe Islands 1 Danish krone (DKr) = 100 øre

Falkland Islands 1 Falkland pound (F) = 100 pence

Fiji 1 Fijian dollar (F$) = 100 cents

Finland 1 markka (Mk) = 100 pennia; euro

France 1 French franc (F) = 100 centimes; euro

French Guiana 1 French franc (F) = 100 centimes; euro

French Polynesia 1 CFP franc (CFPF) = 100 centimes; euro

Gabon 1 CFA franc (CFAF) = 100 centimes; euro

Gambia 1 dalasi (D) = 100 butut

Gaza 1 new Israeli shekel (NIS) = 100 new agorot; 1 Jordanian dinar
  (JD) = 1,000 fils

Georgia 1 lan (Gl) = 100 tetri

Germany 1 deutsche mark (DM) = 100 pfennig; euro

Ghana 1 new cedi (c) = 100 psewas

Gibraltar 1 Gibraltar pound (GIP) = 100 pence

Great Britain 1 pound (£) = 100 pence

Greece 1 drachma (Dr) = 100 lepta

Greenland 1 Danish krone (DKr) = 100 øre

Grenada 1 EC dollar (EC$) = 100 cents

Guadeloupe 1 French franc (F) = 100 centimes; euro

Guam 1 U.S. dollar (US$) = 100 cents

Guatemala 1 quetzal (Q) = 100 centavos

Guernsey 1 pound (£) = 100 pence

Guinea 1 Guinean franc (FG) = 10 francs; 1 franc = 100 centimes

Guinea-Bissau 1 Guinea-Bissau franc (CFAF)
  = 100 centimes; euro

Guyana 1 Guyanese dollar (G$) = 100 cents

Haiti 1 gourde (G) = 100 centimes

Honduras 1 lempira (L) = 100 centavos

Hong Kong 1 Hong Kong dollar (HK$) = 100 cents

Hungary 1 forint (Pt)

Iceland 1 Icelandic króna (IKr) = 100 aurar

India 1 rupee (Rs) = 100 paise

Indonesia 1 rupiah (Rp) = 100 sen

Iran 1 rial (Rls) = 100 dinars = 0.1 toman
Iraq 1 dinar (ID) = 1,000 fils
Ireland 1 Irish pound or punt (1Rf) = 100 pence or pingin; euro
Israel 1 new shekel (NIS) = 100 new agorot
Italy 1 lira (Lit) = 100 centesimi; euro
Jamaica 1 Jamaican dollar (J$) = 100 cents
Japan 1 yen (¥) = 100 sen
Jersey 1 pound (£) = 100 pence
Jordan 1 Jordanian dinar (JD) = 1,000 fils
Kazakhstan 1 tenge (KZT) = 100 tiyn
Kenya 1 Kenyan shilling (KSh) = 100 cents
Kiribati 1 Australian dollar (A$) = 100 cents
Korea, North 1 North Korean won (Wn) = 100 chon
Korea, South 1 South Korean won (W) = 100 chon
Kuwait 1 Kuwaiti dinar (KD) = 1,000 fils
Kyrgyzstan 1 som = 100 tyyn
Laos 1 new kip (NK) = 100 at
Latvia 1 lat (Ls) = 100 santims
Lebanon 1 Lebanese pound (EL) = 100 piastres
Lesotho 1 loti (L) = 100 lisente
Liberia 1 Liberian dollar (L$) = 100 cents
Libya 1 Libyan dinar (LD) = 1,000 dirhams
Liechtenstein 1 Swiss franc (SwF) = 100 centimes
Lithuania 1 litas (L) = 100 centu
Luxembourg 1 Luxembourg franc (LuxF) = 100 centimes; euro
Macau 1 pataca (P) = 100 avos
Macedonia (the former Yugoslav Republic), 1 denar = 100 deni
Madagascar 1 Malagasy franc (FMG) = 100 centimes
Malawi 1 Malawian kwacha (MK) = 100 tambala
Malaysia 1 ringgit (RM) = 100 sen
Maldives 1 rufiyaa (Rf) = 100 lan
Mali 1 CFA franc (CFAF) = 100 centimes; euro
Malta 1 Maltese lira (EM) = 100 cents
Man, Isle of 1 pound (fM) = 100 pence
Marshall Islands 1 U.S. dollar (US$) = 100 cents
Martinique 1 French franc (F) = 100 centimes; euro
Mauritania 1 ouguiya (UM) = 5 khoums

Mauritius 1 Mauritian rupee (MauR) = 100 cents

Mayotte 1 French franc (F) = 100 centimes

Mexico 1 New Mexican peso (MEX$) = 100 centavos

Micronesia, Federated States of 1 U.S. dollar (US$) = 100 cents

Moldova 1 leu = 100 bani

Monaco 1 French franc (F) = 100 centimes

Mongolia 1 tughrik (Tug) = 100 mongos

Montserrat 1 EC dollar (EC$) = 100 cents

Morocco 1 Moroccan dirham (DH) = 100 centimes

Mozambique 1 metical (Mt) = 100 centavos

Myanmar 1 kyat (K) = 100 pyas

Namibia 1 Namibian dollar (N$) = 100 cents

Nauru 1 Australian dollar (As) = 100 cents

Nepal 1 Nepalese rupee (NRs) = 100 paise

Netherlands 1 Netherlands guilder, gulden, or form = 100 cents; euro

Netherlands Antilles 1 Netherlands Antillean guilder, gulden, or form
  (NM. or Ant.f) = 100 cents

New Caledonia 1 CFP franc (CFPF) = 100 centimes; euro

New Zealand 1 New Zealand dollar (NZ$) = 100 cents

Nicaragua 1 gold cordoba (Cs) = 100 centavos

Niger 1 CFA franc (CFAF) = 100 centimes; euro

Nigeria 1 naira (N) = 100 kobo

Niue 1 New Zealand dollar (NZ$) = 100 cents

Norfolk Island 1 Australian dollar (A$) = 100 cents

Northern Mariana Islands 1 U.S. dollar (US$) = 100 cents

Norway 1 Norwegian krone (NKr) = 100 øre

Oman 1 Omani rial (RO) = 1,000 baizas

Pacific Islands, Trust Territory of the, 1 U.S. dollar (US$) = 100 cents

Pakistan 1 Pakistani rupee (Rs) = 100 paisa

Panama 1 balboa (B) = 100 centesimos

Papua New Guinea 1 kina (K) = 100 toeas

Paraguay 1 guarani (G) = 100 centimos

Peru 1 nuevo sol (SI.) = 100 centimos

Philippines 1 Philippine peso (P) = 100 centavos

Pitcairn Islands 1 New Zealand dollar (NZ$) = 100 cents

Poland 1 zloty (Zl) = 100 groszy

Portugal 1 Portuguese escudo (Esc) = 100 centavos; euro

Puerto Rico 1 U.S. dollar (US$) = 100 cents

Qatar 1 Qatari riyal (QR) = 100 dirhams
Reunion 1 French franc (F) = 100 centimes
Romania 1 leu (L) = 100 bani
Russia 1 ruble (R) = 100 kopeks
Rwanda 1 Rwandan franc (RF) = 100 centimes; euro
Saint Helena 1 Saint Helenan pound (ES) = 100 pence
Saint Kitts-Nevis 1 EC dollar (EC$) = 100 cents
Saint Lucia 1 EC dollar (EC$) = 100 cents
Saint Pierre and Miquelon 1 French franc (F) = 100 centimes; euro
Saint Vincent and the Grenadines 1 EC dollar (EC$) = 100 cents
Samoa (Western) 1 tala (WS$) = 100 sene
San Marino 1 Italian lire (Lit) = 100 centesimi; euro
Saö Tome and Principe 1 dobra (Db) = 100 centimos
Saudi Arabia 1 Saudi riyal (SRls) = 100 halalas
Senegal I CFA franc (CFAF) = 100 centimes; euro
Serbia 1 Yugoslav new dinar (YD) = 100 paras
Seychelles 1 Seychelles rupee (SR) = 100 cents
Sierra Leone 1 leone (Le) = 100 cents
Singapore 1 Singapore dollar (S$) = 100 cents
Slovakia 1 koruna (Sk) = 100 haliers
Slovenia 1 tolar (SIT) = 100 stotinov
Solomon Islands 1 Solomon Islands dollar (SI$) = 100 cents
Somalia 1 Somali shilling (So.Sh.) = 100 centesimi
South Africa 1 rand (R) = 100 cents
Spain 1 peseta (Ptas) = 100 centimos; euro
Sri Lanka 1 Sri Lankan rupee (SLRs) = 100 cents
Sudan 1 Sudanese pound (Sd) = 100 piastres
Suriname 1 Surinamese guilder, gulden, or form (Sf. or Sur.f.)
   = 100 cents; euro
Svalbard 1 Norwegian krone (NKr) = 100 øre; euro
Swaziland 1 lilangeni (L) = 100 cents
Sweden 1 Swedish krona (SK) = 100 øre
Switzerland 1 Swiss franc (SwF) = 100 centimes or rappen
Syria 1 Syrian pound (ES) = 100 piasters
Taiwan 1 New Taiwan dollar (NT$) = 100 cents
Tajikistan 1 ruble (R) = 100 kopeks
Tanzania 1 Tanzanian shilling (TSh) = 100 cents
Thailand 1 baht (Bht) = 100 sastangs

Togo 1 CFA franc (CFAF) 100 centimes; euro
Tokelau 1 New Zealand dollar (NZ$) = 100 cents
Tonga 1 pa'anga (T$) = 100 sentini
Trinidad and Tobago 1 Trinidad and Tobago dollar (Tr$) = 100 cents
Tunisia 1 Tunisian dinar (TD) = 1,000 millimes
Turkey 1 new Turkish lira (ii) = 100 new kurus
Turkmenistan I manat (Tm) = tenga
Turks and Caicos Islands 1 U.S. dollar (US$) = 100 cents
Tuvalu 1 Tuvaluan dollar ($T) or 1 Australian dollar (A$) = 100 cents
Uganda 1 Ugandan shilling (USh) = 100 cents
Ukraine 1 Hryvnia (H) = 100 kopiykas
United Arab Emirates I Emirian dirham (Dh) = 100 fils
United Kingdom 1 British pound (£) = 100 pence
United States of America 1 U.S. dollar (US$) = 100 cents
Uruguay 1 Uraguayan peso ($U) = 100 centésimos
Uzbekistan 1 som (Us) = 100 tiyin
Vanuatu 1 vatu (VT) = 100 centimes
Vatican 1 lira (Lit) = 100 centesinu; euro
Venezuela 1 bolivar (Bs) = 100 centimos
Vietnam 1 new dong (D) = 100 xu or 100 hao
Virgin Islands 1 U.S. dollar (US$) = 100 cents
Wake Island 1 U.S. dollar (US$) = 100 cents
Wallis and Futuna Islands 1 CFP franc (CFPF) = 100 centimes; euro
Western Sahara 1 Moroccan dirham (DH) = 100 centimes
Western Samoa 1 tala (WS$) = 100 sene
Yemen I Yemeni rial (YRls) = 100 fils
Yugoslavia 1 new dinar (Din) = 100 paras
Zaire See Congo, Democratic Republic of
Zambia 1 Zambian kwacha (ZK) = 100 ngwee
Zimbabwe 1 Zimbabwean dollar (Z$) = 100 cents

FUTURES AND OPTIONS CONTRACTS TERMINOLOGY

Here is a list of some of the terms used in the trading of futures and options contracts.

Contract Months: Most contracts are traded in all 12 months, but only a group of "active months" are featured in many categories, especially commodities. Although all of these contracts trade constantly, most expire in only certain months of the year. This column presents the active months in those cases, using standard exchange abbreviations.

Daily Price Limit: Many exchanges do not allow prices to rise or fall beyond certain limits within a day. Such limits, if any, are shown first in the increment of the contract, and then as a dollar figure.

Expiration Day: If options are not exercised, they expire. This column details when options expire.

Expiration Month: The month the option expires.

Last Trading Day: The last day trading can occur in a contract.

Price Quote: The unit of value, such as cents per pound, dollars per barrel.

Settlement: The way contracts are settled when they expire. Some contracts provide for the physical delivery of a commodity. Specific rules must be followed on how and where commodities are delivered from seller to buyer. Other contracts involve no physical delivery. These contracts are settled in cash.

Strike Price: This is set both above and below the current market price of the future or index, so puts and calls can be traded in both directions. This column also gives the intervals at which strike prices are set, and when new strike prices are added.

Tick Size: The smallest move, up or down, the contract can make, indicated by the increments in which the contract can move, and as a monetary valuation.

Ticker Symbol: The symbol by which a contract's current price and trading activity can be checked through an electronic price quote service.

Trading Hours: The hours during which a contract is traded, in local time. CST means Central Standard Time, EST means Eastern Standard Time, GMT means Greenwich Mean Time, and PST means Pacific Standard Time. Trading hours for contracts traded on foreign exchanges are expressed in local time.

Trading Unit: The underlying commodity, stock or group of stocks, and the quantity.

The beginning of wisdom is to call things by their correct names.

1035 Exchange: A 1035 Exchange is a process where an annuity owner exchanges a currently owned annuity for one issued by the same or a different insurance carrier. Typically, owners of 1035 exchanges make the change because they are disappointed with the interest they are being paid versus what is being offered by another company. The 1035 exchange is a procedure recognized under federal law with no out-of-pocket expense to the annuity owner; however, the company losing the annuity will impose any remaining surrender charges on the existing annuity before the account value is transferred to the new company, and the new contract may impose surrender charges starting from first issue date.

Active management: The practice of picking individual stocks based on fundamental research and analysis in the expectation that a portfolio of selected stocks can consistently outperform market averages.

Accumulated value: The value of all amounts accumulated under the contract prior to the annuity date.

Accumulation unit: A measure of ownership interest in the contract prior to the annuity date.

Accumulation unit value: The value of each accumulation unit that is calculated each valuation period.

Adjusted death benefit: The sum of all net purchase payments made during the first six contract years, less any partial withdrawals taken. For an enhanced death benefit with a six-year step up each subsequent six-year period, the adjusted death benefit will be the death benefit on the last day of the previous six-year period plus any net purchase payments made, less any partial withdrawals taken during the current six-year period. After the annuitant attains age 75, the adjusted death benefit will remain equal to the death benefit on the last day of the six-year period before age 75 occurs plus any net purchase payments subsequently made, less any partial withdrawals subsequently taken.

Aggressive growth: This term doesn't mean anything except to Wall Street marketing departments that want to describe investors as people being aggressive in the way they grow their money.

Annual insurance company expenses: Annuity contracts include charges for insurance companies' annual expenses. In addition to the asset management fees, there are three other annual charges: annual policy fee, mortality and expense risk, and administrative.

Annual interest income: The annual dollar income for a bond or savings account is calculated by multiplying the bond's coupon rate by its face value.

Annuitant: The recipient of annuity benefits; usually but not always the contract owner. The person whose life is used to determine the duration of any annuity payments and upon whose death, prior to the annuity date, benefits under the contract are paid.

Annuitant's beneficiary: The person(s) to whom any benefits are due upon the annuitant's death prior to the annuity date.

Annuitization: An income-paid-out option is referred to as annuitization.

Annuity: An annuity is a contract between an insurer and recipient (annuitant) whereby the insurer guarantees to pay the recipient a stream of income in exchange for premium payment(s). For example, you give an insurance company $100,000 at age 65 and it might agree to pay you an income of about $800 a month for the rest of your life. That's a typical life income annuity.

Annuity date: The date on which annuity payments begin. The annuity date is always the first day of the month you specify.

Annuity payment: One of a series of payments made under an annuity payment option.

Annuity starting date: The date on which an annuity contract begins to pay benefits; the beginning of the payout period.

Annuity unit: Unit of measure used to calculate variable annuity payments.

Annuity unit value: The value of each annuity unit that is calculated each valuation period.

Asset allocation: A mixture of investments among various classes of financial assets. The goal is to create an efficient portfolio that provides the highest return for a given amount of risk and reduces risk by placing portions of the portfolio in asset classes that move up or down in value in an inverse relationship to one another.

Asset class: Assets composed of financial instruments with similar characteristics.

Asset-class mutual funds: Funds composed of financial instruments with similar characteristics. Unlike managers of index funds, asset-fund managers actively manage costs when buying and selling for funds.

Asset mix: Asset classes within a portfolio that can be invested.

Asset protection kits: Do-it-yourself packages that purport to allow purchasers to create one-size-fits-all asset protection plans. Suffice it to say that the quality of these plans is highly suspect, which is compounded by the fact that the purchasers almost never implement the plans correctly, often leading to negative tax consequences.

Average return: The arithmetic mean is the simple average of the returns in a series. Averages are deceiving. To illustrate: An investor gives a broker $1,000 and one year later it's worth only $500. The next year, it's again worth $1,000. After two full years, how much money has the investor made? Zero, right? But the broker can legally claim that the investor's average annual return was 25 percent! The broker's math works like this: In year 1, the return was minus 50 percent—but in year 2, by going from $500 to $1,000 it was plus 100 percent. When the two returns are added together they total plus 50. Divide that by the two years, and the annual average rate of return is 25 percent, compared to a more conservative program where the investor might get a 10 percent return per year. If the investor gets 10 percent in year 1 and year 2, the average annual return would be 10 percent, less than the 25 percent in the example above. (10 + 10 = 20 ÷ 2 = 10).

Balanced index: A market index that serves as a basis of comparison for balanced portfolios. The balanced index used in the Monitor is comprised of a 60 percent weighting of the S&P 500 Index and a 40 percent weighting of the SLH Government/Corporate Bond Index. The balanced index relates unmanaged market returns to a balanced portfolio more precisely than either a stock or a bond index would alone.

Balanced mutual fund: This term can be applied to any kind of portfolio that uses fixed income (bonds) as well as equity securities to reach goals. Many "boutique" investment managers are balanced managers because it permits them to tailor the securities in a portfolio to specific clients' cash flow needs and objectives. Balanced portfolios are often used by major mutual funds. They provide great flexibility.

Basis point: One basis point is 1/100th of a percentage point, or 0.01 percent. Basis points are often used to express changes or differences in yields, returns, or interest rates. Thus, if a portfolio has a total return of 10 percent versus 7 percent for the S&P 500, the portfolio is said to have outperformed the S&P 500 by 300 basis points.

Bear market: A prolonged period of falling stock prices. Wall Street defines a bear market as a drop of at least 20 percent over two back-to-back quarters.

Beginning value: The market value of a portfolio at the inception of the period being measured by the customer statement.

Benchmark: A standard by which investment performance or trading execution can be judged. The most widely used performance benchmark is the total return of the S&P 500.

Beneficiary: Similar to the beneficiary of a life insurance policy, the annuity contract beneficiary receives a death benefit when another party to the annuity contract dies prior to the date upon which the annuity begins paying out benefits.

Beta: Beta is the linear relationship between the return on the security and the return on the market. By definition, the market, usually measured by the S&P 500 Index, has a beta of 1.00. Any stock or portfolio with a higher beta is generally more volatile than the market, while any with a lower beta is generally less volatile than the market.

Bond rating: A method of evaluating the possibility of default by a bond issuer. Standard & Poor's, Moody's Investor's Service, and Fitch's Investor's Service analyze the financial strength of each bond's issuer, whether a corporation or a government body. Their ratings range from AAA (highly unlikely to default) to D (in default). Bonds rated B or below are not investment grade—in other words, institutions that invest other people's money may not under most state laws buy them.

Bonds—long-term, short-term, and high yield: Debt instruments that pay lenders a regular return. Short-term bonds are five years or less. High yield bonds pay lenders a higher rate of return because of perceived risk.

Book-to-market ratio: Size of company's book (net) value relative to the market price of the company.

Book value: The current value of an asset on a company's balance sheet according to its accounting conventions. The shareholders' equity on a company's balance sheet is the book value for that entire company. Many times when investors refer to book value, they actually mean book value per share, which is the shareholder's equity (or book value) divided by the number of shares outstanding. Theoretically, the book value is what a company could be sold for (liquidation value). The book value number is sometimes used by active managers as a guide as to whether or not the shares are undervalued.

Broker: An individual with a Series 7 license entitled to buy and sell securities, especially stock, on behalf of clients and to charge for that service.

Broker dealer: A firm employing brokers, among other financial professionals.

Bull market: A prolonged period of rising stock prices. Wall Street defines a Bull Market or bull leg as a rise of at least 15 percent over two back-to-back quarters. We define it as a random market movement causing an investor to mistake himself or herself for a financial genius.

Business day: A day when the New York Stock Exchange is open for trading.

Cap: Small cap, large cap: The stock market worth of an individual equity. Large-cap stocks can be found on the New York Stock Exchange. Small-cap stocks are often listed on the Nasdaq.

Capital appreciation or depreciation: An increase or decrease in the value of a mutual fund or stock due to a change in the market price of the fund. A stock bought at $50 that increases to $55 has a 10 percent return from the appreciation of the original capital invested. If the price of the stock falls to $45, it would have a depreciation of 10 percent. Dividend yield is the other component of total return but is not included in appreciation.

Capital preservation: Investing in a conservative manner so as not to put capital at risk.

Captive insurance company ("Captive"): Slang for an insurance company used predominantly to underwrite the business risk of other subsidiaries of the parent company or owner. The term *captive* is not used in any insurance statutes or in the Internal Revenue Code, but is rather a practice term used to describe an insurance company fulfilling the described role.

Cash: Investment in any instrument (often short-term) that is easily liquidated.

Challenge analysis: The process of selecting forms of structures and transfers based upon what creditors know about those structures and transfers, and the level of efforts being made by creditors to penetrate them and set them aside.

Charging order: An order issued by a court to a judgment creditor that essentially compels an entity of which the debtor is a partner or member to direct to the creditor until the judgment is satisfied any distributions that would otherwise have been made to the debtor.

Charging order protected entities (COPEs): Entities that restrict the remedies of a creditor of an owner to a "charging order" that entitles the creditor to distributions made in respect of that ownership interest, but do not allow—at least initially—the creditor to actually take the ownership interest. From an asset protection standpoint, the advantage is obvious: The creditor has no immediate means of getting at the assets in the entity even though the creditor holds a judgment against one of the owners.

Charging order protection: Originally, this protection arose to protect nondebtor partners from the debts of other partners of a business enterprise. Typically, the availability of charging order protection is limited to partnerships and limited liability companies, which is why Family Limited Partnerships are a popular asset protection tool. This prevents a creditor of an owner of a particular type of business interest from reaching the assets of the business and from gaining voting control over the business interest. Rather, the creditor can only get a court order charging the debtor's interest with the debt, meaning that the creditor will receive any distributions made in respect of the debtor's interest. If the person in charge of making such distributions never makes one, the creditor may be out of luck.

Charitable remainder trust (CRT): A trust instrument that provides for specific payment to one or more individuals, with an irrevocable remainder in the trust property to be paid to or held for a charity.

Closely held insurance company (CHIC): A privately held insurance company that is typically owned either by the owner's children or an irrevocable trust formed for the owner's children, to provide additional tax and succession benefits in addition to those of the captive arrangement.

Commission: A transaction fee commonly levied by brokers and other financial intermediaries for buying or selling securities.

Commission of payment received: Payment received for the sales agent for selling an investment product. The commission is split with the broker and the firm.

Company limited by guarantee: A company that has not been capitalized by cash, but rather by the promises of the shareholders to provide a specified amount of cash if required by the company to satisfy liabilities. For example, the traditional Lloyds of London syndicates were essentially companies capitalized by the unlimited guarantees of members to stand behind the syndicates' underwritings.

Complex asset: An asset that is capable of being broken into component parts.

Compound annual return: Geometric mean is another expression for compound annual return. The Geometric Mean is more appropriate when one is comparing the growth rate for an investment that is continually compounding.

Compounding: The reinvestment of dividends and/or interest and capital gains. This means that over time dividends and interest and capital gains grow exponentially. For example, a $100 earning compound interest at 10 percent a year would accumulate to $110 at the end of the first year and $121 at the end of the second year, etc., based on the formula: compound sum = principal (1+ interest rate) number of periods.

Conservative: There is no precise definition of this term. Generally, the term is used when the mutual fund manager's emphasis is on the below-market betas.

Consumer Price Index (CPI): The CPI is maintained by the Bureau of Labor Statistics, which measures the changes in the cost of a specified group of consumer products relative to a base period. Because it represents the rate of inflation, the CPI can be used as a general benchmark for gauging the maintenance of purchasing power.

Contract: The legal agreement between the insurance company and the owner of the annuity.

Contract anniversary: Any anniversary of the contract date.

Contract date: The date of issue of the contract.

Contract owner: The person or persons designated as the contract owner in the contract. The term shall also include any person named as joint owner. A joint owner shares ownership in all respects with the contract owner. Prior to the annuity date, the contract owner has the right to assign ownership, designate beneficiaries, make permitted withdrawals and exchanges among sub-accounts, and guaranteed rate options.

Cookie-cutter plan: A plan of a one-size-fits-all nature sold by promoters, who make enormous profits from selling such plans because their costs to implement the plan are nominal. The effectiveness of such plans is highly questionable, because typically if a creditor is able to defeat one plan, then all similar plans can likewise be defeated.

Corporate shell (corporate veil): Slang for the liability-limiting advantage of a corporation, which limits the liability of shareholders to the equity they have contributed.

Corporation: A fictitious legal entity authorized by statute, created by the filing of Articles of Incorporation with the relevant jurisdiction, and capitalized by issuing shares of stock. A corporation can provide protection to the shareholders against the liabilities created by the corporation in excess of the corporation's capital.

Correction: A correction is a reversal in the price of a stock, or the stock market as a whole, within a larger trend. While corrections are most often thought of as declines within an overall market rise, a correction can also be a temporary rise in the midst of a longer-term decline.

Correlation: A statistical measure of the degree to which the movement of two variables is related.

Coupon: The periodic interest payment on a bond. When expressed as an annual percentage, it is called the *coupon rate*. When multiplied by the face value of the bond, the coupon rate gives the annual interest income.

Currency risk: Possibility that foreign currency may fall in value relative to investor's home currency, thus devaluing overseas investments.

Current return on equity (ROE): A ratio that measures profitability as the return on common stockholders' equity. It is calculated by dividing the reported earnings per share for the latest 12-month period by the book value per share.

Current yield: This is a bond's annual interest payment as a percentage of its current market price. The current yield is calculated by dividing the annual coupon interest for a bond by the current market price. The coupon rate and the current yield on a bond are equal when the bond is selling at par. Thus, a $1,000 bond with a coupon of 10 percent that is currently selling at $1,000 will have a current yield of 10.0 percent. However, if the bond's price drops to $800, the current yield becomes 12.5 percent.

Death benefit: The greater of the contract's accumulated value on the date the company receives due proof of death of the annuitant or the adjusted death benefit. If any portion of the contract's accumulated value on the date the company receives proof of the annuitant's death is derived from the multi-year guaranteed rate option, that portion of the accumulated value will be adjusted by a positive market value adjustment factor if applicable.

Defense: A strategy whereby multiple layers of defenses are created with the idea that even though the creditor might ultimately be able to break through each layer, the creditor will eventually be worn down and settlement will be facilitated.

Deferred annuity: An annuity for which the contract provides that payments to the annuitant be postponed until a number of periods have elapsed, for example, when the annuitant attains a certain age. It doesn't matter if the payments to the insurance company are made as a single premium or a series of premium payments. The "deferred" term refers to when the insurance company begins to make payments to the annuitant.

Devaluation strategy: A method of setting a low value for an asset by repeated sales to third parties at successively lower prices. This may include dissembling an asset with the idea of later reassembling it with the target purchaser.

Deviation: Movement of an instrument or asset class away from an expected direction. In investment terminology, most often associated with asset-class analysis.

Dilution strategy: A method of decreasing a creditor's share or interest in an entity by issuing additional shares or interests to non-creditor shareholders or members.

Directors' and officers' liability (D&O Liability): The direct, personal liability of directors and officers of corporations for acts that adversely affect the corporation (and thus give rise to a shareholders' derivative action) and for the corporation's acts which adversely affect others (as in the case of employment discrimination claims).

Discretionary trusts: A trust that allows the trustee the discretion to make or not make distributions of benefits to the beneficiary, and to make unequal distributions among all beneficiaries.

Dissimilar price movement: The process whereby different asset classes and markets move in different directions.

Diversification: The simplified concept of diversification is: "Don't put all your eggs in one basket." Many investors have a disproportionate percentage of their investment portfolio in one asset class. The true measure of diversification is *not* how many different investments one has, but how *negatively* correlated they are to each other. Investments that move in the same direction will tend to increase portfolio risk and reduce predictability. The basis for *effective* diversification is combining investments that move differently in time, in proportion, and/or in direction (dissimilar price movement). This protects investors from having all their investments go down at the same time, thereby reducing risk.

Dividend: The payment from a company's earnings normally paid on common shares declared by a company's board of directors to be distributed pro rata among the shares outstanding.

Doctrine of disbelief: This doctrine holds that since no sane person would transfer all of his or her assets to a foreign trustee and risk the assets' disappearing, it stands to reason that they still retain some hidden control over the assets, whether they admit to such control or not.

Dollar cost averaging: A system of buying stock or mutual funds at regular intervals with a fixed dollar amount. Under this system an investor buys by the dollar's worth rather than by the number of shares.

Domestic asset protection trust (DAPT): A self-settled spendthrift trust formed in a U.S. state that permits such forms of trust.

Dow Jones Industrial Average (DJIA): A price-weighted average of 30 leading blue-chip industrial stocks, calculated by adding the prices of the 30 stocks and adjusting by a divisor, which reflects any stock dividends or splits. The Dow Jones Industrial Average is the most widely quoted index of the stock market, but it is not as widely used as a benchmark for evaluating performance as the S&P 500 Index.

Dynasty trust: A trust formed in a jurisdiction that has either abolished the "rule against perpetuities" (which limits the duration of trusts) or has statutorily expanded the "rule against perpetuities" for a period in excess of 100 years.

Efficient frontier: A two-dimensional graph that shows the highest potential return from a diversified portfolio for a given level of risk that an investor is willing to assume. The point where the maximum amount of risk an investor is willing to tolerate intersects with the maximum amount of reward that can potentially be generated is the efficient frontier.

Efficient market theory: The theory holds that stocks are always correctly priced because everything that is publicly known about the stock is reflected in its market price. A concept that proposes that all information about a security is available to all interested parties, and that the market price of the security factors in all of that information; hence, the true value of a security is the current market price.

Emerging growth fund: This applies to new companies that may be relatively small in size with the potential to grow much larger. Here, a mutual fund manager is looking for industries and companies whose growth rates are likely to be both rapid and independent of the overall stock market. "Emerging," of course, means new. This implies such companies may be relatively small in size with the potential to grow much larger. Such stocks are generally much more volatile than the stock market in general and require constant, close attention to developments.

Equities: Stocks: Equity mutual funds are made up of many individual stocks. A stock is a right of ownership in a corporation. The shorthand name for stocks, bonds, and mutual funds is equities.

ERISA anti-alienation provision: A provision found in the Employee Retirement Security Act (ERISA) that prohibits a participant in an ERISA-qualified trust from transferring his or her interest in the plan to others, and that effectively prevents a creditor from attacking the assets of the plan while they are in the trust.

Estate freeze: The process of transferring assets to either the children or a trust for the benefit of the children now, so that the future growth of those assets is with the children or their trust, and not within the parent's estate. The asset protection equivalent is known as an "asset freeze."

Excellent / unexcellent companies: Companies with either high (excellent) or low (unexcellent) stock market performances.

Expected risk adjusted return: Calculated as the weighted average of its possible returns, where the weights are the corresponding probability for each return.

Expenses: Cost of maintaining an invested portfolio.

Exchange privilege: This is a shareholder's right to switch from one mutual fund to another within one fund family. This is often done at no additional charge. This enables investors to put their money in an aggressive growth-stock fund, for example, when they expect the market to turn up strongly, then switch to a money market fund when they anticipate a downturn.

Execution price: The negotiated price at which a security is purchased or sold.

Family limited partnership (FLP): A limited partnership that holds the family's business or investments, with the idea that the parents will gift interests in the partnership to their children at a discount, thus potentially saving federal gift and estate taxes. The term is planner's slang, since there is no entity called a "family limited partnership" that is referenced by any statute, nor is any such entity referenced in the Internal Revenue Code.

Fee-based: A manager, advisor, or broker whose charges are based on a set amount rather than transaction charges.

Fee-only: An advisor who charges an investor a pre-set amount for services.

Fixed-income mutual funds: Fixed-income mutual fund managers invest money in bonds, notes, and other debt instruments. They have a broad range of styles, involving market timing, swapping to gain quality or yield, setting up maturity ladders, etc.

Fixed return annuity: A fixed return annuity is one in which the insurance company guarantees to make payments of a fixed amount for an agreed upon term of years or for the lifetime of the annuitant or joint annuitants. In order to make any profit from such an arrangement, the company offers to pay a rate of interest that is less than it expects to be able to earn by investing the funds it receives for the contract.

Forecasts: Predictions of analysts usually associated with stock picking and active money management.

Foreign asset protection trust (FAPT): A self-settled spendthrift trust formed in a foreign debtor haven jurisdiction.

Foreign foundation: A charitable organization typically created in a tax and debtor haven jurisdiction, most often on the model of the Stiftung.

Fraudulent transfer (fraudulent conveyance): A transfer in derogation of the rights of a creditor to satisfy a judgment against the assets of the debtor.

Front-end load: A fee charged when an investor buys a mutual fund or a variable annuity.

Fundamentals: A marketing term referring to the financial statistics that traditional analysts and Wall Street analysts use. Fundamental data include stock, earnings, dividends, assets and liabilities, inventories, debt, etc. Fundamental data are in contrast to items used in technical analysis—such as price momentum, volume trends, and short sales statistics.

Fund ratings: Evaluation of the performance of invested money pools, often mutual funds, by such entities as Chicago-based Morningstar.

Fund shares: Shares in a mutual fund.

General partnership (GP): A partnership that consists only of general partners, all of whom are jointly liable for the liabilities of the partnership, and all of whom have management rights to the partnership. In asset protection planning, general partnerships are usually to be avoided.

Homestead exemption (homestead protection): A statutory exemption against collection given to certain interests in real property being used as the primary residence of the debtor.

Hot tip: Slang for an individual investment, often a stock, that is apparently poised to rise.

Immediate annuity: When the investor gives an insurance company a sum of money and the company immediately begins to make payments for a term of the investor's life or for some other agreed term of years, it is known as an immediate annuity. The benefits begin immediately—or most often within one year.

Income growth mutual fund: A marketing term that is supposed to select securities to achieve a yield significantly higher than the S&P 500. These portfolios may own more utilities, less high tech, and convertible preferreds and convertible bonds.

Index fund: A passively managed portfolio designed to replicate the performance of a certain index, such as the S&P 500. In general, such mutual funds have performance within a few basis points of the target index. The most popular index mutual funds are those that track the S&P 500, but special index funds, such as those based on the Russell 1000 or the Wilshire 5000, are also available.

Inflation: A monetary phenomenon generated by an overexpansion of credit that drives up prices of assets while diminishing the worth of paper currency.

Institutional trustee: A bank, financial services firm, or licensed trust company that acts as a true third-party trustee of trusts.

Insurance manager: A person or entity that has obtained a license from the local insurance commissioner to manage insurance companies in that jurisdiction.

Intentionally defective grantor trust (IDGT): A form of trust where the gift is completed for federal gift and estate tax purposes, but the trust intentionally fails an element to avoid being treated as a grantor trust, so that it is treated as a grantor trust for federal income tax purposes.

International business company: A corporation authorized by the statutes of a debtor haven which (with the exception of banking) can only conduct business with persons or entities outside the debtor haven, and not with the locals. In other words, it is a company incorporated in a debtor haven but required to be used elsewhere.

Intrinsic value: The theoretical valuation or price for a stock. The valuation is determined using a valuation theory or model. The resulting value is compared with the current market price. If the intrinsic value is greater than the market price, the stock is considered undervalued.

Invest: Disciplined process of placing money in financial instruments so as to gain a return. Given the emergence of valid academic research regarding asset-class investment methods, an individual who depends mostly on active management and stock picking may come to be considered a speculator rather than an investor.

Investment discipline: A specific money management strategy.

Investment objective: Financial goals one wishes to reach.

Investment policy: An investment policy statement forces the investor to confront risk tolerance, return objectives, time horizon, liquidity needs, the amount of funds available for investment, and the investment methodology to be followed.

Investment pornography: Extreme examples of investment pandering.

Investor discomfort: Realization that risk is not appropriate and reward is not predictable in a given portfolio.

Irrevocable life insurance trust (ILIT): An irrevocable trust formed for the off-spring of the trust owner, primarily to purchase and hold life insurance outside the parents' estate so that the life insurance proceeds are not subject to federal estate taxes at the parents' death.

Know your customer rule: The New York Stock Exchange rule that requires brokers to know clients' investment objectives and financial conditions before making investment recommendations. The National Association of Security Dealers has a similar rule.

Limited liability company (LLC): A hybrid type of legal entity that combines certain traits of corporations with certain other traits of partnerships and other noncorporate legal entities. LLCs allow their owners (called members) to have the best of all worlds: pass-through tax treatment like a partnership, limited liability as with a corporation, unheralded flexibility in ownership and management structure, and charging order protection.

Limited partnership (LP): A partnership that consists of general partners who are jointly liable for the liabilities of the partnership and who have management rights to the partnership, and limited partners whose liability is limited to their contributions to the partnership and who have no management rights (i.e., general partners are true partners and limited partners are mere passive investors).

Liquidity: Ability to generate cash on demand when necessary.

Litigation expense policies: A form of policy that does not pay the claim or make any funds available to the claimant, but instead only funds the costs and expenses of litigating the claim, and sometimes other ancillary costs.

Living trust: A revocable grantor trust. Because the trust can be revoked, and a court can order a settlor to revoke the trust, the living trust is thought not to provide any meaningful asset protection until the death of the settlor.

Load funds: A mutual fund sold for a sales charge (load) by a brokerage firm or other sales representative. Such funds may be stock, bond, or commodity funds, with conservative or aggressive objectives. The stated advantage of a load fund is that the salesperson will explain the fund to the customer and offer advice as to when it is appropriate to sell as well as when to buy more shares.

Management company: A company formed primarily to act as a manager of another entity, distance control of the other entity from the owners, and absorb liabilities arising from the management function.

Management fee: Charge against investor assets for managing the portfolio of an open- or closed-end mutual fund as well as for such services as shareholder relations or administration. The fee, as disclosed in the prospectus, is a fixed percentage of the fund's asset value, typically 1 percent or less per year.

Market: In investing terms: a place where securities are traded. It formerly meant a physical location, but now may refer to an electronic one as well.

Market capitalization: The current value of a company determined by multiplying the latest available number of outstanding common shares by the current market price of a share. Market cap is also an indication of the trading liquidity of a particular issue.

Market timing: An attempt to base investment decisions on the expected direction of the market.

Market value: The market or liquidation value of a given security or of an entire pool of assets.

Maturities: Applied to bonds, the date at which a borrower must redeem the capital portion of his or her loan.

Migration strategy: A method of transferring assets by repeated sales of the assets to third parties before a final sale to the target purchaser.

Model portfolio: A theoretical construct of an investment or series of investments.

Modern portfolio theory: In 1950, Professor Harry Markowitz started to build an investment strategy that took more than 30 years to develop and which became recognized as Modern Portfolio Theory. He won the Nobel Prize for his work in 1990.

Money market fund: Money market fund managers invest in short-term fixed instruments and cash equivalents. These instruments make up the portfolio and their objective is to maximize principal protection. Even though these accounts have short-term (one-day) liquidity, they typically pay more like 90- to 180-day CDs versus passbook or one-week CDs.

Mutual fund: An investment company that continually offers new shares and buys existing shares back at the request of the shareholders. It uses its capital to invest in diversified securities of other companies.

Mutual fund families: A mutual fund sponsor or company usually offers a number of funds with different investment objectives within its family of funds. For example, a mutual fund family may include a money market fund, a government bond fund, a corporate bond fund, a blue chip stock fund, and a more speculative stock fund. If an investor buys a fund in the family, the investor is allowed to exchange that fund for another in the same family.

National Association of Securities Dealers, Inc. (NASD): The principal association of over-the-counter (OTC) brokers and dealers that establishes legal and ethical standards of conduct for its members. NASD was established in 1939 to regulate the OTC market in much the same manner as organized exchanges monitor actions of their members.

Net asset value (NAV): This is defined as the market value of each share of a mutual fund. This figure is derived by taking a fund's total assets (securities, cash, and receivables), deducting liabilities, and then dividing that total by the number of shares outstanding.

Net income makeup charitable remainder unit trust (NIMCRUT): An income-only trust that provides for any income deficiencies in past years to be made up to the extent trust income exceeds the amount of the specific percentage in later years.

Net trade: Generally, this is an over-the-counter trade involving no explicit commission. The investment advisor's compensation is in the spread between the cost of the security and the price paid by the customer. Also, a trade in which shares are exchanged directly with the issuer.

Nevada corporation: A corporation formed in Nevada pursuant to Nevada's corporation act, which provides debtors some advantages not typically found in the corporation laws of other states. Unfortunately, the advantages are usually grossly overstated by promoters who arrange structures based on Nevada corporations that have very serious flaws from the asset-protection perspective. Nevada corporations are usually the primary part of the "Asset Protection Consultants" scam that is run from Nevada.

No-load fund: Mutual fund offered by an open-end investment company that imposes no sales charge (load) on its shareholders. Investors buy shares in no-load funds directly from the fund companies, rather than through a broker, as is done in load funds. Because no broker is used, no advice is given on when to buy or sell.

Nominal return: The actual current dollar growth in an asset's value over a given period. (See also *total return* and *real return*.)

Nonqualified contract: An annuity that is not used as part of or in connection with a qualified retirement plan.

Offshore limited liability company (OLLC): A limited liability company formed pursuant to the laws of a foreign debtor haven jurisdiction, such as the Nevis LLC.

Offshore management company: A company formed in a foreign debtor having jurisdiction primarily to act as a manager of another entity, distance control of the other entity from the owners, and absorb liabilities arising from the management function.

Operating expenses: Cost associated with running a fund or portfolio.

Opportunity shifting: The process of putting new wealth-creating assets into distanced structures, so that the wealth is created within those structures and not the existing one.

Optimization: A process whereby a portfolio, invested using valid academic theory in various asset classes, is analyzed to ensure that risk/reward parameters have not drifted from stated goals.

Outperform: Any given market that exceeds expectations or historical performance outperforms.

Over-the-counter: A market made between securities dealers who act either as principals or brokers for their clients. This is the principal market for U.S. government and municipal bonds.

Packaged products: Specific types of products underwritten and packaged by manufacturing companies that can be bought and sold directly through those companies. Packaged products are not required to go through a clearing process. Packaged products include mutual funds, unit investment trusts (UIT), limited partnership interests, and annuities.

Panama Foundation: A charitable organization formed in Panama that is modeled after the Stiftung.

Partnership: A partnership is an association of two or more persons carrying on a business venture as co-owners for profit. Partnerships come in two basic varieties: general and limited.

Passive management: The practice of buying a portfolio that is a proxy for the market as a whole on the theory that it is so difficult to outperform the market that it is cheaper and less risky to just buy the market.

Percentage points: Used to describe the difference between two readings that are percentages. For example, if a portfolio's performance was 18.2 percent versus the S&P 500's 14.65, it outperformed the S&P by 3.6 percentage points.

Piercing the corporate veil: When a court disregards the legal fiction of the corporation and imposes liability against the shareholders.

Portfolio: A group of investments held by an investor, investment company, or financial institution.

Portfolio turnover: Removing funds from one financial instrument to place in another. This process can be costly.

Pre-bankruptcy planning: Planning that is done immediately in anticipation of a bankruptcy filing, and which seeks to maximize exemptions and avoid claims of preferential transfers.

Preferential transfer: A transfer that has the effect of alienating property in advance of a bankruptcy filing, and which may usually be set aside by the bankruptcy court within a defined time period.

Price/earnings ratio (P/E): This may be defined as the current price dividend by reported earnings per share of stock for the latest 12-month period. For example, a stock with earnings per share during the trailing year of $5 and currently selling at $50 per share has a price/earnings ratio of 10.

Principal: The original dollar amount invested.

Private annuity: A method of selling an asset whereby the seller (obligee) sells the asset to the buyer (obligor) in exchange for the buyer's agreeing to make certain payments to the seller until the seller dies. To qualify as a Private Annuity for U.S. tax purposes, in addition to other requirements, the buyer (obligor) must not be in the business of issuing annuities.

Private placement deferred variable annuity (PPDVA or, more commonly, Swiss annuity): A variable annuity with annuity payments initially deferred that is offered by a foreign insurance company on a private placement basis, and which is typically customized to the specific needs of the policyholder. From the asset-protection viewpoint, the hoped-for advantage is that the creditor will not be able to garnish payments until the deferral period ceases and the annuity payments begin.

Private placement variable universal life insurance (PPVULI or, more commonly, offshore PPLI): A variable universal life insurance policy that is offered by a foreign insurance company on a private placement basis, which is highly customized for the specific needs of the policyholder.

Private trust company (PTC): A trust company directly or indirectly owned or controlled by the settlor of a trust. The concept is to give the appearance to third parties that the trust has an independent trustee.

Professional corporation (PC): A form of corporation that can have only certain licensed professionals as shareholders and typically does not protect the professional shareholder from lawsuits brought alleging professional negligence.

Promoter: Promoters often attempt to maximize their profits by selling asset-protection kits.

Prospectus: The document required by the Securities and Exchange Commission that accompanies the sale of a mutual fund or annuity outlining risks associated with certain types of funds or securities, fees, and management. At the core of the prospectus is a description of the fund's investment objectives and the portfolio manager's philosophy.

Random walk theory: One element of the efficient market theory—the theory that stock price variations are not predictable.

Rate of return: The profits earned by a security as measured as a percentage of earned interest and/or dividends and/or appreciation.

Ratings: Performance and creditworthiness measurement of funds and corporations generated by Lipper, Moodys, Morningstar, and others. (These ratings, when used to evaluate active fund managers, may be misleading as past performance is no guarantee of future success.)

Real return: This is the inflation-adjusted return on an asset. Inflation-adjusted returns are calculated by subtracting the rate of inflation from an asset's apparent, or nominal, return. For example, if common stocks earn a total return of 10.3 percent over a period of time, but inflation during that period is 3.1 percent, the real return is the difference: 7.2 percent.

Rebalancing: A process whereby funds are shifted within asset classes and between asset classes to ensure the maintenance of the efficient frontier. (See *optimization.*)

Recapitalization strategy: A method of increasing the capital base of an entity under creditor attack by contributing a valuable but illiquid asset to the entity.

Redemption strategy: A method of containing liabilities by an intermediate sale to a party in a debtor haven.

Registered agent: An agent for the corporation who is domiciled in the state of incorporation and is available to receive service-of-process on behalf of the corporation.

Reinvested dividends: Dividends paid by a particular mutual fund that are reinvested in that same mutual fund. Some mutual funds offer automatic dividend reinvestment programs. In the complex equation theoretically used to determine the performance of the S&P 500, each company's dividend is reinvested in the stock of that company.

Re-invoicing (transfer pricing): An offshore tax scheme involving the creation of an intermediate entity or offshore wholesaler in a tax haven jurisdiction for purposes of skimming profits and thus decreasing the amount of U.S. income shown. The IRS has significant powers to combat such arrangements, some of which may amount to criminal tax evasion.

Repatriation order: An order to the debtor to bring assets back within the jurisdiction of the court. If the debtor does not do so, typically the court will order the debtor incarcerated for contempt.

Replication strategy: A complicated strategy for transferring wealth involving mirrored option arrangements and controlled counterparties, and based on particular future assumptions of market volatility.

Reverse alter ego: A developing theory of relief for creditors, which allows creditors of an owner of an entity to invade the entity and get at the entity's assets directly so as to satisfy the creditor's debt against the owner.

Risk: Risk is nothing more than the uncertainty of future rates of return, which includes the possibility of loss. This variability or uncertainty causes "rational" investors to expect higher returns on investments for which the actual timing or amount of payoffs is not guaranteed. A mutual fund portfolio has two types of risk: a measure of the probability of potential outcomes and the potential change in portfolio value as a result of differences in the economic environment between the current time and some point in the future.

Risk premium: The excess investment return above risk-free return on an investment an investor hopes to obtain in exchange for taking investment risk.

Risk systematic: Potential for predictable, quantifiable loss of funds through the application of valid academic research to the process of disciplined asset-class investing.

Risk tolerance: Investors' innate ability to deal with the potential of losing money without abandoning the investment process.

Risk unsystematic: Associated with investment in an undiversified portfolio of individual instruments through active management.

Risk-free rate of return: The return on an asset that is considered virtually riskless. U.S. government Treasury bills are typically used as the risk-free asset because of their short time horizon and the low probability of default.

ROI: Return on investment, the amount of money generated over time by placement of funds in specific financial instruments.

R-squared: A measure of how closely the return characteristics of a security or portfolio match those of a particular market index. R-squared is a measure of a scale from 1 to 100, with 100 being closest to the market index in question. In order to understand the meaning of investment data, it's necessary to know how closely it correlates to the comparative index by measuring the R-squared.

S&P 500: The performance benchmark most widely used by sponsors, managers, and performance measurement services. This index includes 400 industrial stocks, 20 transportation stocks, 40 financial stocks, and 40 public utilities. Performance is measured on a capitalization-weighted basis. The index is maintained by Standard & Poor's Corporation, a subsidiary of McGraw-Hill Inc.

S&P common stock rankings: The S&P rankings measure historical growth and stability of earnings and dividends. The system includes the following rankings: A+, A, and A– (above average); B+ (average); B, B–, and C (below average); NR (insufficient historical data or not amenable to the ranking process). As a matter of policy, S&P does not rank the stocks of foreign companies, investment companies, and certain finance-oriented companies.

Securities and Exchange Commission (SEC): The keystone law in the regulation of securities markets. It governs exchanges, over-the-counter markets, broker-dealers, the conduct of secondary markets, extension of credit in securities transactions, the conduct of corporate insiders, and principally the prohibition of fraud and manipulation in securities transactions. It also outlines the powers of the Securities and Exchange Commission to interpret, supervise, and enforce the securities laws of the United States.

Securities Investor Protection Corporation (SIPC): This is a government-sponsored organization created in 1970 to insure investor accounts at brokerage firms in the event of the brokerage firm's insolvency and liquidation. The maximum insurance of $500,000, including a maximum of $100,000 in cash assets per account, covers customer losses due to brokerage house insolvency, not customer losses caused by security price fluctuations. SIPC coverage is conceptually similar to Federal Deposit Insurance Corporation coverage of customer accounts at commercial banks.

Security: A tradable financial instrument.

Security selection: Process of picking securities, especially stocks for investment purposes.

Self-canceling installment note (SCIN): A method of selling an asset where the buyer provides a promissory note to the seller with a fixed payment period, but which note and obligation to pay the seller is canceled if the seller dies.

Self-settled spendthrift trust: A trust formed for the benefit of the person who created the trust, with spendthrift provisions that attempt to disallow a creditor from invading the trust assets or forcing a distribution to the beneficiary that the creditor would then seize.

Series LLC (cell LLC): A form of LLC allowed by the statutes of only a few jurisdictions (most popularly Delaware) that allow membership interests to be divided into categories or "cells" with liability for particular actions of the LLC theoretically limited to the capital contributed to the particular series in which the operations of the LLC occurred.

Settlor: One who provides assets to a trustee so that the trustee can hold the assets in trust for the beneficiary.

Shares: Specific portions of tradable equity, a share of stock. It generally refers to common or preferred stocks.

Solicited / unsolicited order: A solicited order is a security transaction that results from a broker's recommendation. An unsolicited order results from an investor's request.

Sophisticated investor: Under SEC guidelines, an investor is defined as sophisticated if he or she meets certain income and net worth requirements.

Speculator: One who uses an active management style to invest.

Spendthrift trust: A trust that includes certain language giving the trustee wide latitude to avoid making distributions to beneficiaries where the distribution would go to a creditor, or where the trustee fears the distribution would be wasted by the beneficiary.

Standard deviation: Volatility can be statistically measured using standard deviation. Standard deviation describes how far from the mean historic performance has been, either higher or lower. Mean is simply the middle point between the two historic extremes of the performance of the investment you are examining. The standard deviation measurement helps explain what the distribution of returns likely will be. The greater the range of returns, the greater the risk; the lower the risk, the lower the return expected.

Stiftung: A civil law arrangement that is basically a charitable fund that is created for a particular purpose. It is similar in many respects to a Purpose Trust.

Stock: A contract signifying ownership of a portion of a public or private company.

Stock picker: Someone who is actively trying to select companies whose equity may rise in the short or long term. Valid academic research shows this process is unworkable and results are no better than random.

Sub-account: That portion of the variable annuities separate account that invests in shares of the funds' portfolios.

Swiss annuity programs:

Deferred fixed-term annuity—Annuity payments begin after a deferral period predefined by the owner if the insured person is alive at that date. Payments end with the death of the insured person or, at the latest, at the time fixed by the owner.

Deferred life annuity– Annuity payments start after the end of a deferral period, predefined by the owner (provided the insured person is alive at that date), and continue throughout the lifetime of the insured person.

Fixed-term annuity—Annuity payments are made for a fixed number of years determined by the owner (five years minimum).

Joint and survivor life annuity—Two lives are insured and annuity payments are made until the death of the second person.

Immediate fixed-term annuity—Annuity payments begin immediately and end after a specified period, but not later than the death of the insured person.

Immediate income life annuity—Annuity payments start immediately and continue throughout the lifetime of the insured person.

Life annuity, "X" years certain—Annuity payments are made as long as the insured person is alive. Annuity payments are made for a guaranteed minimum number of years, determined by the owner. If the insured person dies during this period, payments continue to the beneficiary for the rest of the period. If the insured person survives this period, payments continue for life.

Single life annuity—An annuity is paid for life.

Structured financial product: A financial product created to serve a transaction-specific purpose.

Structural methodology: The decision-making process for choosing the type of structure that will be utilized to hold particular assets.

Time horizon: The amount of time someone can wait to generate or take profits from an investment.

Time weighted rate of return: The rate at which a dollar invested at the beginning of a period would grow if no additional capital were invested and no cash withdrawals were made. It provides an indication of value added by the investment manager and allows comparisons to the performance of other investment managers and market indexes.

Total return: A standard measure of performance or return including both capital appreciation (or depreciation) and dividends or other income received. For example, Stock A is priced at $60 at the start of a year and pays an annual dividend of $4. If the stock moves up to $70 in price, the appreciation component is 16.7 percent, the yield component is 6.7 percent, and the total return is 23.4 percent. That oversimplification does not take into account any earnings on the reinvested dividends.

Trading costs: Fees or commissions paid to move money from one financial instrument to another.

Transaction costs: Any fees or commissions generated and paid in the management of a portfolio. Another term for execution costs. Total transaction costs (or the cost of buying and selling stocks) have three components: (1) the actual dollars paid in commissions, (2) the market impact (i.e., the impact a manager's trade has on the market price for the stock) (this varies with the size of the trade and the skill of the trader), and (3) the opportunity cost of the return (positive or negative) given up by not executing the trade instantaneously.

Transfer methodology: The decision-making process for choosing the type of transfer that will be used to move assets to a particular structure.

Treasury bill: A U.S. financial security issued by Federal Reserve for the Treasury as a means of borrowing money for short periods of time. They are sold at a discount from their maturity value, pay no coupons, and have maturities of up to one year. Because they are a direct obligation of the federal government, they are free of default risk. Most Treasury bills are purchased by commercial banks and held as part of their secondary reserves. T-bills regulate the liquidity base of the banking system in order to control the money supply. For example, if the authorities wish to expand the money supply, they can buy Treasury bills, which increase the reserves of the banking system and induce a multiple expansion of bank deposits.

Trust: A relationship whereby one party (trustee) is given assets by another (settlor) to hold for the benefit of a third party (beneficiary).

Trustee: One who agrees with a settlor to hold assets in trust for the beneficiary.

Trust protector: A person or entity who has certain powers under the trust document, usually to discharge (but not appoint) trustees, and to veto (but not make) certain key decisions of the trustees.

Turnover: The volume or percentage of buying or selling activity within a mutual fund portfolio relative to the mutual fund portfolio's size.

Unbundling: The process of breaking an asset into components and treating the components as separate assets.

Underperform: Securities or markets that do not meet expectations.

Value stocks: Stocks with high book to market valuations (i.e., companies doing poorly in the market that may have the potential to do better).

Variable annuity: Insurance-based investment products that like other forms of annuities allow for growth of invested premiums to be free from taxation until withdrawals are made from the contract. Unique to variable annuities are several forms of investment alternatives that vary in their potential for both reward and risk. Variable annuity choices are broad enough that an investor can employ either an aggressive or conservative approach, or a combination of both, while enjoying the benefits of tax-deferred growth.

Volatility: The extent to which market values and investment returns are uncertain or fluctuate. Another word for risk, volatility is gauged using such measures as beta, mean absolute deviation, and standard deviation. Volatility is simply investment jargon for frequency and amount of change.

Wealth preservation: Planning that preserves wealth over time against numerous unforeseen circumstances.

Weighting: A term usually associated with proportions of assets invested in a particular region or securities index to generate a specific risk/reward profile.

Yield (current yield): For stocks, yield is the percentage return paid in dividends on a common or preferred stock, calculated by dividing the indicated annual dividend by the market price of the stock. For example, if a stock sells for $40 and pays a dividend of $2 per share, it has a yield of 5 percent (i.e., $2 divided by $40). For bonds, the coupon rate of interest divided by the market price is called current yield. For example, a bond selling for $1,000 with a 10 percent coupon offers a 10 percent current yield. If the same bond were selling for $500, it would offer a 20 percent yield to an investor who bought it for $500. (As a bond's price falls, its yield rises, and vice versa.)

Yield curve: A chart or graph showing the price of securities (usually fixed income) through time. A flat or inverted yield curve of fixed-income instruments is thought by many to be an indicator of recession. This is because those who borrow at the far end of the curve usually pay more for their money than those who borrow for only a little while. When the yield curve is flat or inverted this means there is little demand for long-term money and this can be interpreted as a signal that there is little demand in the economy for the products that long-term borrowing would generate.

Yield to maturity: The discount rate that equates the present value of the bond's cash flows (semi-annual coupon payments of the redemption value) with the market price. The yield to maturity will actually be earned if (1) the investor holds the bond to maturity and (2) the investor is able to reinvest all coupon payments at a rate equal to the yield to maturity. When a bond is selling at par, the yield to maturity and the coupon rate are equal.

Asset Protection

Adkisson, Jay, and Chris Riser, *Asset Protection, Concepts and Strategies for Protecting Your Wealth*, New York: McGraw-Hill, 2004.

The best book on asset protection covering the legal, technical, and theoretical aspects of asset protection.

Economics

Keynes, John Maynard, *The General Theory of Employment, Interest and Money*, Amherst, New York: Promethius Books, reprinted 1997.

The definitive work of the British economist and government advisor, whose influential theories advocating government intervention (fiscal policy) as a solution to economic problems have become known as Keynesian economics.

McConnell, Campbell R., *Economics: Principles, Problems, and Policies*, 13th ed., New York: McGraw-Hill, 2004.

A highly regarded introduction to the fundamental problems and principles of economics and the policy alternatives available to countries, both from a national and international perspective.

Nelson, Charles R., *The Investor's Guide to Economic Indicators*, New York: Wiley, 1989.

Using plain language and simple charts, a prominent economist provides a guide to reading, interpreting, and using economic and financial news to make better investment decisions.

Samuelson, Paul A., and W. Nordhaus, *Economics*, 16th ed., New York: McGraw-Hill, 2004.

This famous and widely used introductory economics text has been thoroughly revised and updated. It takes students from fundamental to sophisticated levels of understanding of income and production factors, including international trade and finance and current economic problems.

Smith, Adam, *An Inquiry into the Nature and Causes of the Wealth of Nations*, New York: Penguin Classics, 2000.

The definitive work, first published in 1776, of the most famous of the classical economists, who held that economies function best under a laissez-faire system in which market forces are free to operate without government interference.

International Economics, Finance, and Investment

Brandes, Charles H. and Glenn R. Carlson, *International Value Investing*, New York: McGraw-Hill, 1997.
A step-by-step guide to value investing in markets outside the United States.

Christian, Kalin H., *Switzerland Business and Investment Handbook*, London: John Wiley & Sons, 2006.
This is the premier book if you are thinking about investing in anything that has to do with Switzerland. It includes addresses and current information that will help you get around and not waste time.

Lindert, Peter H., *International Economics*, 9th ed., Buff Ridge, Illinois: Irwin Professional Publishing, 2003.
A classic covering aspects of international economics and finance on theoretical and practical levels, plus an examination of larger problems concerning international mobility of people and factors of production.

Walmsley, Julian, *The New Financial Instruments*, New York: Wiley, 1998.
An explanation of sophisticated modern financial instruments used in international finance and investment.

Money and Banking

The Bank Rating Service, Wakefield, Massachusetts: Veribanc.
Veribanc is a service that rates the financial strength of most U.S. banks, savings and loans, credit unions, and bank holding companies and provides short-form or in-depth reports for a fee. Also provides lists of safe financial institutions by state, region, or financial condition. Veribanc also offers default insurance up to $5 million through a program called DEPOSITSURE.

Kaufman, George G., *The U.S. Financial System: Money Markets and Institutions*, 6th ed., Englewood Cliffs, N.J.: Prentice-Hall, 1995.
Assuming a basic knowledge of economics, this text covers in terms of theory and practice the evolution and operations of the national and international financial markets as well as instruments, institutions, and regulators. The Federal Reserve System and other aspects of the economic macrostructure are also examined.

Ritter, Lawrence S., and William L Silber, *Principles of Money, Banking and Financial Markets*, 8th ed., New York: Basic Books, 2006.
A comprehensive introductory text that covers money and banking fundamentals; banks and other intermediaries; central banking; monetary theory; financial markets and interest rates; and international finance.

Updegrave, Walter, *How to Keep Your Savings Safe: Protecting the Money You Can't Afford to Lose*, New York: Crown Publishers, 1994.
How to find the strongest banks, insurance companies, and money market mutual funds. Lists of safe U.S. banks, insurers, savings and loan institutions, and money funds are provided.

Bond and Money Markets

Douglas, Livingston G., *The Fixed-Income Almanac: The Bond Investor's Compendium of Key Market, Product and Performance Data*, New York: McGraw-Hill, 1993.
  Provides a cornucopia of historical performance data for the bond markets, including yield levels, measures of bond volatility, information on ratings upgrades and downgrades, and levels of new bond issuance.

Fabozzi, Frank J., *The Handbook of Fixed Income Securities*, 7th ed., New York: McGraw-Hill, 2005.
  Includes 47 chapters, each by an expert, covering general investment information; securities and instruments; bond investment management; interest rates, and rate forecasting.

Faerber, Esme, *All About Bonds from the Inside Out*, New York: McGraw-Hill, 1999.
  As the title suggests, a discussion of bond basics, including types of bonds, different risk characteristics, methods of valuation, calculating rates and returns, and understanding the yield curve.

Kerzner, Harold, *Understanding Corporate Bonds*, New York: McGraw-Hill, 1990.
  Excellent primer on the complex world of corporate bonds.

Lederman, Jess, and Michael P. Sullivan, *The New High-Yield Bond Market*, New York: McGraw-Hill, 1993.
  How the high-yield (junk) bond market works and how to reduce risk without compromising return. Buying bonds of bankrupt companies.

Stigum, Marcia, *Money Market Derivatives and Structured Notes*, Burr Ridge, Illinois: Irwin Professional Publishing, 1996.
  Like her book, *The Money Market*, an excellent and comprehensive guide, in this case to the more exotic financial derivatives and complex debt instruments invested for modern worldwide money markets.

Stigum, Marcia, *The Money Market*, 3rd ed., Burr Ridge, Illinois: Irwin Professional Publishing, 1989.
  A comprehensive guide, by a working professional, to the U.S. money market. It covers the various instruments traded, how yields are calculated, and the role of the Federal Reserve; the major participants, including Eurobanks; and particular markets, such as those for commercial paper, Treasury bills, and CDs. Includes financial futures.

Mutual Funds

Brouwer, Kurt, *Kurt Brouwer's Guide to Mutual Funds: How to Invest with the Pros*, New York: Wiley, 1990.
  A fine book that explains how mutual funds work and discusses the best strategies for buying and selling them.

Coleman, Aaron H., and David H. Coleman, *How to Select Top-Performing Mutual Fund Investments*, New York: McGraw-Hill, 1993.
  A guide to profitable mutual fund investing, with extensive performance data.

Herzfeld, Thomas J., *Herzfeld's Guide to Closed-End Funds*, New York: McGraw-Hill, 1992.
   Everything you need to know about closed-end funds. Profiles more than 300 fund portfolios with analyses and rankings.

Jacobs, Sheldon, *The Handbook for No-Load Fund Investor*, New York: McGraw-Hill, 1998.
   The definitive book on no-load mutual funds.

Taylor, John H., *Building Wealth with Mutual Funds*, New York: McGraw-Hill.
   A step-by-step guide to investing in mutual funds, including international investing, index funds, variable annuity funds, and socially responsible funds.

Securities Markets, Securities Analysis, and Portfolio Management

Amling, Frederick, *Investments, An Introduction to Analysis and Management*, 6th ed., Englewood Cliffs, N.J.: Prentice-Hall, 1988.
   A text for the beginning investor or aspiring investment professional. Using practical cases to illustrate principles, the book deals with various aspects of fundamental analysis, modern portfolio theory, and technical analysis.

Brown, David L. and Kassandra Bentley, *Cyber-Investing, Cracking Wall Street with Your Personal Computer*, New York: Wiley, 1997.
   Using computer programs and databases to sort for stock opportunities and to time purchases and sales.

Cohen, Jerome B., Edward D. Zinbarg, and Arthur Zeikel, *Investment Analysis and Portfolio Management*, 5th ed., Burr Ridge, Illinois: Irwin Professional Publishing, 1986.
   An introductory text, notable because it is comprehensive and discusses modern portfolio theory and security valuation techniques in a nonmathematical, readable way. It also covers the current investment scene and industry and company analysis.

Dreman, David, *The New Contrarian Investment Strategy*, New York: Random House, 1982.
   An established title and modern classic on contrarian investment strategy by a noted contrarian and Forbes columnist.

Engel, Louis, and Henry L. Hecht, *How to Buy Stocks*, 8th ed., New York: Little, Brown: 1994.
   A highly readable, clear, and informative introduction to investing in the stock market, this book has been a deserved fixture in the literature of investing for several decades.

Graham, Benjamin, *The Intelligent Investor*, 4th ed., New York: Harper Collins, 1986.
   John Train, who wrote *The Money Masters* (below), says this book is "More useful for most readers [than *Security Analysis*] and indeed the best book ever written for the stockholder. One is ill-advised to buy a bond or a share of stock without having read its pages."

Graham, Benjamin, David L. Dodd, and Sidney Cottle, *Securities Analysis: The Original 1934 Edition*, Reprint, New York: McGraw-Hill, 1997.

This classic work remains the bible for students of the fundamentalist approach to securities analysis. It comprises six parts: survey and approach; analysis of financial statements; fixed-income securities; the valuation of common stocks; senior securities with speculative features; and other aspects of security analysis.

Little, Jeffrey B., *Understanding Wall Street*, New York: Tab Books/McGraw-Hill, 2004.

The ubiquitous little green book that provides an education on how to evaluate stocks and bonds and how the brokerage industry works.

Lynch, Peter, and John Rothchild, *One Up on Wall Street*, New York: Simon & Schuster, 2000.

Down-to-earth investment advice from the legendary manager of Fidelity's Magellan Fund.

O'Higgins, Michael B., with John Downes, *Beating the Dow, A High-Return, Low-Risk Method for Investing in the Dow Jones Industrial Stocks with As Little As $5000*, New York: Harper Perennial, 1991.

One of the most influential investment books of the 1990s, this is a clearly written investment primer and discussion of the simple, highly successful, and widely used investment strategy using high-yield Dow Jones industrials.

O'Shaughnessy, James P., *What Works on Wall Street*, New York: McGraw-Hill, 2005.

Investment tools and stock selection strategies are quantitatively tested over a 40-year period and the results discussed in a clear and readable fashion.

Pring, Martin, *Introduction to Technical Analysis*, New York: McGraw-Hill, 1997.

An introduction to the basics of technical analysis by the author of the classic *Technical Analysis Explained,* this chart-filled book explains traditional techniques as well as new analytical tools, such as momentum indicators, made possible by computers.

Schwager, Jack D., *The New Market Wizards; Conversations with America's Top Trader*, New York: Wiley, 1995.

A distinguished group of money managers discuss their secrets and methodologies.

Teweles, Richard J., and Edward S. Bradley, *The Stock Market*, 6th ed., New York: Wiley, 1992.

A revision of a work originally authored by George L. Leffler in 1951. It examines the stock market in five sections dealing with fundamental information, the exchanges, securities houses, regulations, investing practices, and special instruments.

Train, John, *The Money Masters*, New York: Harper Business, 1980.

Interesting stories, by an investment counselor, about the investment strategies of nine distinguished portfolio managers, such as T. Rowe Price, Benjamin Graham, and John Templeton, with commentary on their methods and personalities.

Train, John, *The New Money Masters*, New York: Harper Business, 1994.

A sequel to *The Money Masters* that profiles 10 great contemporary investors, including Peter Lynch, John Neff, and George Soros.

Commodity and Financial Futures Markets

Frost, Ronald J., *Options on Futures: A Hands-on Workbook of Market-Proven Trading Strategies*, McGraw-Hill Trade, Cedar Falls, Iowa: Oster Communications, 1993.
    A clearly written explanation of the complex world of options on futures.

Kaufman, Perry J., *The New Commodity Trading Systems & Methods*, New York: Wiley, 2005.
    An extensive reference guide dealing with individual commodities, including financial futures, and covering markets, forecasting, hedging, risk and money management, along with other technical aspects.

Lass, John P., and Sol Waksman, *Managed Futures Portfolio Strategies; Investment Analysis and the Evaluation and Selection of Commodity Trading Advisors*, Chicago: Probus Professional Publishing, 1994.
    How to evaluate, select, and track the performance of a commodity trading advisor.

Powers, Mark J., *Starting Out in Futures Trading*, 5th ed., Chicago: Probus Publishing Company, 1993.
    A combination of theory and practical information for the beginner; includes history, exchanges, choosing a broker, trading programs, hedging, and forecasting. Covers financial futures.

Schwager, Jack D., *A Complete Guide to the Futures Markets: Fundamental Analysis, Technical Analysis, Trading, Spreads and Options*, New York: Wiley, 1984.
    Assumes a basic familiarity with futures trading, but otherwise provides a nontechnical discussion of various analytical techniques, including regression analysis and chart analysis. Has sample charts and a section on trading guidelines.

Siegel, Diane F., and Daniel R. Siegel, *The Futures Markets*, New York: Harcourt Brace, 1990.
    A comprehensive study of the futures markets. Emphasizing the mechanics of futures trading; the theory of futures pricing; futures trading strategies used for arbitrage, hedging, and speculation; and descriptions of all the major futures contracts.

Options Markets

Ansbacher, Max G., *The New Options Market*, 4th Ed., New York: Wiley, 2000.
    An easy-to-read, yet comprehensive rundown by a professional trader of options and option strategies. For the speculator as well as the conservative investor.

Fabozzi, Frank J., and Gregory M. Kipnis, Eds., *The Handbook of Stock Index Futures and Options*, Burr Ridge, Illinois: Irwin Professional Publishing, 1989.
    Twenty-six chapters by recognized authorities cover strategies for using index futures and options in equity portfolio management and trading the market.

Gastineau, Gary L., *The Options Manual*, 3rd ed., New York: McGraw-Hill, 1988.

Assuming a basic knowledge of options and how they are used, Gastineau discusses option valuation methods and their applications in portfolio analysis and management. The book also covers option investment and trading strategies and tax implications.

McMillan, Lawrence G., *Options as a Strategic Investment*, Englewood Cliffs, N.J.: Prentice-Hall, 2002.

An advanced discussion of option strategies, focusing on which ones work where and why. Includes chapters on arbitrage, mathematical applications, and tax ramifications.

Roth, Harrison, *LEAPS (Long-Term Equity AnticiPation Securities)*, Burr Ridge, Illinois: Irwin Professional Publishing, 1993.

Written in easy-to-understand English with examples and summaries, this book covers the history, the risks, and the strategies possible with long-term options, a 1990s innovation.

Other Securities and General Investor Information

Amerman, Daniel R., *Mortgage Securities: The High-Yield Alternative to CDs, the Low-Risk Alternative to Stocks*, Chicago: Probus Professional Publishing, 1993.

How to invest in mortgage securities, which are the highest yielding of all government-issued securities. Covers mortgage-backed securities mutual funds, buying and selling individual mortgage-backed bonds; how prepayment risk is factored into bond prices, differences among Fannie Mae, Ginnie Mae, and other issuers of mortgage-backed securities.

Calamos, John P., *Investing in Convertible Securities: Your Complete Guide to the Risk and Rewards*, Chicago: Dearborn Financial Publishing, 1988.

A clearly written guide through the sometimes bewildering world of convertible securities.

Goodman, Jordan E., *Everyone's Money Book*, Chicago: Dearborn Financial Publishing, Inc., 2001.

A friendly, readable reference covering virtually every aspect of personal finance, with illustrations and recommended resources.

Lederman, Jess, *The Handbook of Asset-Backed Securities*, New York: New York Institute of Finance, 1990.

Mechanics and economics of asset-backed securities, including those backed by mortgages, credit cards, and auto loans.

Index

Note: page numbers with n indicate a note

About the Author

Darrell Aviss is a founder and the Managing Director o SwissGuard International, GmbH, a Zurich-based financial consulting firm which specializes in international investments that deliver legal tax advantages, protection of assets, and privacy. SwissGuard's clients include physicians, attorneys, accountants, and private business owners who are interested in diversifying their investment portfolios internationally.

For over 23 years, Darrell Aviss has been an internationally recognized expert on international wealth protection strategies that include insurance-based holding vehicles, private banking relationships, and managed accounts.

He is the author of several books, including *Swiss Investing Secrets*; *Retirement Investing*; and *Asset Protection and Wealth Preservation*, and his expertise is sought by many major magazines for articles pertaining to asset protection, asset allocation, and international insurance planning.

Today Mr. Aviss divides his time between Switzerland and the United States. He welcomes questions and inquiries in North America by calling 1-800-796-7496 or by visiting www.swiss-annuity.com.